BUBER'S WAY
TO "I AND THOU"

BUBER'S WAY TO "I AND THOU"

The Development of Martin Buber's Thought and His "Religion as Presence" Lectures

RIVKA HORWITZ

THE JEWISH PUBLICATION SOCIETY
Philadelphia • New York • Jerusalem 5748 /1988

Portions of this book were originally published under the
title Buber's Way to "I and Thou": An Historical Analysis
and the First Publication of Martin Buber's Lectures
"Religion als Gegenwart."
Copyright © 1978 by Verlag Lambert Schneider, Heidelberg
Translation of "Religion als Gegenwart" by Esther Cameron.

This edition copyright © 1988 by The Jewish Publication Society
First American edition   All rights reserved
Manufactured in the United States of America
Library of Congress Cataloging in Publication Data
Horwitz, Rivka.
Buber's way to "I and thou."

List of Book Cited in this Work: p. 237.
Includes index.
1. Buber, Martin, 1878–1965. Ich und du.   2. Life.
3. Relationism.   4. God–Knowableness.   5. Religion.
I.   Buber, Martin, 1878–1965.   Religion als Gegenwart.
II.   Title.
B3213.B83H675   1988   296.3'092'4   87–22607
ISBN 0–8276–0305–3

Designed by Adrianne Onderdonk Dudden

CONTENTS

PREFACE

Buber's Way to I and Thou is a historical investigation into the inception and development of Martin Buber's seminal treatise and an illustration of the emergence of dialogical thought in the early decades of our century. It was a great moment for me when I realized that Buber's lectures "Religion als Gegenwart" ("Religion as Presence"), which I was reading in the Martin Buber Archive of the Jewish National and University Library in Jerusalem, were actually the oral forerunner of the themes that would appear in *I and Thou*. This material allowed me to pursue an investigation into the development of Buber's thought in a manner that otherwise and hitherto would have been impossible. The result of this research was the first edition of this book, published in 1978 by Lambert Schneider in Heidelberg. The book published then presented "Religion as Presence" in the original German; the historical analysis was in English.

However, since there exists a great interest in *I and Thou* in the English-speaking world, I was asked to prepare an English edition. This second edition, then, presents the lectures in translation. The historical analysis has been somewhat revised, with some of the more technical matters deleted. I hope that this work may find favor and understanding in the eyes of God and man.

The greatest reward for me in studying this chapter in the history of ideas was the discovery that Buber's theory of the dialogue was not developed in isolation, written down at a desk in a monological manner. It was, rather, the outcome of a give-and-take, of molding and being molded. There was a living dialogue between Buber and a friend, and perhaps more than one, with whom he spoke about these themes while he was preparing the work. Buber, the great teacher of his generation, was also eager to discuss his thoughts in the classroom. He solicited questions from his Lehrhaus audience that, on occasion, so profoundly stimulated him that they found their way into his masterpiece.

For their help in the preparation of this book, I wish to thank the following individuals and institutions: first of all, Mr. Rafael Buber, the son of Martin Buber, who generously extended his assistance on numerous occasions; the Lakritz Foundation for Research on Buber for supporting the translation of Esther Cameron; Mr. Lothar Stiehm, who gave permission to prepare this English edition; Leo Taubes and Mark Gelber for their suggestions; Nahum M. Sarna, the academic consultant of The Jewish Publication Society, as well as the rest of the staff. It is also important to mention that for the accomplishment of my work I drew support from my son David and my daughter-in-law Ronit, from my daughter Bat Sheva and my son-in-law Meir Cohen, and, most of all, from my husband Josef, a physicist who always has an ear open to the themes of my interest. How much I owe him only the two of us know.

Rivka Horwitz

BUBER'S WAY
TO "I AND THOU"

INTRODUCTION

I and Thou is considered one of the most influential works in modern philosophy and theology. Many books, articles, and commentaries have been written on this masterpiece, which Buber, even in his later years, considered to be his most important work and the starting point of his dialogical thinking. This relatively short book, of some one hundred pages, has been translated into numerous languages, including English, Spanish, Hebrew, Swedish, Danish, Norwegian, Czech, Italian, and Japanese. Today, more than fifty years after its publication, it continues to exert widespread influence, especially in West Germany and the United States.

In *I and Thou*, Buber focused attention on two types of relations, I-Thou and I-It. His treatise has stimulated the investigation of these two types of relationships in the Bible, prayers, theological writing, and poetry. Several generations have evaluated and reevaluated his treatment of these relationships, repeatedly discovering in it new insight into the meaning of individual lives. Certainly, Buber's work is not without its inconsistencies and occasional lack of clarity. But when read as it should be, as an earnest endeavor to open our ears and hearts to the presence of both a human and a divine Thou and to draw us into the depths of dialogue, its message is profound.

Despite the plethora of studies concerning Buber's life and work,[1] there had been no thorough critical study of the sources that nourished his development toward *I and Thou*—a study that did not end with Buber's own published testimony concerning the history of the book but that delved into the rich archival material pertinent to this question. There has been a need for careful study of early plans and versions of the work and for an examination of his personal contacts and correspondence with friends and colleagues while he wrote the book. Since there is little agreement among observers as to Buber's intentions in writing *I and Thou*, knowledge of his personal philosophical and religious struggles during the period (1918–1919) that preceded its publication clarifies the nature of the problems he addressed. His work proposed, in one sense, to resolve those problems. This complicated process is especially important in the case of an existential philosopher, for whom the interaction of life and thought is paramount. In addition, the study of the history of *I and Thou* has significance far beyond that of adding a chapter on a very fruitful period to Buber's biography. It is, in fact, a study of the breakthrough of dialogical thinking in our century, a trend that continues to exert an influence upon social, psychological and religious thinkers.

The existing inquiries into the history of *I and Thou*, such as Bern-

---

1. Hans Kohn, *Martin Buber, sein Werk und Seine Zeit: Ein Beitrag zur Geistesgeschichte Mitteleuropas, 1880–1930* (Hellerau, 1930); the later edition (Wiesbaden, 1979), which will be referred to throughout, includes an afterword by Robert Weltsch. Invaluable notes and bibliographical material are found in Grete Schaeder, *Martin Buber: Hebräischer Humanismus* (Göttingen, 1966), and in English translation as *The Hebrew Humanism of Martin Buber* (Detroit, 1973); Maurice S. Friedman, *Martin Buber: The Life of Dialogue*, 2nd ed. (New York, 1960), which includes a long bibliography; Malcolm L. Diamond, *Martin Buber, Jewish Existentialist* (New York, 1960); Arthur A. Cohen, *Martin Buber* (London, 1957); Michael Theunissen, *Der Andere: Studien zur Sozialontologie der Gegenwart* (Berlin, 1965), and 2nd ed. with new preface (Berlin, 1977), Paul Arthur Schilpp and Maurice Friedman, eds., *Martin Buber* (Stuttgart, 1963), and in English translation as *The Philosophy of Martin Buber* (La Salle, Ill., 1967) (quotations cited here follow the English translation unless otherwise indicated); Simon Maringer, *Martin Bubers Metaphysik der Dialogik im Zusammenhang neuerer philosophischer und theologischer Strömungen* (Cologne, 1936), especially p. 122. Also, philosophically indebted to Buber are, for example: Will Herberg, *Judaism and Modern Man* (New York, 1965), viiff.; Emil L. Fackenheim, *Quest for Past and Future: Essays in Jewish Theology* (Bloomington, Ind., 1968), 5ff.

hard Casper's *Das dialogische Denken*,[2] have relied primarily on Buber's article "On the History of the Dialogical Principle," published in 1954.[3] Neither Casper nor others consulted the important archival corpus that was made available to the public after Buber's death in 1965.[4] This wealth of previously unexamined material makes possible a new understanding of *I and Thou* based on a knowledge of the author's own approach to, or his way toward, the book. Now we can follow Buber's growing dissatisfaction with his earlier philosophy, which had been based on a striving for unity and the "realization of the unconditional" of the Unconditioned, his shift toward intermediary ideas that were different from those of his early philosophy but not yet those of *I and Thou*, and, finally, his first glimpses of the dialogical principle. Most important, these materials permit a close observation of the final stages in the development of the dialogical thinking of *I and Thou*: the influential contacts with others moving in the same direction, as well as the significantly different versions through which the work passed on its way to the only form that readers have previously known—the published version.

Buber's thirteen-page spiritual autobiography of 1954 undoubtedly provides the most significant clues from which to begin any attempt to trace the genesis of *I and Thou*. There he relates that he had formulated a plan for the book in 1916 and that his new direction had grown out of his interpretation of Hasidism. In 1919 he had already described true Jewish teaching as a two-directional, reciprocal relationship between the human I and the divine Thou: In the fall of that year he wrote a first rough draft of *I and Thou*. Then, according to his testimony, there ensued an interruption of two years during which he concentrated solely on Hasidism and read scarcely any philosophical

---

2. Bernhard Casper, *Das dialogische Denken: Eine Untersuchung der religions-philosophischen Bedeutung Franz Rosenzweigs, Ferdinand Ebners und Martin Bubers* (Freiburg i.Br., 1967).

3. Martin Buber wrote "Zur Geschichte des dialogischen Prinzips" in Jerusalem in 1953; the work was first published as an epilogue to *Schriften über das dialogische Prinzip* (Heidelberg, 1954), and was also included in Martin Buber's *Werke*, vol. 1 (Munich/Heidelberg, 1962), 291–305. Maurice Friedman added this essay as an afterword to *Between Man and Man* 2nd ed. (New York, 1967), 209–224.

4. Martin Buber died on June 13, 1965, at the age of 87. In accordance with his will, the Martin Buber Archive (MBA) has been made public and belongs to the Jewish National and University Library in Jerusalem.

works. His activities at the time were part of a larger spiritual asceticism to which he was committed. Thus, he records that he read the books of his forerunners and contemporaries in dialogical thinking "belatedly." The works he mentioned in this context are: Hermann Cohen's *Religion of Reason from the Sources of Judaism* (1919), Franz Rosenzweig's *The Star of Redemption* (1921), and Ferdinand Ebner's *Das Wort und die Geistigen Realitäten* (The Word and the Spiritual Realities, 1921). Buber gave his own thoughts their final form in the spring of 1922, after having first presented them in January and February 1922 in a course at the Freies Jüdisches Lehrhaus in Frankfurt, which was then under Rosenzweig's direction.

There is a striking similarity between passages in the works by Rosenzweig and Ebner, both of which appeared in 1921; in turn, Buber's *I and Thou*, which appeared in December 1922, has points in common with the two earlier works. The significance of these parallels became clear only after examining certain correspondence between Buber and Rosenzweig concerning the galley sheets of *I and Thou*.[5] The exchange of letters shows unmistakably an active relationship between Buber and Rosenzweig at the time *I and Thou* was being written, and it encouraged me to pursue what has proved to be a most rewarding search for other pertinent sources.

The new material supports Buber's testimony that already from 1918 he was working intermittently on themes for *I and Thou*. The evidence from 1918 to 1921 is, however, rudimentary and includes only a short plan written in 1918 and mention of this work in letters from 1919 and 1920. No evidence of the 1919 manuscript has been discovered. The material makes clear that Buber's philosophical point of departure was not the coining of the terms I-Thou and I-It, as so many have assumed, but rather a grappling with religious issues that required abandoning philosophical monism and embracing existential confrontation. Initially he spoke of *I and Thou* as "Prolegomena to a Philosophy of Religion."[6]

---

5. This correspondence is housed at the MBA. An important part of it has been published by Grete Schaeder.

6. The name "prolegomena" was undoubtedly inspired by Kant. Buber's great interest in Kant's treatise can be seen in the lectures he delivered at the

An early plan, which Buber dated February 5, 1918, outlines a work on "The Confronted and the Between" ("Das Gegenüber und das Dazwischen"), which was to have been a book or an essay. An analysis of this document, together with Buber's correspondence regarding his work, provides a much clearer picture of the intellectual origins of *I and Thou* and of the inception of dialogical thinking.

The majority of the new material, however, dates from 1922, the period in which the book was born out of an "overpowering inspiration." On the basis of all the new evidence, I submit that Buber's lecture course, "Religion as Presence," given between January 15 and March 12, 1922, was his attempt to present the themes of *I and Thou* orally, before committing them to final, written form. Two typewritten copies of the lectures exist in excellent condition.[7] And indeed, a comparison of parallels in the lectures and in *I and Thou* reveals that they are, in fact, an early version of the book; the stenographer's manuscript served as the basis for the writing of *I and Thou*. One is thus afforded the rare opportunity to trace the stages of a book's composition, in this case,

---

Hebrew University in 1943, later presented in essay form as "Das Problem des Menschen," in *Werke* vol. 1, p. 328, and in English as "What is Man?" in *Between Man and Man*). When describing his boyhood thoughts on the infinity and finitude of space and time, Buber commented: "Salvation came to the fifteen year old boy in a book, Kant's *Prolegomena to all Future Metaphysics*." To the best of my knowledge, Buber's prolegomena first received the title *Ich und Du* formally on May 2, 1922, in the contract with the publisher. Prior to that date and even later, Buber referred to the work as a "Prolegomena to a Philosophy of Religion" or "Religion as Presence"; the title of the lectures at the Lehrhaus may well have been the planned title for the future book. On January 2, 1922, when sending "Der Grosse Maggid" to Richard Beer-Hofmann, Buber wrote: "I hope to be able to follow soon with the prolegomena to another work, which is more important to me than any other" (MBA, MS Var. 350/83).

7. The stenograph is mentioned in two unpublished writings: in a postcard from Buber to Rosenzweig dated December 18, 1921 (MBA, MS Var. 350/59), in which Buber writes, "And something else: It would be good if someone reliable could write it down. Do you know of anyone?" She is mentioned again in a letter from Rosenzweig to Buber of January 15, 1922, in which Rosenzweig apparently enclosed her bill and praised her (see infra, p. 176). On the existence of the stenogram, see also Grete Schaeder, ed., *Martin Buber: Briefwechsel aus sieben Jahrzehnten*, vol. 2 (Heidelberg, 1973), 98.

to note its amplification and remolding and the shift in Buber's ter-minology during the months after the conclusion of the lectures.[8]

Although the lectures "Religion as Presence" are mentioned by Buber in his article "On the History of the Dialogical Principle" and by Rosenzweig in his letters, unfortunately no serious study of them had been undertaken until now. They are being published for the first time in English in the present volume. Although they evidence a shift toward the concept of confrontation, their contents tend to represent an intermediary point between the thought of *Daniel* (1913) and *I and Thou*.

Furthermore, the lectures suggest the impact on Buber of the Aus-trian thinker Ferdinand Ebner—whose influence has not been seriously considered by any scholar other than Ebner himself. The new historical data, although admittedly not abundant, provide a basis for my con-tention that Buber's encounter with Ebner's thought may have marked a turning point in the early stages of the writing of *I and Thou*. One finds that the similarities between Buber's lectures and Ebner's writings are not merely structural and thematic but also linguistic.

Most interesting is the new historical material concerning Buber's relationship with Rosenzweig during 1922, that is, precisely during the period of the final stage of development of *I and Thou*.[9] Buber's cor-respondence attests to crucial meetings and conversations with Rosen-zweig prior to the publication of the book. The active relationship between the two had its inception at a meeting on December 4, 1921.[10] A correspondence immediately ensued, during the course of which the lecture series was arranged. Subsequently, the two were in frequent

---

8. Nahum Glatzer, "The Frankfort Lehrhaus" (in *Leo Baeck Institute Year-book*, vol. 1, 1956), p. 112, seems to suggest that Buber was writing *I and Thou* while lecturing, whereas Buber is quite specific that he *first* lectured and *then* wrote. Glatzer says, "at the time Buber was writing his philosophical work *I and Thou* and agreed to make this the basis for the Lehrhaus lecture, to start together with the Hasidic text seminar in January 1922." Buber, in "Zur Ges-chichte des dialogischen Prinzips," in *Werke*, vol. 1, p. 298, stated that he gave it final form *after* the course. See also, Franz Rosenzweig, *Briefe* (Berlin, 1935), 437 n. 1, which says that *I and Thou* was developed out of "Religion as Pres-ence," and also 462: "As he presented orally the first volume of his five-volume life's work in January and February 1922—before he wrote it down—now he will present the second one."

9. See infra, p. 208.

10. Rosenzweig, *Briefe*, pp. 46off.

contact: Rosenzweig attending Buber's course, and Buber calling on
Rosenzweig regularly. Before beginning his course, Buber read *The Star
of Redemption*, an exposition of Rosenzweig's theological system that
included his treatment of dialogical thinking.

It is the correspondence from the summer of 1922, when both were
ill and could not meet personally, that sheds the greatest light on the
sort of conversations they had, the themes they discussed, and the
nature of their relationship. The letters of August 1922 deal with the
theme of a second volume to follow *I and Thou*, which was first to be
presented as a course at the Lehrhaus during the following school year,
winter 1922/1923.

The correspondence from September 1922 deals with the galley
sheets of *I and Thou*, which Buber had asked Rosenzweig to critique.
Rosenzweig's letters raise a number of serious questions regarding the
systematic structure of the book. This entire correspondence leaves no
doubt that Buber's book on dialogue was written in the midst of a most
significant living dialogue on its themes.

The Martin Buber Archive of the Jewish National and University
Library in Jerusalem holds two carbon copies of the stenographer's
transcription of Buber's eight lectures, clearly typed from shorthand
notes.[11] The copies were brought to Palestine by Buber in 1938; the
original, which has not been found, was presumably used by Buber in
preparing *Ich und Du* and probably contained the corrections, deletions,
and additions that eventuated in the final version of the book. Thus,
the bulk of Buber's revisions are lost. Nevertheless, one of the copies
has several corrections, which have been identified by Margot Cohn,
who worked with Buber for years, as being in his own handwriting.
Buber's corrections, approximately twenty in the Lecture Four and
fewer in Lecture Seven, include several changes that are crucial to the
development of his thinking. The copies have additional corrections,
apparently made by readers of the manuscript. We have evidence that
the transcription was read by Ernst Simon and that it was in Franz
Rosenzweig's home in 1922;[12] one may perhaps assume that it was read
and commented upon by additional associates of Buber.

The eight lectures comprising "Religion as Presence" can be divided, with regard to their importance to the writing of *I and Thou*,

---

11. "Religion als Gegenwart," in MBA, MS Var. 350-/B 29.
12. Schaeder, *Briefwechsel*, vol. 2, p. 98, and infra, p. 181.

into two groups: Whereas one group was scarcely used, the other, containing much parallel material, became the very source of the book.

The lectures of secondary importance are the first, second, third, and seventh, of which only limited portions were incorporated in the book. The first three lectures, involving Buber's criticism of the philosophical trends, form a unit of sorts. From their critical point of departure, it becomes apparent that Buber had sharpened his thoughts in a living debate with such predecessors as Otto, Schleiermacher, and Scheler.

The fourth, fifth, sixth, and eighth lectures are the source of *I and Thou*. The fourth and the fifth lectures, dealing with "the world of It" and "the world of Thou," constitute parts of Book One of *I and Thou*. The end of the fifth and the sixth and the eighth lectures, involving Buber's treatment of God, the absolute presence, comprise segments of Book Three. In the way Buber developed his ideas in the lectures, and can discern an order comparable to the progressive rungs of ascension in mystical thought. At its base is the It-world, the world of knowledge, experiencing, and using, without which we cannot live, although living within it is not real living. Over and above it stands the Thou-world, the moments of real confrontation that are the height of human existence and that exist only when rooted in the Absolute Thou. This opposition of two worlds, an It-world and a Thou-world, tends to give Buber's work an entirely different emphasis: Whereas the completed book stresses *relation*, the lectures exhibit a much stronger *metaphysical* character.

In Lectures Five and Six he speaks of "the difficulty in constructing a Thou-world." Thou-moments, which are otherwise disconnected and transient, gain strength only when anchored in the Absolute Thou. Buber is thus compelled, in Lecture Seven, to return to a discussion of religion as presence, as opposed to other understandings of religion in which God becomes an It or a He. Finally, in Lecture Eight, he reaches the culmination of the ascending structure of his lectures when he describes the absolute community of believers whose center is God, thus uniting his religious and social ideas.

One of the most rewarding insights of this study was to discern the impact of the audience on Buber: At times it helped him to formulate his thinking in difficult matters. For example in Lecture Six, Buber was asked: "Can I say instead of Thou 'my other I'?" To this Buber replied: "What you say is not at all what this depends on. It does not depend on what you call the Thou. When I say 'I' I mean something quite different from when I say 'Thou.' So if you disarrange these very clear, meaningful basic words, it seems that what is meant loses something of its immediate clarity. For what it is to say 'I' and 'Thou' we know from our whole life with a distinctness that we could never gather from another person's words." Very probably encounters of this sort helped Buber to crystallize this thought and penetrate deeper into the meaning of the dialogue. He later placed the phrase expressed here—"basic words"—at the beginning of his book.

The title "Religion as Presence" for lectures on *I and Thou* appears surprising. One may be tempted to say that Buber wished to offer a religion for all men at all times, based on His presence. And, indeed, he explained his understanding of religion as presence at the outset of Lecture One. Critics whose own social orientation led them to interpret Buber as, first and foremost, a social philosopher, have assumed that this thought developed in the order in which *I and Thou* develops, that Buber's point of departure was, as the book would suggest, the social idea of overcoming the I-It in favor of life rooted in the I-Thou relation. They may, therefore, consider Book Three of *I and Thou*, in which God and religion play a central role, less essential to the work as a whole. The present research reveals, however, that the social aspects of *I and Thou* were, in fact, additions to a work whose original and primary concern was the attempt, prompted by the disillusion with mysticism, to reformulate the concept and position of religion.

As we shall see in Part Two of the present volume, manuscript evidence shows that the attempted reformulation was begun in 1918, or, if we follow Buber's testimony, as early as 1916. The meaning given to "religion as presence" in the lectures of early 1922 nonetheless indicates that Buber's break with his earlier mystical approach to religion was gradual; some elements—such as the preoccupation with the mystical experience—have been abandoned; others are yet apparent.

The milieu of the first decades of the twentieth century, in which Buber undertook his reformulation, has been characterized by his biographer, Hans Kohn,[13] as one in which attempts were made to restore religion to its prior status of autonomous supremacy. From its position in the Middle Ages as a force that ordered all of life, religion had been reduced in the Age of Enlightenment to one of many disparate, interdependent spheres that comprise the atomized life of modern man. The endeavor to return religion to its paramount position is, for example, apparent in Georg Simmel's book *Die Religion*, which appeared in 1906

---

13. Kohn, *Martin Buber*, pp. 213–214, 352.

in a series edited by Buber.[14] Viewing religion as the highest expression of social unity, Simmel maintained that modern man, torn by conflicting norms and values, must fix religion "as the deciding factor in life."

In defining religion as "presence," Buber, too, lamented the loss of the depth and richness of religion, as it became an auxiliary of other spheres of existence. He attacked, in particular, those schoools of thought that view religion as an aid to man in his biological survival, in the sociological persistence of the group, and in the achievement of national unity as depicted in Dostoevsky's *Devils*.[15] Regarding this point, Buber was even critical of Kant, who posited religion as a means to ethics. In the first lecture he decries that "religion," which is but a function of other spheres, as the shattering of man's spiritual life into autonomous and often contradictory realms, as a "suicide of the spirit." In its place he advocates "religion as presence" as the source of meaning for all of life. True religion cannot be that whose growth and diminution is dependent on something other; it must be the determining absolute. Clearly in this context, Buber is not depicting religion in its historic form; he, in fact, criticizes historic configurations of religion as the transference of God into the It-world. Nor does he even describe man's relation to absolute, but the Absolute itself. Religion as presence, as that which precedes all life, can, in the end, be identified only with God.

The treatment of religion as presence in the lectures, like Buber's earlier interest in mysticism, is thus an attempt to overcome the narrow rational and functional interpretations of religion that prevailed in the nineteenth and early twentieth centuries. In "Religion as Presence," however, Buber abandons his earlier advocacy of "experiencing God" and denounces the pursuit of moments of psychological or mystical ecstasy: Buber himself, then,—he who inserts precious experiences into Being—the target of his own criticism. Continuing a theme already taken up in "Herut," he admonishes those who tear reality into moments of the soul, adding that "of all the fictions made of religion, this is the worst." Truth lies not in mystical union, for one can never achieve complete union, but in encounter.

Secondly, Buber shifts the emphasis from his former interest in the pantheistic Unconditioned Divine of Far Eastern religions to the bib-

---

14. Georg Simmel, *Die Religion* (Frankfurt a. M., 1906), 8.
15. Kohn, *Martin Buber*, p. 177.

lical God of the burning bush, the *ehyeh asher ehyeh*, whom he calls the Absolute Thou. It is with the Absolute Thou that religion as presence is identified. Here the break with mysticism is less apparent. Religion is described as that which cannot be past but only present—just as he later depicts the Eternal Thou as ever-present. Employing Spinoza's definition of substance, he speaks of religion as presence as "that which is in itself"; conditioned by no other, it is neither preceded nor brought into being. And taking an Augustinian approach, he asserts that religion "is not only in man's soul, but that in which man dwells"; in the same vein, he states in *I and Thou* that "nothing is next to God, but all is in him."

For Buber it is typical that a pantheistic view is compatible with a concept of God as Eternal Confronter, as the Absolute Thou. For Buber in 1922, God is both the Confronter and the all-encompassing and ever-present; religion as presence is an eternal reality for all men at all times.

Buber's particular attempt to return religion to its prior position of supremacy did not go uncriticized, especially inasmuch as his concept of religion lacked clarity; he did not specify his demands. Already in a letter of September 19, 1919, the same year in which Buber's "*Herut*: On Youth and Religion" was published, Samuel Hugo Bergman wrote to him: "I see the central meaning of the religious now as before. But do things become religious by our writing about them and by our debating them? And what did we do besides this until now? And moreover in a foreign tongue [i.e., not Hebrew]!"[16]

Shortly before Buber began his course, Rosenzweig—who disliked the term religion—noted that for Buber's audience, religion, that vague "foxhole" with its many exits for escape, may be preferable to the "exitless lion's den," God. But he perceived that the course entitled "Religion as Presence" would, in fact, deal with *God* as presence. His discernment is confirmed in Lecture Seven, where Buber explicitly identifies religion with God.

Perhaps the clearest and most forceful expression of the themes of the first three lectures is found in an article that Buber wrote the following year:

> As often as religion has appeared once again in history, there was also in it a force that—not in a doubtful manner like the profane forces,

---

16. Schaeder, *Briefwechsel*, vol. 2, p. 58.

but with the appearance of the highest legitimacy—diverted man from God. That it thereby enjoyed a great success was caused for the most part by the fact that it is far more comfortable to have to do with religion than to have to do with God who sends one out of home and fatherland into restless wandering. In addition, religion has all kinds of aesthetic refreshments to offer its adherents, whereas God transforms for man even formation and vision in a sacrifice that is offered, to be sure, by a joyful but not by an enjoying heart. . . . But either religion is a reality, rather *the* reality, namely the *whole* existence that unites all that is partial; or it is a phantom of the covetous human soul, and then it would be right promptly and completely to replace its rituals by art, its commands by ethics, and its revelations by science.[17]

The present edition is composed of two parts. Part One presents the first English translation of Buber's lectures, "Religion as Presence." Part Two consists of an examination of the history of the development of Buber's seminal work, *I and Thou.*

---

17. "Reply to My Critics," in Schilpp and Friedman, *The Philosophy of Martin Buber*, p. 742.

CHRONOLOGICAL
TABLE

1916	Brief sketch mentioned by Buber (not extant).
February 5, 1918	A plan for a work: "The Confronted and the Between" ("Das Gegenüber und das Dazwischen").
1919	Rough draft mentioned by Buber (not extant).
1919–1920	Buber's letters speak of a prolegomena, a work that can be identified with *I and Thou* (*Ich und Du*).
1919	Hermann Cohen's work *Religion of Reason from the Sources of Judaism* was published (*Religion der Vernunft aus den Quellen des Judentums*).
1920	Parts of Ferdinand Ebner's book *The Word and the Spiritual Realities* (*Das Wort und die geistigen Realitäten*) appeared in *Der Brenner*.
March 1921	Franz Rosenzweig's *The Star of Redemption* (*Der Stern der Erlösung*) appeared.
April 1921	Susman asks Buber to review *The Star* (*Der Stern*) in *Der Jude*.
September 1921	Ebner's work, *The Word and the Spiritual Realities* (*Das Wort und die geistigen Realitäten*) appeared.

(For the convenience of the reader the titles of the books are given in English first.)

Fall 1921	The "answer" on the train: Never refer to God in the third person.
December 4, 1921	Rosenzweig visits Buber in Heppenheim; a friendship ensues.
From December 6, 1921	Arrangements are made for Buber to teach a course at the Lehrhaus: "Religion as Presence" ("Religion als Gegenwart").
January 4, 1922	Buber has by now read *The Star* (*Der Stern*).
January 15–March 12, 1922	Buber's weekly Lectures "Religion as Presence" ("Religion als Gegenwart"), an early version of *I and Thou* (*Ich und Du*).
April 1922	Buber begins negotiations with the publisher of *I and Thou* (*Ich und Du*).
April 19, 1922	Buber visits Rosenzweig with Ernst Simon to discuss with them "Religion as Presence" ("Religion als Gegenwart").
May 1922	The handwritten manuscript of *I and Thou* (*Ich und Du*) written (date in notebook).
July 15, 1922	Publisher's acknowledgment of receipt of first part of *I and Thou* (*Ich und Du*).
July–August 1922	Correspondence with Rosenzweig on the volume to follow *I and Thou*, "The Primary Forms of Religious Life" (*Ich und Du*, "Die Grundformen des religiösen Lebens"), also planned first as a series in the Lehrhaus.
September 1922	Buber sends the galley sheets of *I and Thou* (*Ich und Du*) to Rosenzweig and to Florens Christian Rang for criticism.
December 1922	Publication of *I and Thou* (*Ich und Du*).

PART ONE:

The Lectures

LECTURE ONE

January 15, 1922

Dr. Franz Rosenzweig wishes to remind the participants, in the name of the Lehrhaus and also on behalf of the speaker, that they are requested to let their teachers know about any questions that arise immediately or that occur to them later. Questions may be asked orally or in written form at all lectures.

Religion as an Absolute

Already, from the request that has just been made in my name as well as in that of the Lehrhaus, our concern here emerges. It is not a communication, so to speak, from above to below, but a collaboration, a way[1] on which we will set out and travel together. It is a reconnaissance, a way of exploration. Together we shall explore the question of the extent to which there is religion as presence.[2] That is, religion not as

---

1. "Way" (*Weg*) is a very important concept of Buber and recurs in many of his writings. Its meaning is very close to that of Tao. See Buber's "The Spirit of the Orient and Judaism" and "*Herut*," in *On Judaism* (New York, 1967), 59ff., 162.
2. Cf. Buber, "*Herut*" (1919) and "The Holy Way," in *On Judaism*, pp. 151–155, 109.

remembrance and hope but as lived presence. This question cannot be posed for exploration, cannot be undertaken with respect to this age in which we are living, however urgently this particular age poses this question for us; rather, we must necessarily pose this question for all time. We cannot ask to what extent religion is presence in this present of ours; rather, we must ask to what extent religion is absolute presence, absolute present that can never become past and must therefore become present and be present in every time and for every time. For otherwise this question would be placed in the problematics of our time and again in those of every time; it would always have to be asked anew and could never really be answered. Only by asking it absolutely, and thus for all time, do we ask it completely, once and for all. We must ask ourselves: First, to what extent is religion absolute present that can never become past? To what extent is religion a presence that cannot be limited by any other and that therefore cannot be superseded by any other? Second, this means, at the same time: To what extent is religion unconditional actuality that nevertheless does not border on anything actual, does not stand out against anything actual, cannot be corrected by anything actual—but that is unconditionally actual of itself, in itself? And third, to what extent is religion presence for everyone? To what extent is it something that is there for everyone?

I would like once more to try to make these three things plain to you. First, I said that we are concerned with the extent to which religion is a presence that cannot become past. All presence, as we know it, must, by the very fact that it is present, become the past in the next moment, the next present. This occurs because all presence is a concept of the soul; every presence is a moment of the human soul that is followed by another moment. An absolute present that did not become past would have to be one that did not merely exist in man as a moment of his soul, but one in which man stood, something in which man lived, yet which he could fulfill only in his inner being, by the dedication of his entire inner being.

Second, I said that presence in this sense means that we are concerned here with what is most actual, something that cannot be limited by anything else that is actual; that does not border on any actuality of the actualities known to us; that does not stand out against it, so as

20

to be superseded or corrected by it. For all actuality that we know is actual precisely because it stands out against other actual things. It is precisely because of the borderlines that divide it from other things that it preserves its own actuality, which is conditioned thus and not otherwise. But here we are concerned with something that does not have its place beside other actual things as one of the component parts of a collective actuality, with something that is purely and simply actual, that cannot be corrected, superseded, by other actual things. We are concerned, then, with something absolutely actual.

And in the third place: Presence in this sense must be for all. It cannot be intended that somewhere one part of humanity, one division of spiritual beings, possesses this actuality, lays claim to it, as it were, has a monopoly on it by virtue of its chosenness, by virtue of its greater participation in the spirit. Rather, the meaning of an absolute presence requires that it be everywhere there is spirit—not that men find it out of some special spiritual talent but that every man can unlock for himself the power of the phenomenon "spirit" in which he himself is.

Question: Then one is not religious in the same way one is musical?

Answer: Quite right, it is not a gift among other gifts that one has or does not have. One is not religious in the same way as one is artistic or even in the same way as one is moral.

Because religion is unlocked for all, it is a phenomenon upon which an invisible humanity is founded. This is the third result of the fact that, and the extent to which, religion is absolute presence. I said: an invisible humanity. For this is the only way and the only possibility of conceiving of humanity, that the phenomenon of the spirit in which humanity stands expresses itself in an absolute actuality and presence that is in each of us and that can be unlocked in each of us.

Question: Is one religious if one is moral?

Answer: I shall speak of this at length later. I, certainly, am not of this opinion; at least I do not believe that whoever is moral is thereby religious.

Question: But is being religious not also at the same time the same as being moral?

Answer: In any case I would like to dispute that whoever is moral is thereby religious and has thereby unlocked that which is religious in himself. Only in this sense are we permitted to speak of being religious, not in the sense of a privilege that one has and another has not.

I said before that we cannot put the question to our age alone. Rather, we must pose it in relation to time as such. And yet, in posing the question, we pose it from the standpoint of our time, conditioned by the fact of this age with all its limitations. And, therefore, we must start by asking to what extent a wholly specific attitude toward religion or a particularly intensified attitude toward religion makes itself known in this age. This attitude, which, it seems to me, corresponds to the character of our time as that of being on the edge. Or perhaps one could say more vividly, as a time of being in a narrow hollow, of being in the deepest trough between two upward curling worlds of the word, of law, of world-possession.

Religion as Relative

To this age, which has this character—one could also call it the character of silence—that character of baited breath, in this sense I speak of the trough. To this age corresponds a definite attitude—or an attitude that is intensified in a definite manner—toward religion, an attitude one might, at first glance, call the striving toward relativization, that is, toward making everything that in itself is or can be unconditioned, conditioned, or letting it appear conditioned. But probably this would not yet be a sufficiently accurate designation. Relativization is something that necessarily clings to religion at all times. All religion, to the extent that it portrays itself in time, includes relativization in the sense in which we may perhaps say that actuality is a relativization of God. In that sense we may probably say that religion in its temporal manifestation necessarily includes a relativization of our relation to the absolute. This is not what we mean by speaking of relativization in this age; rather, another tendency makes itself felt here with particular acuity, specifically in all the domains that we may (in order to set them off from this general fact of relativization) perhaps designate as functionalization. I use "function" here in the mathematical sense. Thus all religion is grasped, or an attempt is made to grasp it, not as an independent quantity but as something dependent on another quantity, increasing and decreasing along with it. We are dealing, then, with a tendency to undermine the independence of the religious sphere. It is a matter—in all domains, as I will try to demonstrate—of robbing religion of its independence, of its autonomous totality, and of making it into a dependent function of another sphere, one of the spheres of the cosmos.[3]

Evolution and Religion

Perhaps the sphere that in our times has pressed its claim most strongly in this functional sense is biology. Biology demands that religion should not be something that exists in its own right but, rather, that it be a function of life. Religious concepts would then be among the means by which life preserves and elevates itself. The individuals and groups that have religious concepts would develop and use them in order to assert themselves in life against other individuals and groups and to elevate their own existence within life. In no other domain, perhaps, does this biologism of our time assert itself so clearly and emphatically. I would like to add here that religious concepts as a result become a fiction to be used primarily as a means of asserting life, heightening life. Here I cannot, whether in response to questions from you now or afterwards, discuss in detail the various forms of relativization or functionalization of which I speak. But I should like to say this much now: This degradation—I cannot put it any other way—this degradation of religious concepts to fictions useful to life is a process leading to a real suicide of the spirit.

Spirit builds up its world by virtue of the fact that it is rooted in it. If it did not know at the deepest level that it is rooted in a world, if it did not know at the deepest level that what it produces is precisely

---

3. Cf. Georg Simmel, *Die Religion*, 2nd ed. (Frankfurt a. M., 1912), 87–88. This book was published in the series *Die Gesellschaft* edited by Buber.

that from which it emerges, then all that it creates would be caprice and falsehood. Precisely the fact that spirit cannot make anything save what it discovers, that it cannot create anything save what it finds, elevates it as a phenomenon of all time and all space, as one lifted out of the conditionality of times and spaces. This is because spirit is not a phenomenon of a definite phase of cosmic evolution, such that, at some definite moment in time, spirit evolved from cosmic matter or cosmic matter unfolded spirit. Rather, spirit is in truth, and the spirit that is merely unfolds itself in these forms of spirit that cosmically have become. I say that spirit inevitably overstrains itself on this its primal phenomenon; it treats its highest concepts as fictions in the service of life, which many may thus use and manipulate, which are at the mercy of his caprice, and which he can now spin, and spin out, and tear apart at whim or according to the demands of life. Of course, this relativization of which we are speaking here contains a peculiar paradox that may well console us even beyond its problematics. For if, as the representatives of this biologistic theory of religion intend, religious concepts should be recognized as fictions useful to life, then they would no longer be usable for life. For they are only useful to life since they do not appear as fictions. They aid the preservation, assertion, and elevation of life through man's believing in them unconditionally and thereby being able to concentrate his strength in a manner that would be impossible for him without this belief and to give himself to the thing he wills with a fervor that he would not be able to muster without this power of belief. Thus biologism contains its own annulment. Biologism, biologism in the theory of religion, annuls itself. And perhaps we can already say at this point that the biological sphere, too, already teaches us that religion is not something that stands in this sphere and receives its laws from it, but, on the contrary, religion is something that must determine the laws for this seemingly so autocratic biological life. Religion stands at the edge of life and in the face of life. It does not speak out of life but to it, commanding not as something that stands at the edge outside life but as something that stands before life and as something that at the same time encompasses it in an embrace. For this reason, religion determines the border, the edge, the wall, the dam beyond which life may not extend its power.

Nationalism and Religion

From the biological sphere to the one that I suppose I may call the social, from the claim of life to the claim of society and community, leads a way that may easily be taken in at a glance. These, again, are spheres that naturally touch each other at many points, so that those of society and community appear completely embedded in that of life, yet nevertheless they confront it with their particular aspects and their particular demands. The relativization of religion in this domain means that religious concepts are, as I suppose the expression goes, a projection of social life, a projection of the life of the social group. In the history of religion one expresses this by saying: A group makes its particularity—its particular life and its particular claim—into a god by projecting this claim onto the superhuman sphere.

This god is nothing other than, so to speak, the personified consciousness of this social group. That is how the history of religion expresses it. In the theory of religion, the same thing is expressed by Dostoevsky. In his revolutionary novel *The Possessed*, he says in one place that the nations have their gods, each nation its own god, and in the unconditional devotion to the god, in the absolute intolerance toward others, lies each nation's strength and vitality. When the nations fought with one another over their gods, the gods of these nations, so to speak, fought with one another, each one relentlessly asserting and maintaining his right and his existence against all others. Basically, this particular way of relativizing means simply that man, who stands probably by empirical necessity in a group, participates in the life of his group and cannot separate himself from it without separating himself from a vital element of his own self. Precisely with the kind of nationhood Dostoevsky describes, it is absolutely clear that this empirical, historical necessity of human life is made into an inevitability, into something that no longer forms man's freedom but becomes his barrier. Man, in this instance, can go only so far as his group allows, for the group is now not something that stands beside something else and can demand its right as other things demand theirs. Rather, the group is ruled by the god that demands that it should serve him against all other groups and gods in an unconditional and never-ending struggle, in a never-wearying striving to annihilate other groups and their spirits. This terrible limitation of man and the accompanying relativization of religion mean at the same time an absolutization of the social group, an absolutization that annuls for all time the idea of an invisible humanity. There is now no humanity; there is no possible humanity. And therefore there can be in truth no united spirit because there exists no spirit that is divided into absolute groups, in which each has its own untranslatable, untransferable nature that can only be expressed in battle. Groups can unite with one another; groups that have group gods cannot.[4]

Question: Can one express that by saying that religiosity has replaced religion? Can one express social relativization in this way?

Answer: That I would not like to say. The distinction between religiosity and religion, which is very important to me personally, belongs in that other sphere of which I first spoke, to which we shall have occasion to return, and which is the real theme of these lectures. It belongs to the sphere of the necessary, the historically, temporally necessary relativization of religion. Religiosity always relativizes itself—and must necessarily relativize itself—to religion. For to this extent it has duration and represents human continuity. If it did not relativize itself, men would be enclosed, each in his own religiosity, and would have nothing to do with one another, and would have nothing to do in time or in the continuity of generations. They would have something to do with one another in everything, and in this last, strongest thing they would have nothing to do with one another. Thus I do not mean this necessary relativization of religiosity; rather, I mean the specific striving to grasp religion merely as an exponent of existence, as the assertion of social groups, not that religion is a social phenomenon—it has to be that—that represents itself again and again by a

---

4. Buber developed this idea in a separate article, "The Gods of the Nations and God," in *Israel and the World*, 2nd ed. (New York, 1965), 195–213 (first published in 1948). In this article Buber referred to the nineteenth-century Jewish philosopher Nachman Krochmal and utilized the idea that he had developed earlier in the lectures in relation to *The Possessed*.

social phenomenon but that religion is nothing but a function of social life.

Question: Then we end up at the same point as before with biologism?

Answer: Not quite, the difference being that the concept of life is not individualistic but completely general. Individuals and groups are bound up in it; it is life itself, so to speak, that asserts itself. You are right, there is indeed a parallelism. But the same would probably be true for the other spheres of which I must now speak.

Culture and Religion

The sphere of which I now wish to speak perhaps borders more closely on that of the sociological than on that of the biological. I mean the sphere of so-called culture, that is, the claim that one can call cultural-historical and cultural-political. In this sphere, religion is understood as only one function of culture, forming a part of this culture as a specific manifestation. Within the many expressions of cultural life there is also this one: that man makes religious world views for himself. So that you will see most clearly what I mean, I will remind you of a historical view,[5] quite well known today, according to which cultures are something like organisms: Both come into being and pass away according to definite law, and both have their definite phases of life. These phases of life are the same with all cultures, and so one culture after another goes through the cycle of development. When the culture of one nationality or group of nations has reached the end of its development, some other nationality or group of nations has already begun building up a culture, and so forth. I suppose that this process will continue as long as there are still uncultivated nations and groups of nations. It is not that I want to polemicize against this view, although

---

5. This may be a popular description of Oswald Spengler, *Der Untergang des Abendlandes*, vol. 1 (Vienna, 1918).

I have a great deal against it. I should merely like to speak about what place religion has in this view. Really, none. That is, religion has a place in this view only insofar as it is, so to speak, static, insofar as it has developed a definite dogma and a definite ritualism so that the whole of religious life has put itself into these forms of thought and action and no longer lives for itself. This means that only those epochs in historical religion that were not creative epochs can have a place in this cultural-historical configuration, in other words, not those epochs that represent man's deepest consciousness of the meaning of the self and of God. There is no way in which those epochs can be pressed into this world view, into this view of world history. For in every age it has happened that when a culture seems to have reached the end of its development, and when it seems that one must appeal to another rising culture and wait for its works, suddenly, from some nameless source, from what is unforeseen and unmediated, a force arises that changes the face of the earth, the face of history: the religious force. Of all the so-called revolutionary forces, religion is the greatest revolutionary force in history. Even if everything else could be fitted into this scheme of a foreseeable development after the model of the organism—of the coming into being and passing way of organisms—the religious force could not be fitted in; its world is not foreseeable. Even if one knows enough of the history of cultures to be able to say that we are now at a certain point in our cultural development and now such and such will happen, this force need only arise to overturn all such calculations. Thus religion is by its very nature, by its innermost nature, something that does not always fit in. One could also say here that just as religion did not receive its law from life but must dictate law to life, just as it did not receive its law from society but must prescribe it for society: Your rights and laws extend to this point. You can tell a person, up to this point, how to live. But beyond that he is taken up into my being—that's how matters stand here. In the face of culture, religion again and again speaks its culture-critical, culture-annulling, and culture-renewing word. It is not that a culture replaces another; it is rather that cultures are reawakened again and again by the religious force.

I have to close for today, but I should like you to think over those things for next time, so that I will not have to go into so much detail with the next sphere, for I do not want to dwell too long on the negative side nor on the premises of this age. I should like to indicate to you what the other spheres are: the aesthetic, that is, the concept that religion is a free artistic creation; the ethical, that is, the concept that religion is but a necessary superstructure of the ethics of moral life, the formulated absolute sanction of the ethos; the logical, that is, the concept that religion is either a variety or a continuation of or a supplement to science that proceeds according to logical and methodological principles; and finally that view whose deeper fundamental error is perhaps at the bottom of most of what I have to discuss in this section: psychology.

January 22, 1922

Art and Religion

I had begun to speak of the subordination of religion, that is, those attempts to make religion dependent on various spheres of life, to force it into a dependency on them, to portray it as a function of this sphere of life. I spoke of this tendency toward functionalization, at first specifically within the spheres in which the spirit, the personal spirit, is still embedded in the concrete, the objective, the general, in the objectivity of life, of society, of culture. I should like now to demonstrate the same thing within the spheres where the personal spirit is no longer embedded but appears creatively, personally—first of all, within the sphere of the aesthetic, of art. The aesthetic way of looking at things, or let us say the application of the aesthetic viewpoint to nonaesthetic things, is something that you have probably encountered very fre-

---

1. The lectures were given weekly on Sundays, beginning January 15 and extending through March 12. There are nine Sundays in this inclusive period, but only eight lectures were given. Lecture Two is undated. Lecture Three is dated February 5. Thus three weeks elapsed between Lectures One and Three. It is possible that Lecture Two was given on January 22 and that Buber did not speak on January 29 because of the death on January 25 of Rabbi Nehemiah Nobel, one of the founders and leading teachers of the Lehrhaus.

quently in our time. It is a peculiarity of a certain philosophical style of our time to let philosophies and religions pass before one like landscapes, like works of art, like plays; that is, to look at them as a surface, to fail to enter the very dimension that is their own peculiar and decisive dimension, to leave their mystery uncontemplated. This way of looking at things has its counterpart in the way religious concepts and formations are often viewed today as "free creations of the human spirit," as the expression goes. But this expression "free creation" does injustice even to art itself. For every art stands under a law. Every artistic act follows the law of the form that this act intimates or, it would probably be more correct to say, that is intimated by this act, that will be realized through it. But the expression "free creation" does greater injustice to religion. Probably, both religion and art are action under a mandate. But art, artistic creation, originates in the mandate of something that strives to come into being, something formlike that is not yet actual, that is still dormant and latent in the actual, and that wants to be brought to life, to be actualized. I repeat: It is the mandate of a thing that strives to come into being.

The mandate in which the religious concept originates is something else. So different is this mandate that here we can no longer speak of a creation in the human sense, let alone of a free creation in the all too human sense. For this is the mandate of a being, the mandate of *the* being. All religious concepts rest on the foundation of a bond of being, a bond with being, and without this foundation, religious concepts are not the same, they are nothing. This bond of being is often wrongly called faith. For faith implies a certain kind of duality: There is something that is believed, and someone who believes it or who holds it to be true. What is meant here by faith would at least have to be enormously delimited against everything. This bond of being is quite necessarily inherent in all concepts and formations of the religious. Without this bond to being they would be merely another subspecies of art, that is, a less formlike and therefore objectionable subspecies. For never—in no other human enterprise—can what is formlike be so purely attained as in the work of the artist.

But there is something besides what is formlike. There are other actualizations. Of course, one can look at religious forms with an eye to what is artistic about them. But their real, decisive dimension thus remains unexplored. If, for instance, prayer is considered to be an artistic form, it is not more but less than a poem. If a religious celebration is considered to be an artistic form, it is not more but less than a theatrical performance. In this way, as I said, the true dimension of these things is not entered into at all. All these things acquire their decisive sense and existence through their bonds with something, that is, through the bond with what is, through the fact that they originate in the mandate of something that is. And therefore it is perhaps the very greatest folly of our time to drivel about a God in process of becoming. Of course, God is drawn by us into this life, into this actuality—we shall have occasion to speak about that. In a sense that I can only allude to at this moment, God is actualized by us. But: *God* comes into being; that which is comes into being. It is the mischief and libertinism of our time to overstrain itself on this mystery by saying that man, the human spirit, has at some time and at some place to bring forth God.[2] Obviously, this tendency originated in certain scientific theories, then took on a form through the tremendous spiritual passion of Nietzsche, and finally degenerated into—I cannot change the name I have given it—a highly unedifying kind of claptrap.

There is another point on which the religious distinguishes itself fundamentally and unconditionally from the artistic. All arts and all artistic creations exist according to their meaning in plurality, in multiplicity. That there are many arts, many arts in the sense, as it were, of many languages that exist one beside the other; that there are many arts that touch one another without disturbing each other; that within each art there are many works and many new works always being created; that the spirit is always putting many new and different things into the world of things; and that these works, again, touch one another without disturbing each other—these phenomena belong to the final,

---

2. This is Buber's way of criticizing his own earlier thinking; cf. Buber's 1911 article "Judaism and Mankind," in *On Judaism* (New York, 1967), 27: "And this God Himself had emerged from striving for unity."

unalterable meaning of art. It is not so with religious concepts. They, too, stand in a plurality, a multiplicity. But this multiplicity has necessarily the character of something provisional. Every religious concept, just by existing, at first confronts the other concepts as something exclusive. But at the same time each religious concept exists in the will toward a universality, toward a future universality of religion that is in the process of perfecting itself, in which the multiplicity of religious concepts is annulled. Here multiplicity is a stage, a transition, the way. Regarding art, it was the basic condition itself, and here, as in every earlier sphere, there was contrast to, distinction from, the religious; yet there was contact. So it is with religion too: With its inwardness, with its creative experience of self, the artistic touches the religious. And here again, as at the edge of every sphere, religion stands at the edge with open arms, embracing and ordaining boundaries. Here, too, religion stands at the edge of form and of the realm of form, pointing to what is formless and, despite all the eternal attempts at formation, nonformable. Perhaps I may quote here a statement by Goethe, which does not entirely coincide with what I mean but which does touch upon it. He says: "The highest, the most perfect in man is formless. One should beware of giving it form save by noble deed." This touches at the same time upon the other sphere of the spirit of which I wish to speak here: the ethical.

Ethics and Religion: Kant

All of you know the attempt—it comes up again and again—to regard religion as a function of the ethical, as something that is postulated, demanded by ethics as, so to speak, its prerequisite or its sanction. In its crudest form this attempt is represented by the well-known saying that religion must be preserved for the sake of the people, to keep them from degenerating and going astray. I think we can leave this crudest form undiscussed here. But from this form an almost unbroken line leads to that most sublime form, which is represented by Kant's postulates of practical reason. This is not to say that Kant viewed the postulates as a list of fictions, the way a certain school today seems to have made a practice of adapting these things to people's understanding by enclosing them in the parentheses of "as-if."[3]

This is not the case. What Kant meant is not that we have to posit God for ourselves because the moral law demands the highest sanction, the highest unconditionality. Rather, Kant meant that only by starting from the moral law can freedom and immortality and God be deduced. But even this form of the foundation of religion on the ethical robs the religious element of its independence and thus of its genuine existence.[4] For the religious relation that still remains is an indirect relation. It is a way of deriving it through the moral law. It is deduction from what is directly given or immediately posited—morality—and all indirectness annuls the religious element. Religion is either directness or it is nothing. It crystallizes around the direct relation or it is fiction. Furthermore, if access to the religious, the sole and indispensable access, is the moral, if the religious only serves as a foundation and a crown to this morality, then certainly the religious has a home in some niche or it has no home at all. But then the religious has nothing more to do with actuality. Then it has to do only with this narrow slice of actuality that is delimited by the moral, which can fit into the polarity of good and evil. Then God is only a God of this part of the world; then creation—I think one can also say it this way—is no longer revelation; and thus the existence of the religious breaks down. I should like to make it quite clear: There would probably still be revelation, but creation would no longer be revelation. Certainly the person who is religiously alive, religiously opened up, has even in his actions a dedication, a solemnity, that no one else, no one who is not religiously opened, can have. But this dedication does not result from raising morality to the religious plane. It results from man's standing upon a

---

3. Allusion to Hans Vaihinger and his philosophy of "as-if."
4. Cf. Buber's statement of 1918 in "The Holy Way," in *On Judaism*, p. 111: "Thus the special character of Judaism resides in neither the religious nor the ethical realm but in the unity of both realms." On Buber's attitude toward Kant, see "Elements of the Interhuman," in *The Knowledge of Man*, ed. Maurice S. Friedman (London, 1965), 84.

ground that cannot be shaken. And I would like to say that this dedication does not arise in response to a demanding God; rather it comes from God's sustaining this life. Not from a God of moral law but from a God of creation. This dedication results from the fact that to the religious person life, all life, necessarily has meaning: a meaning that cannot be expressed in words, that likewise cannot be expressed in an ought, a commandment, a law, a morality of attestable meaning, *the* meaning.[5] This shows itself most clearly, perhaps, in that domain of morality that touches upon the religious, that touches directly upon the sphere of the religious, indeed, I may say, that reaches up into it— in the domain of decision.

Good and Evil

In the domain of decision it becomes entirely clear that it is not as if decision were somehow strengthened in its reality, as if it were then truly decision, when the religious sanction lives and is present over it in its consciousness, resides in it as an element, when the moral law as something demanded by God is included in, drawn into the elements from which decision grows upward. I might even say quite to the contrary: What is valid is not as the representatives of the philosophy of fiction think. What is valid is not: Act as if there were a God. But I might almost say—I think I can't make it clearer to you in any other way than by saying: Act as if there were no God. And precisely because the religious sanction is not included at all in the elements of decision, precisely because of this, the person who is religiously opened does not, in deciding, bring the sanctioning, demanding, legislative force of religion into the element of his decision. The decision can be based entirely on freedom; indeed, when the religiously opened person seems to be stepping out of the religious sphere, he in truth remains most

---

5. On the search for meaning, see Buber's *Daniel* (New York, 1965), 91, 92; and also *I and Thou*, trans. Walter Kaufmann (New York, 1970), 158–159.

deeply within it and thus assures it of autonomy. It is precisely through this that in his very decision he touches the sphere of religious being. Precisely through freedom, which does not have elements of absolute dependency and absolute determinacy as its prerequisites but, rather, bases itself on nothingness, the man who decides touches divine freedom.

Truly, it might be expressed in this way: By not concerning himself with God, the man who acts touches upon the divine. Of course, that means above all truth, unreservedness. This freedom cannot be gained by speculation; this freedom must not be caprice. In contrast, one might perhaps point to the person, who seemingly does not stand in decision and yet does the right thing, to the so-called beautiful soul, the person who, as they say, instinctively does what is good and right. That could be and that is a misunderstanding. The person thus portrayed is one in whom the decision takes place in those elemental depths of the soul that are closed to reflection and inaccessible to analysis. That is a person of pure, ultimate unreservedness of decision and of the ultimate (in the sense of which I have spoken), the innermost unconsciousness of God as one who makes demands. This, however, is something that perhaps cannot be brought to its ultimate clarity at this moment. But I believe that you have probably understood that we are dealing here with a polarity and also with knowing and nonknowing. Here, in the sphere of decision, in that domain of the moral, which, as I said, touches upon religious being, there is no good or evil. For the person who decides, there is no good and evil. He does not decide for *the* good or *the* evil. Instead there is only, if one can say it in a specific sense, the just and the unjust, that is, the directed—directed by decision and choice—and the undirected. And here, to be sure, a comet arises with which we cannot concern ourselves at this moment but with which we shall yet have to concern ourselves: the great problem of the Law.

I wish merely to have mentioned it at this point. Good and evil,[6]

---

6. For the later development of Buber's ideas on good and evil, see "The Question to the Single One," in *Between Man and Man*, trans. Ronald G. Smith (Boston, 1955), 79; "Images of Good and Evil," in *Good and Evil: Two Interpretations*, trans. Ronald G. Smith (New York, 1953), 63–143.

however, exist and are valid in the other sphere of the ethical, the sphere in which moral judgment rules. Here there are indeed two kinds of being, two kinds of reality, whereas in decision, there is only the actual, which is done, and then the nonactual, which is simply not decided upon, not done. Here in the sphere of judgment, this limitation operates. But when one makes the religious into a function of the moral, when one draws the religious sanction into this sphere as its necessary foundation, then this duality is raised to an absolute. We spoke of decision. For decision there is no delimited reality. For decision there is only the unlimited, within which the decision is taken. The only limitation of this unlimited is the eternal recurrence of the act of decision. In the world of judgment there is a world delimited, divided into good and evil, separated. But this separation is right in some human sense. I say human, although really it goes against what is human; and yet is right in some human sense, simply because it is relative, because it is fluid, because it remains human.

If the religious is not viewed as something overarching but instead is made a function of this sphere, drawn into this sphere so as to serve as its prerequisite or sanction, then precisely the negation of evil and the affirmation of good becomes something rigid, inadequate, unbreakable, inhuman. Because God is not opened up in immediacy but through the good, because God is nothing more than the hypostatization of the good, the raising of it to a substance, not only the human soul falls apart, but the whole. As in the sphere of society, in the sociological sphere of which we spoke last time, the invisible humanity fell apart, so the whole falls apart here into a good and an evil world. This of course is always happening, even in religion(s), but this is precisely the point at which religions have again and again experienced their crises, to which I can merely allude here. I should like to elucidate what I mean through one example, perhaps the clearest example, the Avesta religion. The Persian religion Zoroastrianism seems to have done just that of which we are speaking; it seems to have divided the world into a good one and an evil one. Here the ethical and the religious do seem fused precisely in this manner. And yet, whoever follows the history of this religion will notice that that is not so. For in this religion there are two phases. In the first, evil is not an equal of the good, confronting it, but God is in truth the God of good and evil, the God of the All, and evil is the turbidity, the demonic element that has crept in and that is to be combated in the name of God. Of course, this religion develops more and more toward a situation in which evil itself is absolutized; the good God is confronted more and more by an evil god. It is in this way that God becomes the good God, the good God as exclusive, God as counterpart [?] to evil.[7] Thus this duality arises. But the more strongly this duality solidifies, the more strongly the demand arises in this religion for an overarching, uniting Deity. This second phase of the Avesta religion is characterized by the fact that the image of an aeonic[8] God enthroned in unity over duality emerges more and more distinctly, whether interpreted as infinite time or in some other way.

What is meant is probably best conveyed, in its space-time quality, by this expression or by the Hebrew expression *olam*.[9] Precisely here in this second phase, religion reveals its character as overarching unification of all duality. For the man enclosed in his moral sphere, affirmation of good and negation of evil, reception of good and rejection of evil, is valid. For the man who has been opened to religion, who also acts out of his religiosity, what is valid is precisely love for evil, living with evil, being with evil. Thus here, too, at the edge of this world, at the edge of the moral law, where this world flows into it and is enclosed by it, stands religion. And third: the claim of the logical sphere, or to put it more clearly, of the scientific-philosophical sphere. Perhaps I may be brief here, because we shall yet have occasion to speak of these things. I should like merely to point to a few things which are of particular current interest.

---

7. The text is corrupt.

8. Buber uses the Greek term *aeon*, meaning an age of the whole duration of the universe, an immeasurable period of time. Buber's interpretation of the Hebrew term *olam* may have originated from the Greek *aeon*. See the following note.

9. The stenographer had written *ola*, misspelling *olam*, which Buber translates in this lecture as *Raumzeit* (space-time); in the Bible translation, however, he translates *olam* as *Weltzeit* (world-time).

Science and Religion

An attempt is being made today to let the religious, religion, appear as a continuation of science, specifically by saying something like this: "Up to here is the object of science, here in the realm of the empirical; and now here the sphere of religion begins, and, moreover, the same logical principles are also valid for this, so to speak, higher empirical realm as for science. But the methods of science are no longer valid for religion. Instead, new methods particularly suited to this purpose are valid, such as exercises, visions, meditations of all kinds. And thus is attained a scientific knowledge of the supernatural, or whatever one calls it, which finally makes it possible to project a complete topography, a complete geography of the mystery.[10]

I should like merely to indicate that in this respect one can rest easy—although these tendencies will become even more powerful in the future. Nonetheless, it must be said that such a process would mean the breakup of science. For a separation of logical principles from the methods derived from them—so that the one and not the other could still rule—annuls science; and it would also break down science. It is an objective delimitation of science, a delimitation of the right of science in the sense of saying: Your object reaches so far and no farther; it is with this object that you must deal from within your methods, and from there on is an object for which your methods are no longer valid.[11] Through this process science would break up over religion. For what is really happening with this whole enterprise, this whole procedure beyond the sphere of scientific methodology, is a carrying over of the scientific coordinate system, not onto an object over which it has no jurisdiction, for there is no such thing, but onto the nonobjective.

The world with which science deals, and rightly so, and within which it can rightly demand that nothing should be withheld from it—

---

10. Cf. Buber, *Daniel*, p. 91: "Orientation . . . is thoroughly godless; godless also is the theologian who fixes his God in causality, a helping formula of orientation, and the spiritualist who knows his way about in the 'true world' and sketches its topography."

11. The syntax of the original sentence is incomplete.

that there should be no distinction made between sensual and super-sensual experience—is the world of orientation. That is the world that we have fabricated for ourselves around our self-assertion in the infinite and in the human spirit, the enormous spatial-temporal coordinate system in which we have to enter the things and occurrences and by means of which we have presumed to order them. And this coordinate system exists by right. But it must not be falsified into a system of being. It must not be reapportioned from a schema to a substance, to *the* substance. And just as senseless and pernicious as this whole enterprise are all those attempts to (. . .) science, not by inaugurating another sphere alongside it but by scrutinizing everywhere within it for little gaps through which religion or the religious can slip in.

Question: With the first point you are referring to Steiner's philosophy?[12]

Answer: To that, among other things.

Question: And with the second?

Answer: I don't want to localize it like that. I have intentionally avoided pointing to such phenomena of the time. If necessary we could reserve that for discussion in a special hour after the lecture. I do not mean only these things, but above all the things that are to come, above all the things that have as yet no name and that I see coming. I don't mean the gaps at which I can point a finger but the gaps that I can only intuit as the signature of a time toward which we are advancing. To localize would constitute here an anticipation of things, enormously

---

12. This is a reference to Rudolf Steiner, who write numerous books expounding anthroposophy, a system of thought related to theosophy and much preoccupied with the occult. Although Buber opposed Steiner's views, Hugo Bergman, Buber's friend and disciple, accepted them. See Bergman's introduction, "Rudolf Steiner as a Philosopher," to Rudolf Steiner, *The Philosophy of Spiritual Activity* (West Nyack, N.Y., 1963), 11–26; see also Bergman's article "The Need for a Courageous Philosophy," in *Scripta Hierosolymitana* 6 (1960): 115. Gerhard Wehr wrote a book, *Martin Buber in Selbstzeugnissen und Bilddokumenten* (Reinbek bei Hamburg, 1968), in which he tries to show the affinity of Buber's thought with that of Steiner. This misinterpretation of Buber was criticized by Ernst Simon in "Ein bedenkliches Buber-Buch," *Neue Zürcher Zeitung*, May 11, 1969.

greater and more pernicious and more poisonous, that are to come. And I admit that a call to arms against these things is one of my main intentions, which occasions my speaking about all these things.

I would merely like to note in addition that all these attempts to supplement science by religion by saying something like: Religion really is the same as science, only not in the form of the concept as in Hegel, but of mental image. All who indicate that religion consists of symbols that say the same thing as science only in another language, who make of religion, as it were, a huge metaphor, already fall into the category of the artistic, of the aesthetic sphere. The aesthetic perspective means, as I said earlier, viewing religion as a free creation, as a metaphorical way of expression. In the scientific sphere too, the religious stands at the edge of the assertion, the assertion determined and ruled by logic, within which logical principles and scientific methods should hold unlimited sway and at whose edge religion stands, admonishing and pointing outward and to the other side. This is not to be misunderstood as though religion were somehow removed as the object of science. Not at all. Religion is also an object of science. The study of religions, the philosophy of religion, the psychology of religion—whatever these disciplines may be called—are justified, for nothing can be cut out of science as the object of science. But religious being, of which we are speaking here, remains untouched by this treatment of religion in the world, in the structure of orientation. And so, starting from there, I would like to give you a view of the final problematic of the tendencies of dependence, of psychology, in order to take up again after these digressions the real question that I indicated at the beginning.

February 5, 1922

Response to Questions

Before beginning to speak about our subject, I should like to have a brief discussion with you concerning the questions that some of you have directed to me, orally and in writing. Some of those who asked the questions may have felt the lack of an answer to them in my subsequent remarks. If so, they should ask themselves whether the question was put in the right way. I said at the outset that you should ask questions if at some moment what I said was not sufficiently clear and intelligible; if you felt some sort of doubt or uncertainty in the face of it; if in order to go further with me you needed, so to speak, to get past this dark, uncertain spot. I did not, however, mean that you should in some way anticipate what I have to say. What I must term an anticipation, as revealed in several questions that have been put to me, is the application of a specific concept of religion, a fixed traditional concept, or something read or heard to what I have been talking about; and that is not right. For you cannot take in what I have to say if you approach it with a fixed concept of religion and then apply that concept to what I have been saying—which so far has been negative—by way of rejection and elimination. For then we are not really traveling together on the way that these lectures should represent. For I am trying to arrive, together with you, at an adequate concept of what we call religion. But if we anticipate and introduce into this first stage something fixed, rigid, and closed, then it will not work out, at least not with us here together.

Therefore I would like to request that you ask questions and, at the same time, that you not apply the questions to something that you know or think you know and then set the questions up in opposition to the lecture, to measure the one against the other. Instead, simply ask: How is this meant? How is it to be understood? Because I cannot go on here; I am in the dark about it. This way you will not only further understanding between me and you, but you will be furthering the whole, what we are doing here as a whole. To this I would like to add that it has also been pointed out in some of the questions that religion is connected in such and such a way with the spheres of which I have spoken. But it seems to me that it goes without saying that religion is most intimately connected with all these spheres, that mutual influence is the rule in all these domains. If, for example, I have negated the dependence of religion on art, I of course did not mean to deny that religion has always exercised the strongest influence upon art, that it expresses itself with a very special distinctness in art, and that art, too, in its creativity, touches again and again upon the religious. Here and there I have indicated something of this reciprocal action, but of its immense domain I have not wanted and do not want to speak here. My sole concern here is the refutation of this one idea: that religion is in any way dependent on one of these spheres, that it is in any way a function of one of these self-enclosed activities of the human spirit. In this sense I have spoken up until now of the sphere of life, of society, of culture, of these objective spheres, if one wishes to call them that.

Critique of Psychology: Schleiermacher and Rudolf Otto

Last time I spoke of the spheres of the personal spirit, the aesthetic, the ethical, the logical. All that remains for me now in this introductory exposition is to speak of the one sphere that is apparently the foundation of all of them and through which, over and over again, the attempt is made to designate religion as something dependent on it and rooted in it. I mean the psychological sphere.[1] What is this sphere really, what

---

1. Cf. an address on psychology that Buber presented in Zurich in 1923: "On the Psychologizing of the World," in *A Believing Humanism: Gleanings by Martin Buber*, trans. and ed. Maurice S. Friedman (New York, 1969), 144–145.

is its real meaning? Here it seems to me more difficult than with any of the other spheres of which I have spoken to draw the limits exactly. This is because the concept on which the psychological sphere is based—the concept of the soul—is full of pitfalls. It is not as clear as the concepts on which the other spheres are based; however, the term "soul" as used in the psychological sphere has a very specific meaning, which we have to clarify for ourselves first of all. Perhaps the best way of doing this is to clarify in what sense one does *not* speak of soul when one engages in psychology. For if soul, as it seems to me, means nothing other than the relation of the human being to the world, to things, to beings, to humans, to being, to oneself, then soul is this relation insofar as it is known to humans in an unmediated way, insofar as the human being has knowledge of it without having to ask others, insofar as soul means simply this relation. In other words, it is something into which the human being is inserted, which establishes itself again and again between the human and all being, and which the human being, as person, knows in this unmediated way. If soul means this bridgelike being between human and world, insofar as the human knows of it in an unmediated way, then, of course we do not need to "defend" religion—if I may use that expression—against dependence on it. For soul in this sense does indeed form an essential prerequisite of the religious— not the religious itself but an essential prerequisite of it. But this soul is not the object of psychology. Psychology is concerned with something that has been lifted out of, isolated from, set off from the human relation to the world. The object of psychology is, so to speak, the isolated portion of the human being, which is contemplated as if it existed in itself, as if it were a closed apparatus, a self-enclosed domain in which one knows one's way around. The same holds in any other part of the world that is similarly isolated and contemplated in itself (and in which one now distinguishes different species, different groups of phenomena) and that one marks off into various subdivisions: thought, emotions, will, whatever one calls those things in which one knows different modes of perception and the like. All of that is certainly interesting and significant within the sphere of an orienting science, but it is not of immediate importance for that which concerns us here.

But before proceeding I would like to ask whether I am being understood. If something is unclear here, I request that you ask me now.

By "unclear," I mean regarding this distinction between the soul that
is nothing other than the human being's relation to the world, insofar
as he knows of it in an unmediated way, and the soul as object of
psychology, that is, something set apart from the world, something
that takes place within the human being, a process enclosed in the
human being. And here there are various groups, kinds of phenomena,
that stand in different relations to one another and about which it is
possible to make various statements concerning their kind, the course
they take, and their connections. It is on the soul, in the psychological
sense, that people want to make religion functionally dependent. As I
said last time, what I am saying is not directed against the scientific-
psychological treatment of religion, not against the science of the psychology of religion, which has its definite place within the world of
orientation; rather, it is opposed to making religion dependent in its
essence on this sphere, so that it is not seen as an independent existence
but as an existence conditioned by this sphere. Perhaps what I mean
will become clearer if I give you an example of how this functionalization, this psychology, works. Within this apparatus of the soul, the
psychic apparatus, different groups of phenomena are distinguished.
Thus the religious, if it is made dependent on psychology, must necessarily be assigned to one of these groups, let us say the group of
feelings.

And of course you know how the religious, specifically in German
religious philosophy, has been conceived especially as feeling, for instance, as "the absolute feeling of dependence," or, to use the somewhat
different formula recently proposed, "creature-feeling."[2] Now, I shall
disregard the fact that in every such definition only a small part of the
extent of the religious, a specific part with which the philosophizing
human is familiar, is included. I shall merely indicate that, instead of
an absolute feeling of dependence in religion, one could speak with

---

2. Cf. *I and Thou*, trans. Walter Kaufmann (New York, 1970), 129: "The
essential element in our relationship to God has been sought in a feeling that
has been called a feeling of dependence or, more recently, in an attempt to be
more exact, creature-feeling."

equal justification of an absolute feeling of independence; and in great religions, not merely personal religiosities, it is precisely the fact that the spirit becomes independent of everything that it is accustomed to call its own.[3] Of course that is another feeling of independence, understood quite differently from the feeling of dependence of which I spoke and differently related.

But it becomes evident how dangerous, how narrowing and impoverishing it is to make a feeling, a specific feeling, the essence of religion. Since feelings necessarily stand in some polarity, every feeling necessarily has some corresponding opposite feeling and becomes clear to itself only in relation to this opposite feeling: Pain is clarified by pleasure, pleasure by pain; tension by relaxation, and relaxation by tension. So it is in the case of religion that one of these polar feelings is taken out of some such polarity and termed the religious.[4] But even disregarding this, what does feeling really mean for the psychology of which we are speaking?

Like everything else in this psychology, feeling can basically be defined only negatively. It constitutes that aspect of a psychic phenomenon that cannot be grasped as an external. What cannot be assigned to some part of the so-called external world, that is, the external world set off from the soul, is called feeling. When everything about some psychic process that cannot be related to this or that thing is removed, then something is left that corresponds to the No-Thing, and this is called feeling. Indeed, from the standpoint of this psychology, I know of no more adequate definition. Perhaps one of you could suggest one. But from the standpoint of this philosophy of dependence of which we are speaking, I at least know of no other definition. Of course I know that those who make the definitions of which I am speaking,

---

3. Cf. ibid.: "While the insistence on this element and its definition are right, the onesided emphasis on this factor leads to a misunderstanding of the character of the perfect relationship."

4. Cf. ibid.: "Above all, every feeling has its place in a polar tension; it derives its color and meaning not from itself alone but from its polar opposite; every feeling is conditioned by its opposite."

such as that of the feeling of dependence, do not invoke psychology in this way, but all their definitions are inevitably, ineluctably drawn into this basic attitude of psychology as such.

Of course, it may be emphasized that this feeling of dependence is not meant psychologically but metapsychologically: What is meant is not something that clings to something rooted in subjectivity, that varies according to individual differences, but something that transcends individual difference, something in common, something general, substantial, or however one chooses to call it. But this distinction can only be formulated, never really postulated and unfolded—because within the psychological sphere there is simply nothing but this, the pieces of this apparatus constructed in this way. Because where one speaks of feelings nothing metapsychological exists. Feelings exist within a plurality of feelings and other things. One feeling borders on another; one is limited by another, corrected by another, surpassed by another, annulled by another. And now in this world of feelings there is supposed to be something that has the religious as its essence or its object. Indeed, I do not know how one would go about removing the religious feeling from the whole, from the narrowness of subjectivity. It is and remains something cut off; it is and remains something that does not really happen to and with the human being but that allegedly takes place in the human being, that is squeezed into this happening inside the human—delimited by his compartments, circumscribed and confined on all sides by his other processes. And that is supposed to be the religious. That is supposed to comprise the relation to the absolute.

Nor does it help matters to take another category instead of feeling. It does not help matters to speak of mental images[5] or of drives, rather than of feelings, in the way a religious drive has recently been spoken of, as if "drive" in the psychological world meant something other than the striving for the removal of a lack, and as if lack could be grasped in the psychological world in any other way than in opposition to hav-

---

5. *Vorstellungen.* Kaufmann translates *Vorstellung* as "notion," giving as alternatives "representation" or "idea." (*I and Thou*, p. 141).

ing, to possessing. And, of course, this psychology fails completely when called upon to point to the existence somewhere in its world of this correlative, this opposite, this necessary counterpart to a lack, this having, this possessing.

In answer to a question: You are making the same mistake that I indicated earlier. But now let us go into the language, the conceptual language of this attitude. We shall not speak of how this attitude might be overcome, but ask: Can one, starting from this attitude, grasp the religious in an adequate way? And here I would like to ask those who think that the religious can be grasped from this attitude to state it from this psychological attitude.

"He has experienced God"

This attitude has in our time been carried to extremes, I might say, by a concept that I unfortunately cannot avoid discussing here, although I feel a definite aversion to uttering it. I mean the concept of "living experience." I can assure you that in general I am a patient person. But I once became very impatient and very intolerant—I cannot put it any other way—when someone said to me concerning a rather well-known writer: "He has experienced God."

I am somewhat accustomed to the hell that the misuse of this word signifies. I know exactly how things go in this world, in this hellish world in which we live, to whose torment we are exposed with each new day.

But there I felt something uncanny. There the misuse had, evidently, reached its limit. Indeed, it had to go that far. Experience, yes, the word "experience"[6] no doubt had and has even now its justification: when it is a matter of emphasizing subjectivity in life, in the course of

---

6. It is interesting to trace the development of Buber's attitude toward *Erlebnis* (religious experience). In the story "A Conversion," in which Buber relates an incident that occurred around 1914, he describes a religious experience positively and as the exception to everyday life: an "otherness which

life; of pointing out that confronting this life, or we should rather say within this life, there are moments when we feel our relation to our I particularly strongly. When we cannot simply take for granted, as usually, that it lives with us, that it lives this I. And not only that it lives this substantive I in the nominative case, that this our life is simply being lived, but rather that we are compelled to feel particularly, and also perhaps to consider, that we are living it. And this relation to the I sometimes crystallizes around single events, so that we can no longer say: I live, but rather: I am living this experience, I am pulling this out of myself as something that now vibrates as utter subjectivity. Something is occurring to which, in order to do it justice, I can give no other name but "living experience." These intimate matters of subjectivity are actually there, and I myself have advocated calling them "living experience." But I almost regret it.

For what has been called "living experience" since that time really means the opposite. It means that life is subjectified, that life, from a great constancy, a space-time constancy in which we stand and into which we are inserted, is transformed into a pulling out of things for the use and to the taste of our subjectivity in such a way that the constancy is utterly torn apart and nothing remains but inconstant moments—not even events that are inserted into being but "experiences," gems of the soul, as people call them. And religion is made into one of those gems, so to speak, into a real refinement of this elevated life.

This, then, is the final farewell to continuity, to actuality, to some-

---

did not fit into the context of life. . . . The 'religious' lifted you out [and was an] . . . illumination and ecstasy and rapture held without time" (cited in Paul A. Schilpp and Maurice S. Friedman, eds., *The Philosophy of Martin Buber* [LaSalle, Ill., 1967], 25.) However, in 1918 Buber began to criticize his earlier attitude toward religious experience. See "The Holy Way" (1918) and *"Herut"* (1919), in *On Judaism* (New York, 1967), 109–110, 153: "But it may happen, by some odd perversity, that an individual entertains the illusion that he has surrendered himself to the unconditional, whereas in fact he has evaded it: he interprets the fact of having been affected by the unconditional as having had an 'experience' . . . He has savored his hour of exaltation. He does not know the response; he knows only a 'mood' (*Stimmung*). He has psychologized God." Cf. also infra, p. 86 (*Erleben*).

thing in which one stands, in which one is enfolded and interwoven. Here religion is totally included in transience, in unconnectedness, in the disjointedness of moments of the soul. Of all the fictions into which religion has been converted, this is the most fictive. It is no longer the ascription of the religious to some sphere, it is the annihilation of the religious.

Max Scheler

In recent years people have begun to sense this, and one of the attempts to react to this nonsense is still and all a very interesting psychological attempt—it remains a psychological attempt, although it is not meant as such. I am referring to the attempt by Max Scheler[7] to grasp the religious in its essential process as an act. A distinction is made between two different kinds of psychic acts. He says the following: It is not that the religious is located there, somewhere among those groups of psychic phenomena; nor is it a feeling of a drive or a mental image; whatever you call it, it is all the same. Instead we need a completely different attitude. All psychic phenomena, whether processes, feelings, or strivings of the will, can be either religious or nonreligious acts; and now such an act is not to be limited merely to the psychic side, but, rather, it demands, so to speak, its object as a necessary complement, as a necessary foundation of the act. This, in my view, is a definite improvement on the psychological formulations. Nevertheless it seems to me that this formulation remains caught in the psychological.

It is not possible to deal with the topic exhaustively in this context; still, I would like to clarify it for you with one point. This view assumes that within the psychic there are, so to speak, two things—religious

---

7. See Buber's criticism of Scheler in 1943: "The Doctrine of Scheler," in *Between Man and Man*, ed. Maurice S. Friedman and trans. Ronald G. Smith, 2nd ed. (New York, 1967), 181–199. See also Max Scheler, *Vom Ewigen im Menschen* (Leipzig, 1921), 559; and Walter Kaufmann's note to the English translation of *I and Thou*, p. 153.

and nonreligious acts. What seems to be meant by nonreligious acts is that they are always directed to something limited, to some specific object one may encounter, to the world or some part of it; religious acts, by contrast, are distinguished by their absolute transcendence over the world and all that can be situated within the world. Now, it is difficult to grasp how there could be in psychic life two different kinds of things, one beside the other. But it soon turns out that it is not really two different kinds, since Scheler also says: Every human being really performs the religious act. But this religious act relates either to God or to an idol. This idol may have one of many names: power, possession, woman, money, or anything else.[8] And it would be quite sufficient if one were to show a person that he is directing his religious act to an idol. It would be quite sufficient to direct this act to God, in order to bring this religious act to its fulfillment, so to speak. For instance, a person might perform the religious act with respect to the idol of money, and now one takes this idol from him by showing him that money is the idol.

But precisely this shows that the division is, after all, not ultimately serious. For if the religious act is not necessarily founded in the one absolute bond of being but can relate, although falsely, to an empirical object, then there are not two kinds of act. But, in actuality, the religious act is simply a certain heightened psychic act.

And it is impossible to see how the transcendence of the object, the soaring above the world and all that is worldly, belongs to the religious act. This is exactly what is presupposed, and then the act can attach itself to any untranscendent object and make do with that until one enlightens it as to the inappropriateness of this object. But then, even in this formulation, the religious remains within the psychological,

---

8. Cf. *I and Thou*, p. 153: "A modern philosopher supposes that every man believes of necessity either in God or in 'idols'—which is to say, some finite good, such as his nation, his art, power, knowledge, the acquisition of money, the 'ever repeated triumph with women'—some good that has become an absolute value for him, taking its place between him and God."

although it seems to extricate itself from the psychological. I do not know of any more decided attempt, starting from the world, from the psychological method, to overcome it. But even this attempt inevitably fails. It remains true that if the religious is embedded in the psychological world it will inevitably also be dependent, caught in subjectivity, and it will remain necessarily caught in inconstancy, in the discontinuity in which the events of the soul begin and end. And the religious is then one of these events, which, as such, begins and ends and is limited by other events, set off from them and annulled by them. In this version, the religious event is necessarily something correctable. It is bounded by other experiences and can be corrected, annulled, and surpassed by other experiences.

All these conceptions have in common, necessarily in common, that the religious occurs *within* the human being, that is, in this being-cut-off that psychology calls soul, in this encapsulation within the human being that it calls soul. Here the religious does not occur, as it occurs in truth, to the human being, *with* the human being. Seen psychologically, it clings to him as a rightful or unrightful experience, but it is not in him as in a presence, in an actuality. As I said before, of all presuppositions this is the most dangerous. For, aside from everything else, it is this most of all that leads to the real perdition of our age, namely intermixture—here, to the intermixture of the religious occurrence with illusory and hallucinatory psychological and psychopathological processes.

And thus we may, as it were, place religion in opposition to this sphere too, at its edge, truly at the edge of the soul as thus understood. If soul is the human being's disjunction from the world, if it is the inner dispensation of the human being, the division of the human being into various phenomena and events, then religion stands as admonisher and warner at the edge of this soul, embracing it and showing it its boundaries. All this detachment and separation does not extend into the religious. Here only wholeness and bondedness are valid. And if the soul finds entrance here too, then it is only the soul of the present, actual human being, not the soul of the psychological human being.

Conclusion

Thus we have traversed the circle of functionalization. And once more, before I seek to paraphrase the results—the provisory results—I ask of you: If something has remained unclear, please ask questions. For soon we shall have to take a mighty step beyond all these Noes. We have found that religion stands at the end of all spiritually partial worlds, at the edge of all of them, embracing each single world and showing each one its boundaries. Therefore it cannot be a partial world. Religion, which encompasses all the spheres of the spirit, cannot be a sphere of the spirit. It is therefore not enough to find for it an independent sphere beside the others. It is not enough to free it from all these dependencies and then to place it upon one of these thrones, to find a place for it beside the others. Rather, if it is, it must surround, envelop, embrace all of them. Not as something complex, but as something simple. Certainly it bears elements of all of these spheres, of all these things, within itself, as we have seen and shall yet see. You yourselves, if you think back on the single spheres, one after the other, clarify to yourselves the way all these elements dwell together in religion. And still it is not based on these elements.

And one more thing. For the most part these attempts at functionalization, these attempts to make religion dependent on some spiritual sphere, were intended, among other things, to demonstrate the universality of religion. That is, to call forth in religions, in the plurality of religions, the common religiosity that is immanent in all of them alike. And indeed, if *the* religious exists, if there is *one* religiosity, then it must be possible to demonstrate and to contemplate it in all religions and religiosities. And yet it must be not as something general, not as something vague and colorless, which would then exist within the colorful plenitude, the explicitness, the plasticity of the religions, as some general concept that one could point to, saying: This exists here and here and here, that is, not as a Nothing, but rather a great, living, visible, lived presence.

The religious has necessarily the character of vitality and necessarily the character of actuality, of what cannot be given up. All this together means—we can now take this up again, now that we have traversed the circle of negations and rejections—absolute presence. How this is the case is what we shall be inquiring about from now on.

LECTURE FOUR

February 12, 1922

It-Experiences

As I said before, now that we have examined the various attempts to make religion a function of some spiritual domain, now that we have examined these attempts and rejected them,[1] we shall, so to speak, begin at the beginning. Now that we have established all this No, we can begin at the beginning to inquire after the Yes, as if we had not even spoken of all that. And, in an ultimate sense, if it were not for this very specific moment in time, we would not have had to speak of it. But on this new stretch of the way that we want to walk together,[2] some you will, I suspect, find the going hard or less comfortable—not because the things that we now have to discuss are getting more complicated but rather precisely because they are simpler. So simple are they, in fact, that a certain conceptuality, a certain philosophical terminology that has become firmly set in most people's heads, conflicts

---

1. Lectures One, Two, and Three form a unit whose theme is the definition of religion as distinct from other spheres of life; Lectures Four, Five, Six, Seven, and Eight are devoted to the development of Buber's own philosophy.
2. Cf. the beginning of Lecture One; and unpublished motto of *Ich und Du* reads: "This book presents the beginning of a way in which I intend to persevere and to continue to lead others."

with them, and if I proceed one step at a time I am afraid that many of you will ask, out of this conceptuality, how what I am going to say relates to this or that. I should therefore like to request that, insofar as possible, you refrain from juxtaposing what I have to say to ready-made, traditional formulations and instead that you juxtapose it only to your self-experience, to what you know from yourself about these things, and forget other formulations as far as possible. Do not start out by assuming that a particular philosophical formulation is right, but suspend judgment on it completely for the time being and ask yourself, starting from the very beginning, what these things actually mean, as if there were no terminology and no formulation at all.

Once, in a book, I stumbled upon a sentence that went something like this: "And since our conscious life consists of experiences (*Erfahrungen*) . . . ," and it went on from there. And this sentence seemed a little strange to me. What does that really mean,[3] that our conscious life consists of experiences? Either it is a tautology and means nothing more than that our conscious life consists of conscious events—but then the sentence says nothing at all, or it is more than that; for then it means that our conscious life consists of events in which we experience something. Experiences would then be events in which something, some thing, an object, is experienced. You know how this word, this remarkable world *erfahren* (to experience) arose. *Erfahrungen* (experiences) is a very late plural. Originally the word existed only in the singular, *Erfahrung*, meaning that which one acquires when one travels (*fährt*), when one goes over the surface (*befährt*) of the world, or, I would almost like to say, when one goes over the surface of things. One experiences (*erfährt*) things and in so doing extracts experience (*Erfahrung*) from them; one extracts a knowledge of things, so to speak, out of things, and this knowledge then has things as its object. One experiences what things are, what there is to things.[4] Thus it is always a matter of some-

---

3. Cf. *I and Thou*, trans. Walter Kaufmann (New York, 1970), 55: "We are told that man experiences his world. What does that mean?"
4. Cf. ibid., p. 55: "Man goes over the surface of things and experiences them. He brings back from them some knowledge of their condition—an experience. He experiences what there is to things . . . I experience something."

thing that is experienced. One comes to know the condition of things; one grasps something knowable and assertible.

Thus, if that statement that our conscious life consists of experiences is to mean anything, it would have to mean this: Our conscious life consists of events in which we experience something knowable and assertible about the condition of things, that is, of outer and inner things.[5] For of course inner experiences also belong to the region of experiences. The things we experience by no means have to be things of the outer world. They can also be things of the inner world. And this statement would merely be displaced if it were true that we also have some experiences that exceed the limits of the senses and the narrower [   ].[6] If what people usually call occult experiences, or whatever the term, were true (I should like to suspend judgment on this), these would still only be events in which we experience something from some domain—something knowable and assertible. And now the basic question with which we will start is this: Does our conscious life indeed consist of such events? Do such events, such experiences, indeed constitute our conscious life? And here I would like you to ask yourselves, quite independently of any ready-made formulas: What is the case with this? If you reflect on yourselves, not under the influence of any conceptuality but in a completely unbiased manner, does your memory indeed reflect your conscious life back to you as a series of experiences and nothing more? Or are there things, moments, events in your life that you cannot designate as experience?[7] Are there events in your life in which what is brought to you is not something, the

---

5. Cf. ibid., p. 56: "All this is not changed by adding 'inner' experiences to the 'external' ones."

6. The stenographer may have left a space for a missing word.

7. See *I and Thou*, p. 55: "But it is not experiences alone that bring the world to man." See also *I and Thou*, pp. 81–82: "Only It can be put in order. Only as things cease to be our You and become our It do they become subject to coordination. The You knows no system of coordinates. . . . There are moments of the secret ground. . . . These moments are immortal." The contrast between *Erfahrung* (experience) and *Augenblick* (moment) is found in his early philosophy. See his *Daniel* (New York, 1965), 54, 61–63.

condition of something, something knowable and sayable, but in which you confront something or other, a so-called inner or a so-called outer thing, differently from the way you would confront an experienceable object, an object about whose condition I can know and say something, about which it is given to me to know and say something? Is my question clear to all of you? For we cannot go on unless it is.

Question: Is there also a distinction to be made between lived experiences (*Erlebnissen*) and experiences (*Erfahrungen*)?[8]

Answer: Yes. I have already discussed the concept of experience once. This concept seems to me very indefinite and inadequate because it refers to something psychic that occurs in me and not to an event in which I participate. And second, because "experience" does not say anything definite, comprehensible. I can call experiences "lived experiences" if I wish. "Lived experience" means merely that I ascribe a certain piece of my life, so to speak, to myself as a subject; I relate it to myself. But this does not convey what it actually is, so I avoid this expression because of its fluctuating, vague character.

But I believe there is a much simpler and more accurate word to designate what there is besides[9] experiences in our conscious life. But before I get to this, I would like to approach the matter from another angle. It would gratify me if you could arrive by yourselves at the point I mean. What is meant by experience, in the sense of which we spoke just now, could perhaps be designated somewhat more narrowly as It-experiences. I always experience something, a content, an object, something that is situated as an It in the world of things, outer and inner. In this sense I can perhaps say that these experiences mean It-experiences. And if we want to hold onto the word "experiences" a moment longer before giving it up, we could perhaps start by asking: Is there

---

8. Cf. *I and Thou*, p. 157: "The moment of encounter is not a 'living experience.'" On Buber's negative attitude to *Erlebnis* (living experience), see Lecture Three. The question from a person in the audience is based on his knowledge of *Daniel*; the listeners are unaware that Buber had changed his position.

9. This word (*aussen*) was written into the manuscript with a red pencil by Buber. In the following pages there are numerous other corrections made by Buber in red pencil.

perhaps another kind of experience? Are there only It-experiences? Are there only such events in which things are brought to us as an It, as a something in the world of things? Or are there events in which a thing or being of the outer or inner world confronts us in a different manner?[10]

Question: Feeling, perception through feeling (*Erfuhlen*)?

Answer: Feeling is also a kind of experience, one in which we still have an It, although a psychic kind, whether it is a feeling of tension or relaxation, of pleasure or pain.[11] We do not locate it in an external world, but still it is a definite content that we experience in this manner. We can describe this feeling somehow; it is a feeling among other feelings, so that we can say of it: Such and Such is the case.

Question: I think, though, that all experiences are It-experiences. Whether It-experiences are sayable is the second question. The thought has occurred to me that It-experiences may be connected with assertible experiences.

Answer: By "assertible" we of course do not mean assertible by this individual at this moment but assertible in general.

Question: Yes. Then there would still be the question whether this It is assertible in its entirety, or whether some final remnant is left over, whereas experience is of course always It-experience.

Answer: That is quite true. Now the question would be whether this remnant is actually experienced as an It. I admit that really there are only It-experiences, but apparently one would like to say that there are still other experiences.

---

10. Buber's didactic method is apparent; first he speaks of *Erfahrung* (experience), then of *Es-Erfahrung* (It-experience), and finally of the limitation of the It-experience.

11. Cf. *I and Thou*, p. 54: "I feel something. . . . The life of a human being does not consist merely of all this and its like. All this and its like are the basis of the realm of the It."

Question: They are not experiences; rather they are an original knowledge, a knowledge of, a becoming manifest.[12]

Answer: I mean something quite simple.

Question: Is there only object-experience or is there experience from the subject as such without an object?

Answer: That would be a psychic experience. I experience something, a psychic fact.

Question: From the inside of the thing outward, not passing beyond the outer world.

Answer: You mean then it would be limited to something that occurs in the subject itself.

Question: No, then this word no longer applies.

Answer: I mean something simpler. Not some very special compartment that is entered only in particular moments of grace[13] but something that each of you has lived and lives again and again.[14]

Question: Of I and Thou?

Answer: Quite right, that's it. This is indeed the perfectly simple matter that is different in kind from an experience, that we can at first, just for a moment, call Thou-experience. That is the simple fact of being confronted by a Thou. Perhaps you can make present to yourselves, out of your own self-knowledge, your memory, how these things stand.

---

12. Cf. ibid., p. 56: "And all this is not changed by adding 'mysterious' experiences to 'manifest' ones, self-confident in the wisdom that recognizes a secret compartment in things."

Kaufmann here translates *offenbaren* as "manifest" and adds that this term does not have religious overtones. Note also that in this case Buber incorporated a student's question into the book.

13. Contrast with Buber's statement in *I and Thou*, p. 62: "The You encounters me by grace." See also *Daniel*, p. 51.

14. This is a fundamental idea in the lectures. See the beginning of Lecture One: "Presence in this sense must be for all. It cannot be intended that somewhere one part of humanity . . . has a monopoly on it by virtue of its chosenness."

Four Examples of Encounter

THE HUMAN

I confront a human being—to give the clearest example—whom I love. What does that mean? What kind of event is it when I actually confront this person as a Thou? Does it mean that I am experiencing something about this person's condition, that this person is now given to me somehow as a He or a She in the world of things and that I now perceive this person as an aggregate of qualities that I can know and express?[15]

Whoever is acquainted with this very simple fact of relation (I think every human being is acquainted with it) knows this. It is something that is totally separate from It-experiences. Or, in other, more accurate words, these are not experiences at all or anything at all that we can designate subjectively—experience still sounds subjective—but something we can designate only objectively as an event in which we participate; in a word, these are relationships.

Our conscious life, to take up the statement again, consists not only of experiences but of relationships.[16] And if you now go one step further in this introspection to which I invite you, you will note that these relationships, the relations to a Thou, to the Thou, are the primal, essential occurrences of life. I should like perhaps to clarify this by a few more examples.

We started with the relation to a beloved human being. This person can of course also become an object of experience for me. I can put him into the world of things and thus come to know, to experience, to

---

15. Cf. *I and Thou*, p. 59: "When I confront a human being as my You and speak the basic word I-You to him, then he is no thing among things nor does he consist of things . . . nor a condition that can be experienced described, a loose bundle of named qualities." Note that in the parallel section in the lectures the central motif of speech is still absent. In the early plan of 1918 (see infra, Part Two, chap. 1) and in the lectures, Buber speaks only of encounter.

16. Cf. *I and Thou*, p. 56: "The world as experience belongs to the basic word I-It. The basic word I-You establishes the world of relation.

assert something of him, of his qualities. He can become for me a complex of qualities, a thing among things, an experience. But in this moment, or to put it more accurately, for this moment, I have lost the decisive relation to him. And I can only recapture it when it once again confronts me as a Thou, as something to which I stand in relation and that I do not experience.[17]

NATURE

Now let us proceed one step further to an example that is perhaps not quite so self-evident. How is it with nature? What are our decisive relations to nature? What do they look like? What are the decisive moments in which we take something of nature into our lives?[18] Are they the moments in which we take component parts of nature, if I may use the expression, into our experience? Or are they the moments in which we confront nature as a Thou that confronts us and to which we have this unique, unprecedented, incomparable relationship, which in its essence can only be lived, whose essence cannot be converted to experience, and which we can of course step out of, time and again, to enter the domain of experience in order to know, experience, and assert something about that to which we stood in relation. But this, obviously is after we have turned, turned away, after we have turned back.

Question: Could one then apply the adjective "nonconscious" to the word "relationships"?

Answer: I should not like to say that. When you say "nonconscious," it sounds as if you were talking about the unconscious life.

Question: That isn't really what I mean.

---

17. Cf. ibid., pp. 59–60: "The human being to whom I say You I do not experience. But I stand in relation to him, in the sacred basic word. Only when I step out of this do I experience him again." And a few lines above: ". . . the human being, to whom I say you. I can abstract from him the color of his hair or the color of his speech or the color of his graciousness: I have to do this again and again; but immediately he is no longer You."

18. In the lecture, Buber gives the example of nature in general; in *I and Thou*, however, he uses the specific example of a tree.

Answer: Of course not, but it sounds a little that way. Nonconscious, yes, not conscious—to the extent that we mean consciousness as knowing in the sense of knowing something. But we should not say "nonconscious." I avoid the expression because it sounds like unconscious. We want to fix this in our minds at this point: It is something that belongs very much to our conscious life, and I might say, to put it paradoxically, we know it but not as an It. We know the beloved person and nature to which we stand in relation—but not as an It that we experience.

THE CREATIVE CONCEPTION OF A WORK OF ART

Another example concerns the act of the artist.[19] I mean the actual creative conception. The work, what the artist calls with a very primal, very accurate word the idea of the work, in the sense of the primal form of the work, appears to the artist. The work appears to the artist not as an It in the world of things, for example, of inner things, not at all, but as a Thou pure and simple: just like the beloved person, just like nature, as something exclusive. Just as in the relation to the beloved human being, it is not that there are now all sorts of things around this person among which he stands as one of them. Rather in the exclusivity of the relationship—I shall come back to this—he is, as it were, the world, the Thou pure and simple, to which one stands in an exclusive relationship. Exactly as we have actual relationships with nature only insofar as we relate to nature and to nothing else, actual artistic conception exists only when the idea of the work, or I would prefer to say the work, is encountered as a Thou in the exclusivity of relationship, which has eliminated everything experienceable. Here you can already see that it would be wrong to grasp the Thou from the point of view of the It. That is, to say the Thou is an object with which we enter into relation.

---

19. The idea that the conception of a work of art confronts the artist is found in *I and Thou*, pp. 60, 61: "This is the eternal origin of art that a human being confronts a form that wants to become a work through him. . . ." See the entire passage and its parallels in Lectures Five and Six.

For this work, if grasped from the objective point of view, is, so to speak, not yet there at all. From the point of view of the experienceable world I still have to create it. And yet I stand in relation to it. It is present to me in the relationship. Thus you see that the whole level of the experienceable world is no longer at all adequate here. For from the point of view of the experienceable world one would have to designate this conception of the work as a fiction, as something fictive, which is merely given to me in imagination. But in the world of Thou, this contemplated work to which I stand in relation as to a Thou has a thoroughly immediate and unconditional reality. In other words: The creation of which we are speaking here, the creation of this work that confronts me as a Thou, means nothing other than a discovery, an uncovering of this Thou, a bringing over of this Thou—though a bringing over that, as we have seen, necessarily makes this Thou also into an It. We shall yet come to speak of this process—the process of the Thou becoming It.

DECISION

And one more example. (It will be good to clarify these things again and again by examples; otherwise they threaten to fall into a rigidity that would contradict the essence of this recognition.)

Here is one more example, which will perhaps make still clearer with what level we are dealing. We have spoken of the decision of the person who acts. Decision, the moment in which a human being decides to do thus and so, is also an event of relationship.[20] For just as in the artistic, creative conception the work approached the artist as a Thou with the exclusivity that causes everything else to sink from sight, so the person who decides is confronted by his deed, the deed that he chooses. The deed becomes present for him as a Thou in an exclusivity

---

20. Cf. *I and Thou*, p. 60: "The deed involves a sacrifice and a risk. The sacrifice: infinite possibility is surrendered on the altar of the form; all that but a moment ago floated playfully through one's perspective. . . . None of it may penetrate into the work." Buber discussed the concept of decision at length again in the manuscript of *I and Thou* but reduced it considerably in the book.

that causes all other possibility of action to sink from sight, just as in the artistic conception all other possibilities of the artistic act sank from sight.[21] Everything else is, as it were, rejected by the exclusivity of this relation, and this one thing is chosen. Even though here, even more than in the artistic event, it looks, from the viewpoint of the world of objects, of experience, like something fictive, something that is not yet there. In actuality, seen from the viewpoint of the Thou itself, it is definitely something that has being and to which I stand in relation and that I have now to actualize.

For this is something that all these relations have in common: The Thou that encounters me is not something I must experience—it is something I must realize.[22] By entering into a relationship with it I do not make it an experience; rather, I make it an actuality, a presence, or, to put it more correctly, it becomes a presence for me, through me, in confrontation with me. This is what all relationships have in common.

I should like now to pause for a moment and ask you please to tell me if there is something that is not yet clear or if other formulations are still interfering with this way of thinking. Otherwise, I would now like to try to make this clear to you once more from another standpoint.

Human Development

What is the case with human development? Or to put the question more accurately: How does the I of the human being begin, and how does it develop? We can grasp the question in two ways: in the de-

---

21. Cf. ibid., pp. 124–125.

22. Cf. ibid., p. 61: "The form that confronts me I cannot experience nor describe; I can only actualize it." This is perhaps related to Job 4:16, which reads (as translated here from Buber's translation, *Die Schriftwerke*, 4th ed. [Heidelberg, 1976], 283): "One stands, I know not his appearance, as a form confronting my eyes; what I hear is silence and voice." It is interesting to note the similarities between Buber's discussion of inspiration and Job's description of prophecy.

velopment of the particular human being, of the individual, and in the development of the human race. The form that is directly given to us is that of the individual human being. We do not know the beginnings of the human race; and what we can deduce by analogy from the lives of the so-called primitive peoples is also rather problematical, for we really do not know in what stage of development these so-called primitive peoples are.[23] On the other hand there is the infinite fact of the child. The beginning of the I in the particular human being is impossible to overlook; it is always being given to us anew. Now, usually the response to this is: "The I begins in this way"; and I would merely like to insert here that the beginning of the I and the beginning of the consciousness of I are one and the same thing. "I" means precisely that the human being confronts the world as a subject.

Thus people usually interpret this beginning of the I by saying that the human being, the child, learns to set himself off from the world. In this way, by noticing that this body of his is the carrier of sensations, of his sensations, the other things that are not carriers of his sensations are set off from himself. And the self is placed in that privileged position that it designates, that the human being designates, with the word "I."

But is this description actually correct? Is it true that the I develops in this way, or only in this way, so that the human being, the child, sets himself off from things, beings, and persons, in a certain sense places the things around himself as an It, It, It, It from which he sets himself off?[24] Is it true that this is the whole picture of the development of the I? Thus, it is, please understand, the setting off of the I against the background of a world of It, against an It-world. Or is there not a quite different essential setting off of the I?

Now, whoever has observed children, especially in their first year, will have noticed that, both in the manner of looking and in the manner

---

23. This contradicts *Daniel* and *I and Thou*. In *Daniel*, Buber idealized the child and the primitive society (p. 71). In *I and Thou* the emphasis is on both primitive man and child; cf. *I and Thou*, pp. 69–73. In the lectures, Buber discusses the child more than primitive man.
24. The syntax of the original sentence is unclear.

of certain motions—we can go into this more specifically later—there exists a very specific kind of, one cannot express it otherwise, relationship to a Thou. And not only to a Thou that is essential for the child, for instance, for his self-preservation, such as the mother or the bottle of milk, but to something that often seems quite arbitrarily "lifted out," sometimes indeed to something that we cannot even see, that seems to be in the air, yet toward which the child nevertheless seems to grasp and strive.[25] If we then continue contemplating where conscious expressions are already involved, then we notice that the child is not merely and perhaps not even essentially setting himself off from an It but that he is setting himself off from a Thou to which he stands in relation. Or to put it even more precisely: The essential life of the child fulfills itself in relationships with a Thou.[26] And this way of setting oneself off from a Thou, of confronting a Thou—this is what first creates the feeling of the I, although of course the more the I then tries to orient itself, to affirm itself, to affirm itself through knowledge in the world, the more it sees itself as inserted into a world of It. We shall discuss later how this occurs. What I want to go into at the moment is the fact that the I begins in this relationship; the consciousness of the I begins in the relationship to a Thou. If we take the earliest life of the child to be an undifferentiated state in which the I and the other are bound together in an indistinguishable unity, the I at first lifts itself out as one that confronts a Thou and only afterwards as one that confronts a plurality of He, She, It, of things. This Thou that confronts the child at first need not, of course, be a living being. It can be any-

---

25. Cf. *I and Thou*, p. 77: "The innateness of the longing for relation is apparent even in the earliest and dimmest stage. Before any particulars can be perceived, dull glances push into the unclear space toward the indefinite; and at times when there is obviously no desire for nourishment, soft projections of the hands reach, aimlessly to all appearances, into the empty air toward the indefinite." See entire passage.
    26. Cf. ibid., p. 76: "The prenatal life of the child is a pure natural association. . . . What this longing aims for is the cosmic association of the being that has burst into spirit with its true You." On the unity that precedes man's life see also Buber's *Daniel*, pp. 130–135.

thing, as long as the child confronts[27] it as a Thou, that is, with the exclusivity of relationship that causes everything else to sink from sight, so that this one thing, as it were, represents the world of the Confronted, the Thou pure and simple.

Even from this point, we can say that there is not one layer or one world of conscious life, but two: an It-world and a Thou-world. Moreover, this does not result merely from the external world that approaches the human being; rather the Thou, the Thou-relation, is inherent in the human being himself. The Thou is inborn in the human being, and it is not so, it cannot be so, that the Thou-relation begins when some piece of the external world approaches the human being. Rather, this Thou-relation is somehow inherent in the human being himself,[28] the Thou is inborn in him and develops in the Thou-relationships.[29]

All the elementary emotions of the child and, as far as we can infer, of primitive man are built upon Thou-relationships. Thus we have on the one hand an It-world, which tends toward a pure separation between the human being and the world; and on the other hand we have a Thou-world, which tends toward a pure connection of man with the world—connection, but not union.[30] This face-to-face confrontation of I and Thou always means a connection, a linkage, but not a union.

To formulate this in terms of the world and of cosmology, one might say that there are three layers of world.[31] There is the layer of nondifferentiation, the world of creation, which is not even an object

27. Cf. *I and Thou*, p. 78: "It is not as if a child first saw an object and then entered into some relationship with that. Rather, the longing for relation is primary."

28. These last two lines were crossed out by Buber.

29. Cf. *I and Thou*, p. 78: "In the beginning is the relation—as the category of being, as readiness, as a form that reaches out to be filled, as a model of the soul; the *a priori* of relation; the *innate You*." Cf. Buber's *Daniel*, p. 52: "inborn direction."

30. *Vereinigung*. This is in contrast to *Daniel*, pp. 141, 143: "I was the unification" (*Vereinigung*) or: "This I is the I of the world. In it unity is fulfilled."

31. This theme of "three layers of world" recurs in Lecture Five. This paragraph in the lectures is reminiscent of Buber's early work.

of our consciousness; but it is something we grow out of, as the non-individualized world, as the We; as individuals we ascend out of it. Then there are two aspects of the world, two layers of world, that are accessible to us in a conscious life: the world of perception, of perceiving, of taking out and making true of objects, of It-contents, of experiences, and the world of actualization, the Thou-world of the relation to a Thou that we actually make present or that actually makes us present. This second world, I should like to indicate here already, this second world is the true world of the spirit.

I should like to stop here and ask that before the next time you make these things present to yourselves in a quite unprejudiced manner, from your own life. These things are quite simple, but they seem difficult because the conceptual framework that is drilled into us is of another sort. When you have done this, it will perhaps be easier for us to proceed together. I just want to indicate what steps we shall be taking next.

We shall now speak of the extent to which this inherent Thou, the inherent relationship, entails a task for the human being, for the human spirit, and the extent to which the construction of the It-world, which the human spirit carries out, confronts the construction of a Thou-world, of a possible Thou-world, and what hinders the construction of this Thou-world. I can perhaps indicate this even now—namely, the fact that every Thou by its own nature, the limitation of its own nature, again and again threatens to become an It, again and again becomes an It. Every Thou of which we have spoken, every finite Thou to which we stand in relation, again and again becomes an It, is drawn into the context of the experienceable world.[32] Thus it seems that a continuum of a Thou-world is impossible. Perhaps you can continue to make these things present to yourselves in the following days.

---

32. Cf. *I and Thou*, p. 84: "The individual You *must* become an It when the event of relation has run its course." This idea recurs in Lecture Five.

February 19, 1922

A Review

The line of thought that I presented last time is for the way that we want to walk together of such decisive importance that I want to communicate it to you once more, though again partly from another standpoint. Contrary to the widespread view that has been disfigured by academic philosophy, life is not a uniform progression of experience. The widespread view has it that we live in an experiential world that is continuous, continuous in time, and that this experiential world is the basic mode of existence, the sole material, I might say, of our lives. We are always experiencing some thing, whether this be outward or inward experience—this whole terminology is false, by the way, like the whole basic view, but let us keep to it. One can go beyond this and speak of an experience that is to a certain extent not experienceable, of so-called extrasensory experience,[1] thus attempting to widen the boundaries of what can be experienced and draw more into the world of experience. But it always remains the same; it always remains a "having of the object." One experiences something; one goes over the

---

1. The term "extrasensory experience" is used by Buber in reference to Rudolf Steiner in Lecture Two.

surface of it. Last time I already pointed out that this word *erfahren* really means going over the surface of things; one makes, so to speak, a journey through things and each time pulls out of them what one thinks one knows about them.[2] Of course only philosophy has attempted to build on top of this It-world, this It-world of experiences, another world, the world of the idea, the world of values.[3] But this world, curiously enough, is marked by the fact that we have nothing to do with it, that we have no traffic with it, that it is not immediately there for us, that it is not actual, that it only manifests itself to us in some way. And this means that it does not concern us as living beings truly possessed of an I. I can only indicate it now, but in the last part of this lecture we shall probably have occasion to speak of it: This whole world with which we have no immediate continuity is a world not only of nonactuality but truly a world of spooks, of the nonactual in this quite specific sense. Morever, aside from this philosophical superstructure: Is it indeed true that our immediate life is a uniform life of experience, of experiencing something, a continuous It-world, that is, a world that is made up of so many Its joined together, of so many things that may also be called He and She? Is it indeed true that this is our life, that this is our world?

---

2. Cf. *I and Thou*, trans. Walter Kaufmann (New York, 1970), 55: "Man goes over the surfaces of things and experiences them. He brings back from them some knowledge of their condition."

3. Cf. ibid., pp. 64–65: "This essential twofoldness cannot be overcome by invoking a 'world of ideas' as a third element that might transcend this opposition. For I speak only of the actual human being, of you and me, of our life and our world. . . .

"To be sure, some men who in the world of things make do with experiencing and using have constructed for themselves an idea annex or superstructure in which they find refuge and reassurance in the face of intimations of nothingness. . . .

"But the It-humanity that some imagine, postulate, and advertise has nothing in common with the bodily humanity to which a human being can truly say You. The noblest fiction is a fetish, the most sublime fictitious sentiment is a vice. The ideas are just as little enthroned above our heads as they reside inside them; they walk among us and step up to us. Pitiful are those who leave the basic word unspoken, but wretched are those who instead of that address the ideas with a concept or a slogan as if that were their name!"

It suffices to answer that it is true if each one will make present to himself what his life contains in the way of, let us say for now, just moments that he himself has felt and preserved as decisive, authentic, as the substance of life. If he questions himself with ultimate honesty, he will be able to understand all these moments not as moments of experience, for they have a peculiar quality of their own. They all have the peculiarity that what is experienced is not something, something that is composed of qualities and that can be pointed to as having these qualities. It is rather that in these moments the human being stood in relation to a Thou, and this was precisely the essential character of this relationship, which, as long as it lasted, left no room for an I and manifested this Thou only as Thou, but not as It, not as He, nor as She.

Remoteness from God and Nearness to God

Thus there are two qualitatively different states in life. There are two modalities of world: There is the It-world and there is the Thou-world, the world of relation.[4]

I say "qualitatively different," although I would like already to indicate that these two worlds are different in the way proximity and distance are different. We shall see, and I would like merely to indicate this now, we shall see that these two worlds lead toward something that one can designate as nearness to God and distance from God.[5] And yet in the actuality of our life these two basic attitudes are qualitatively, essentially, different—not quantitatively, not by degrees. I

---

4. See ibid., pp. 53, 82: "The world is twofold for man in accordance with his twofold attitude." In *Daniel* (New York, 1965), 64, Buber writes: "There is a twofold relation of man to his experience."

5. Cf. *I and Thou*, p. 60: "Experience is remoteness from You"; see also ibid., pp. 147–148, and *Das verborgene Licht* (Frankfurt a. M., 1924), 18: "For, as the wise man says, 'Where can I find you? And where can I not find you?' And the Seraphim, too, answer: 'The earth is full of His glory.'" Buber relates this Hasidic tale to a poem by Judah Halevi; see *Das verborgene Licht*, p. 193.

would like to recall for those who attended the last lecture the memory of their life, the examples, the basic examples of relationship to a Thou, the most distinct forms, such as the relationship to a human being— in the clearest example of all, to a human being one loves.

Four Basic Examples

I mean, however, the pure, truthful relationship in which one confronts this person, truthfully, as his Thou. In this relationship one does not experience anything about this person. One confronts this person truly as his Thou. Here this person appears not as an aggregate of experienceable qualities; he is not an object that I can come to know, of which I then know something, about which I could now probably assert something. Rather, he is nothing more or less than my Thou, and in this exclusivity of the Thou—the Thou unlike the He and She and It is never juxtaposed to others but is always exclusive—the essence of the relationship is a world in itself.[6] Or, the same is true in a relationship with some confrontation, some piece of nature. If I do not place nature, or what I can grasp of nature in this moment, in a temporal-spatial world that is in such and such a condition and takes such and such a course, but rather if I confront (nature) in this thing or being as a Thou and actually say Thou to it in an unmediated way, then this thing is for me not a content of experience. But it is something exclusive, unique, unfolded only in this relationship, present only in this relationship.[7] And it cannot, it need not, however, by any means belong to the sphere that can be immediately translated into experience.

---

6. Cf. *I and Thou*, p. 69: "The human being who but now was unique and devoid of qualities, not at hand but only present, not experienceable, only touchable, has again become a He or She, an aggregate of qualities." See also Lecture Four.

7. Cf. *I and Thou*, p. 68: "Genuine contemplation never lasts long; the natural being that only now revealed itself to me in the mystery of reciprocity has again become describable. . . . And even love cannot persist in direct relation."

It is as if we make present to ourselves the artist who has the conception of his work and confronts his work as a Thou, as his Thou, in such a manner that he knows nothing of earlier works that may already surround him in the It-world: He knows only this one work—has, so to speak, a relationship only with this one, so that it becomes a world. This work, as it were, fills the entire horizon, and yet he does not know it in such a way that he could say something about it, describe it, demonstrate its place in space and time but only in such a way that he can actualize it. And even so, one would be laboring under a delusion fostered by academic philosophy if one were to interpret this as though the work were a psychic process, a fiction, something that this human being thinks up and only then makes actual. The truth, in this world of the actual of which we speak, is rather that the work *is*, just as much as the beloved person, or as nature when addressed as Thou. This relationship is not a relationship to something fictive but to something that is there, as Thou, not It.

To put it still more plainly:[8] For the person who decides on a deed—I have already spoken of him when I spoke of the relation of the religious to the ethical—for the person who decides on a deed, this deed is truly present for him as something that confronts him in such a way that, in the decision, it excludes. So that, all that is thinglike, all that can otherwise be met with and experienced, falls away, and nothing remains except this worldlike Thou of the deed that he has to do, that he has decided to do. And this, too, is not something fictive, not something that has yet to become actual; rather, in this moment of decision it is thoroughly actual and present—as something that confronts, as a Thou.

To make this elemental relation plainer, we may perhaps designate it with an objective expression, contrasting it to what has elsewhere,

---

8. Cf. ibid., p. 100: "Here I and You confront each other freely in a reciprocity that is not involved in or tainted by any causality; here man finds guaranteed the freedom of his being and of being. Only those who know relation and who know of the presence of the You have the capacity for decision. Whoever makes a decision is free because he has stepped before the countenance." See also ibid., p. 60.

for instance, in natural science or in psychology, been designated as polarity. What this bound polarity is, I shall now try to explain. Could one designate this relation as free polarity? By bound polarity I mean that both poles of the relation are objectifiable: They are fixed and can be objectified. Everything in natural science or psychology that is called polarity is of such a kind that we can and must grasp both poles as objective; both have been, so to speak, pegged down. Polarity in physics or biology or philosophy or psychology always means that two opposites, as one may call them, face each other in a certain relation of reciprocity, of transition, of flowing into each other and that this whole reciprocity has a thoroughly objective or objectifiable character. Concerning the polarity of which we are speaking here, it is not so. Rather, it is a free polarity; That is, the other pole, the Thou, is not objectifiable as long as the relation exists. The polarity is free. Only the one point, the point of the so-called It, is fixed. The other is floating, not objective, but present. I believe that by now you understand the attitude to which I refer sufficiently well so that I do not have to explain more clearly what I mean by I. Still, I would like to indicate it once more.

I most definitely do not mean any psychological I or any epistemological I, not anything that must first be abstracted from actual life. I mean simply the human being who says "I."[9] I mean each of you; I mean the present, actual human being who says "I" to himself and "Thou" to another, whether this other is a human being or a part of nature, a being or a thing, a work or a deed. I ask you always to keep this in mind; otherwise the level of actuality of which we are speaking cannot truly be entered into.

---

9. Cf. ibid., p. 65: "For I speak only of the actual human being, of you and me, of our life and our world, not of any I-in-itself and not of any Being-in-itself."

The Thou

What, then, does one experience of the Thou?[10] One experiences nothing. It is not an aggregate of qualities; it is not an object; it is not anything that I—not that either—not something that I know but cannot assert because my language is too weak, too inadequate. It is not an object at all. I experience nothing of it. What, then, does one know of the Thou? Only everything. That is, nothing, no particulars, nothing objectifiable, only everything.

Can one then fulfill the Thou-relation, the relationship, through knowledge? No. Only through actualization. If you have followed me to this point, then in this moment you already understand what I meant by calling these lectures "Religion as Presence." Now at last we have arrived at the first meaning of this word.[11] There is presence in life to the extent and only to the extent that there is relation, that there is Thou, that there is relation to a Thou. From such relation, from such relation alone, presence arises. When something confronts us and becomes our confronter, our exclusive confronter, by the fact that something becomes present to us, presence arises; and only on the strength of this is there presence.

To put it still more plainly: All these things of which we spoke, everything that confronts us as a Thou, can, even must, become an It. The very person we love—who in the Thou-relation was not an aggregate of qualities for us, who did not have such and such a character but who was thoroughly unique and devoid of characteristics—was only present, exclusively present, not to be known but only to be lived, to be actualized. This very person must necessarily—because of the finiteness of all the Thou of which we have spoken, the finiteness of all things—cross over into the It-world. He becomes a He or a She,

---

10. Cf. ibid., p. 61: "What, then, does one experience of the You?—Nothing at all. For one does not experience it.—What, then, does one know of the You?—Only everything. For one no longer knows particulars."

11. See ibid., pp. 83–84: "The world . . . it is your present; you have a present only insofar as you have it."

of whom one can indeed know all sorts of things, all sorts of characteristics, of whom one can and must state all sorts of qualities.[12]

That very part of nature that in the Thou-relation did not border on any other parts becomes a content that can be experienced, that is subject to the so-called natural laws and can be considered under their aspect, observed and ascertained.

The next example enters perhaps even more deeply into the particular, perhaps one may say tragic, connection[13] and entanglement of these things, into which the work of the artist enters by its very actualization, by the very fact that he creates it. That is, he makes it from a presence into an objective reality; by this very fact it enters into the actuality of things, becomes a thing among things that one now, indeed, cannot help knowing. Even the artist cannot help knowing all kinds of things. But now, of course, it is something that he can already describe, of which he knows something, that is composed of qualities.

And the deed done by a person who decides has entered, by the very fact that it is done, into the world of It, of the experienceable. It has become objective.

Thus presence becomes object,[14] and I would like to ask you to confront yourselves with these words in a very immediate way. Then you will find that the one, which designates something, which one usually uses for something that is apparently quite transient, which only exists in the moment and passes away with the moment—that the word presence in truth designates that which is lasting, that which,

---

12. Cf. ibid., pp. 68–69: "And even love cannot persist in direct relation; it endures, but only in the alternation of actuality and latency. The human being who but now was unique and devoid of qualities, not at hand but only present, not experienceable, only touchable, has again become a He or She, an aggregate of qualities, a quantum with a shape."

13. Cf. ibid., p. 68: "This, however, is the sublime melancholy of our lot that every You must become an It in our world."

14. Cf. ibid., p. 63: "For the real boundary . . . runs . . . between presence and object."

one may well say, leads one across, that which waits in truth, which lastingly confronts me, which is eternal.[15]

The word "object" (*Gegenstand*) is the stoppage, the breaking off, the becoming fixed, dense, flowing away to something that is now squeezed, forced into the It-world. Objects exist only in the past. The past is object. By becoming object, presence becomes past.[16]

Development of the Child

We can also express it in this way: Beings live in the present; objects exist in the past. I have pointed out, and I should merely like to repeat it briefly, that this duality corresponds to the development of the human being and probably also to the development of the human race, and that it (shows) itself in the life, in the immediate life, of the individual. And I repeat, this is what we are talking about. We are not talking about something conceptual but only about life, about the actual life of each one of us, just as in immediate life it shows itself in the development of life. If, for instance, we look at the development of the I in the child, we see that the development of the I is the same as the development of the consciousness of I, so the two cannot be separated at all. The development of the I occurs in two different ways. The I comes into being only by being set off. In the beginning there is no I. The primal, undifferentiated life, the natural life out of which the human being grows, in which he grows up—this life knows no I and, of course, no Thou and no He either.[17] It is merely undifferentiated

---

15. Cf. ibid., pp. 63–64: "The present—not that which is like a point and merely designates whatever our thoughts may posit as the end of 'elapsed' time . . . And the object is not duration but standing still, ceasing, breaking off."

16. Cf. ibid., pp. 63–64: "The I of the basic word I-It . . . has only a past and no present. In other words: insofar as a human being makes do with the things that he experiences and uses, he lives in the past, and his moment has no presence. . . . But objects consist in having been."

17. Cf. ibid., p. 76: "Every developing human child rests, like all developing beings, in the womb of the great mother—the undifferentiated, not yet formed primal world." See also ibid., p. 77.

life; it is creation. Out of this undifferentiatedness of the world of creation, when the human being is born, the I forms itself in two ways: [in one way,] by setting itself off from a world of He, She, It, as one usually assumes. Indeed, one usually considers this setting off as the only one; one usually says: "I come to consciousness."[18] This is again the false attitude that believes that it can separate consciousness from the coming-into-being of the I by saying: Thus the I comes to consciousness by setting itself off from other things. But precisely this attitude, which ˙ regarded as the decisive one, is merely secondary; the primary anu decisive formation of the I, the setting off of the I, occurs not as a setting off against an It but as a setting off against a Thou.

The primary act of the child, who reaches over the undifferentiated creation and so to speak out of and away from it, is the reaching for a Thou—and not only for a certain Thou that is experienced, such as the mother or an object, but for the Thou, for the still nameless, still unknown, undetermined Thou pure and simple.[19] The more strongly this Thou confronts the child, the more strongly it learns to set itself off against it as an I, that is, as the one who reaches for it and who is not this Thou-being as the one who stands in relation to it. Even in this early stage these two worlds are inherent: the world of Thou, which tends toward pure connection, connection not union, for relation is connection; and the world of It, which tends toward pure separation, severance.

Objectively formulated, there are three layers of world: the world of nondifferentiation, the world of creation, the world of It; that is, the experiential world, or, as one usually says, the world of perception (*Wahrnehmungswelt*) (one takes [*nimmt*] something to be true [*wahr*]) and

18. Cf. ibid., pp. 73–74. The similarity is one of content only.
19. Cf. ibid., pp. 77–78: "The innateness of the longing for relationship is apparent even in the earliest and dimmest stage . . . and at times when there is obviously no desire for nourishment . . . soft projections of the hands reach . . . into the empty air toward the indefinite. . . . But this 'imagination' is by no means a form of 'panpsychism'; it is the drive to turn everything into a You."

80

the Thou-world, the world of realization. And this Thou is not something that approaches the human being after the fact, that is merely superimposed; it is not an empirical fact that is presented to man. Rather, it is something that is already inherent in man. There is an innate Thou. This innate Thou unfolds by confronting the child, and therefore it is already clear at this point that all this cannot be grasped from the experience of particular objects, but it is something that exists in itself and merely presents itself in the so-called objects.

And I should like merely to illustrate what can be insofar inferred in the case of the primitive man as well as in the child, all the elemental events of the life of the child and of the primitive human being, that is valid to the extent that the human being is still close to the Undifferentiated, to all the elemental processes. Then all the elemental convulsions of this life are based on the relation to a Thou, on the tremendous thing that thus happens to the child, to the primitive human being when this innate Thou confronts him bodily. And this may even be a dream—or what one must call a dream; that is, localized in the world of experience, it can be a dream, an image.

For in the world of the child and of the primitive human being the corporeal is simply not determined from the standpoint of experience. And, therefore, an image is as corporeal for him as anything that we have established as corporeal by experiential criteria.

The Thou and the Absolute Thou

Are Thou-relations only isolated moments? I think that since every Thou, because of its finiteness as a thing or its being delimited as a thing (I remind you of the work and the deed), must change from a Thou into an It. Therefore the relations are necessarily moments of life that come and go, lightning flashes in the sky of life that disappear, among which there is no continuity.[20] If this were true, and it seems

---

20. Cf. ibid., p. 163: "The moments . . . are no mere flashes of lightning in the dark but like a rising moon on a clear starry night."

to be, then a Thou-world would be impossible. Only an infinity of Thou-moments, world-moments, would be possible, and the continuous world would remain the world of It, the world of orientation,[21] the world in which there are things, qualities, objects. What could this reality of the innate Thou then mean? Could this be merely something that is inherent in us, that has been placed in us, suggesting a task that we are unable to perform? For how is a world of Thou, a world of immediate truth, to be built up if nothing of it enters our life except moments without continuity, transitory moments? If we juxtapose the two elemental basic attitudes of which I have spoken, then we may well feel first of all that the construction of an It-world means somehow a betrayal, a falling away, a distancing of ourselves from the task that is inherent in us. This is the task of constructing the world out of the Thou—a distancing that is of course necessary, and that is ordained by our human nature but that nevertheless remains a distancing, a falling away, a betrayal.[22] But if in actuality the Thou-relationships were isolated moments, then this falling away would be not only inevitable but eternally insuperable. Then we could never raise ourselves from the world of orientation to a true world, at least as long as we were beings, human beings.

There are always attempts to make the world as a whole, the It-world, independent, to detach it from relation, to know it as that which is, to fathom its secret. And from the standpoint of the Thou, from

---

21. "Orientation" is typical of Buber's thought when he wrote *Daniel*; it does not appear in *I and Thou*.
22. This section, though well prepared, was excluded from *I and Thou*. Cf. *I and Thou*, pp. 82–85, in particular 84: "The Thou-world does not hang together in space and time." The negative attitude toward the world that Buber displays here is unusual for him. It may show the influence of Ferdinand Ebner; see Ebner, *Schriften*, vol. 1 (Munich, 1963–1965), 91, 92, 304.

In *Das verborgene Licht*, p. 17, Buber takes a different position. He quotes a Hasidic saying: "For there is no level of being on which one cannot find God's holiness, everywhere and at every time." (Hasidic stories incorporated into that book were the theme of a seminar Buber led at the Lehrhaus in conjunction with these lectures.) Cf. also his *Daniel*, p. 95: "to live so as to realize God in all things."

the knowledge of the Thou, we grasp that all these attempts are in vain, that all this so-called world is nothing other than a creation that has run away from God. But if the Thou-relation consists of isolated moments, then our fate would be insuperable, then this flight from the Thou would be the only possibility of remaining in life. If all Thou, by the nature of each of these Thous, becomes objective, becomes It, then there is apparently no continuity of the Thou-world, that is, no present that does not become past. Then there is no presence that lasts and fulfills life. This is the basic issue in the light of which we can, I believe, alone grasp what may rightfully be called religion. It is the question of the continuity of the Thou, of the unconditionality of the Thou.

God is the absolute Thou, which by its nature can no longer become It. When we address as Thou not any limitable thing that by its nature must become an object but the unconditional—Being itself—then the continuity of the Thou-world is opened up. The human being's sense of Thou, of every innate Thou that is latent in him and unfolds in the relationship, which must again and again experience the disappointment of the Thou becoming It, strives through and beyond all of them toward its adequate Thou. There is in truth no God-seeking; rather, one discovers something, beyond all obstacles, that was with one from the very beginning.

It is not a seeking but a finding. It is a finding without seeking: It is a discovery of that which is the most primal and most immediate. The human being's Thou-sense, which is insatiable until it finds the Thou as such, had this Thou present in itself from the beginning and needed only to bring out this presence and make it wholly actual.[23]

---

23. Cf. *I and Thou*, p. 128: "It is a finding without seeking; a discovery of what is most original and the origin. The You-sense that cannot be satiated until it finds the infinite You sensed its presence from the beginning; this presence merely had to become wholly actual for it."

In the lectures, Buber called God "das Du an sich" (the Thou as such), Kant's expression, which he had used earlier in "*Herut*," in *On Judaism* (New York, 1967), 150. In *I and Thou* he changed it to "das unendliche Du" (the infinite Thou).

It is not that this Thou must be inferred from something else, for instance, from nature as its cause, from history as that which reigns in it and over it, from the subject as its final subjectivity and I-quality, which can be inferred from pure thought. It is not that something else is primary and this Thou is then inferred from it, but even what is immediate and first for us and present before all and in confrontation with everything, which is assertion, means necessarily a limitation, an overstraining, an attempt at falling away.[24]

The pure relation, which is the truth of life, finds here its fulfillment and also its continuity. Here lies the guarantee of the construction of a world from the Thou.

Our next task will be to survey, from this point that we have reached, that sphere that I designated at the beginning as the necessary relativization of the religious, that is, the sphere that one generally calls religion.

---

24. Cf. *I and Thou*, p. 129: "It is not as if God could be inferred from anything—say, from nature as its cause, or from history as its helmsman, or perhaps from the subject as the self that thinks itself through it. It is not as if something else were 'given' and this were then deduced from it. This is what confronts us immediately and first and always, and legitimately it can only be addressed, not asserted." Cf. Ebner, *Schriften*, vol. 1, pp. 97, 256.

LECTURE SIX

February 26, 1922

Religion as Presence

Last time I spoke of what it is that hinders the construction of a Thou-world, the construction of a world out of Thou-relations, and what it is that made and makes it so difficult to confront the It-world with a Thou-world, namely, the apparent discontinuity of the Thou-moments. And in the face of this question arose whether an actual continuity of the Thou-moments in the depth of actuality is possible, whether there exists a Thou-world that is hidden and has to be lifted out. We asked whether it was characteristic, necessarily characteristic, of all relations that they change from presence, immediate present, to past, according to the nature of each Thou, and whether it was necessarily characteristic of all of them that they change from presence to object, so that every Thou must necessarily become an It, a He, or a She, a thing or being in the It-world. And to this question we found the answer that there is one relation, the decisive one, of which this is not characteristic, that is, the relation to the absolute Thou, which by its nature cannot become It.

This absolute Thou, which is not inferred from natural history as a subject but which is immediately present, this absolute Thou in our relation to it is the inviolable core of a continuous Thou-world. From this vantage point the continuity of the Thou-moments can be established.[1]

We can call this relation—in contradistinction to all others in whose nature the germ of their transition to the It-world lies, in contradistinction to everything else—the pure relation. And I repeat what I said at the beginning, what I ask you to keep in mind constantly during our journey together: All that we are contemplating here is not to be grasped psychologically.[2] This goes for all the relations of which we have spoken. I remind you of the examples of which we spoke last time: the relation to a beloved human being, the relation to nature as a Thou, the relation to the work one has conceived, to one's own creation as to a Thou, the relation to the deed in the decision as a Thou. All these are not to be grasped psychologically, not as something that occurs *in* the human being but that occurs[3] between[4] the human being and a Thou that has being. Otherwise we do not have anything whole in our hands, only a fragment with which we can do nothing.

This Thou has being; however, its being is not like that of something at hand, which we may encounter. Rather, it is the Being that unfolds only in relation. And this applies with particular, incomparable strength to the pure relation. This relation, too, more than any other, is not to be grasped psychologically but as an event in which we stand, a relation so real, grasped as immediate presence, just as we are capable of grasping any relationship.

As when we walk our way and encounter a person who comes

---

1. Cf. *I and Thou*, trans. Walter Kaufmann (New York, 1970), 128; see also Buber, *Daniel* (New York, 1965), 91, on the theologians who deduce God from His causes.

2. Here Buber says, "cannot be grasped psychologically." At the corresponding point in *I and Thou*, he quotes his criticism of psychology regarding Schleiermacher and Otto in Lecture Three; see *I and Thou*, p. 129. Buber probably had these *two* lectures in front of him when writing *I and Thou*.

3. Cf. the shorter version in *I and Thou*, p. 129: "What has been said earlier of love is even more clearly true at this point: Feelings merely accompany the fact of the relationship which, after all, is established not in the soul but between an I and a You."

4. This is one of the rare cases where the important term *zwischen* (between) appears in the lectures.

toward us and is also walking a way, we know only our part and experience the other only in the encounter—that is the way it is here.[5]

Every actual event of the spirit is first and foremost an encounter, a going forth and an encounter. We know—in the way of having lived we know our going forth, our having gone forth—this part of our way. The other part merely happens to us; we do not know it. It happens to us in the encounter.[6] This other we may call grace.[7] But we try to encompass more than we can if we speak of it as an It, something other than what exists in the encounter.

What concerns us in the encounter, that is, what we know of it from our life, from our own standpoint, is not a waiting, not a being open, not what one calls receptivity. Rather, from our standpoint, it is concentrated activity. Unified, whole activity. But it is an activity that is not felt as such because it is essentially different from the feeling of activity that we know from all other activities, because it is essentially different from the feeling of activity that we know from all dividing, dichotomous activity, in short, from all the activities of all our days.

That is the activity of the human being who has become whole, the activity that in particular religions has been called not-doing, in which nothing particular, nothing partial is at work in the human being. And, thus, nothing of him intrudes into the world. Rather, the whole human being, self-contained and calm, is active here, goes forth, where the human being has become a whole that acts and goes forth.[8]

---

5. Cf. *I and Thou*, p. 124: "When we walk our way and encounter a man who comes toward us, walking his way, we know our way only and not his; for his comes to life for us only in the encounter."

6. Cf. ibid., p. 124: "Of the perfect relational process we know in the manner of having lived through it our going forth, our way. The other part merely happens to us, we do not know it. It happens to us in the encounter."

7. Cf. ibid.: "Our concern, our care must be not for the other side but for our own, not for grace but for Will. Grace concerns us insofar as we proceed toward it and await its presence; it is not our object." This idea is developed more extensively in *I and Thou*.

8. Cf. ibid., p. 125: "This is the activity of the human being who has become whole: it has been called not-doing, for nothing particular, nothing partial is at work in man and thus nothing of him intrudes into the world. It is the whole human being, closed in its wholeness, at rest in its wholeness; that is active here, as the human being has become an active whole."

For only something whole can be the I of the pure relation; only something whole can say Thou to the absolute Thou. To this end one does not have to abandon the world of the senses as a world of appearances. There is no world of appearance; there is only our adequate or inadequate relation to the world.[9] Our inadequate relation to the world is the experience of which we have spoken, having the world as an aggregate of It-contents. Only this is to be annulled, not the world. There is no need to "go beyond sense experience," as people say. Every experience, whatever its character, could only give us an It. There is no need to turn to a world of ideas and values, for this world of ideas and values can only be the superstructure of an It-world and not Thou, not presence, not that which confronts us in immediate, present relation.[10] All this is not needed.

Can one say what is needed? Yes and no. Not by way of prescription. All the prescriptions that have been excogitated and invented in the history of the human spirit, over and over throughout the ages, all the preparations, exercises, and meditations that have been suggested have nothing to do with the perfectly simple and decisive matter of which we are speaking. All the advantages gained by knowledge or art, by power or the effect of one or another exercise—they all remain inadequate, senseless, and actually foolish in the face of what we are speaking of; they do not approach it. All this is valid only in the world where it has meaning, and everything that is gained in this manner has its place only in the It-world and does not take us one step—does not take the decisive step—beyond it. The going forth is unteachable in the sense of prescriptions, and yet it can be pointed to. But it can only be pointed to in this very simple way, in the way all these things we are speaking of can be indicated: by drawing, as it were, a circle that

---

9. Cf. ibid., p. 125: "To this end one does not have to strip away the world of the senses as a world of appearance. There is no world of appearance, there is only the world."

10. Cf. ibid.: "Nor is there any need to 'go beyond sense experience'; any experience, no matter how spiritual, could only yield us an It. Nor need we turn to a world of ideas and values—that cannot become present for us. All this is not needed."

excludes everything that does not belong here, by demarcating and pointing out this exorcising circle.[11] With this, of course, the human being, the particular person, is given each time the hint that then of course has to be actualized, fulfilled, by that person with his own personal actuality[12]—that actuality that can neither be prescribed nor grasped in general but that is present only in the life unique to him. This is what I mean by saying that the aim is not to go out of the world but to go with it, not to let it become an It-world, not to let it congeal into an It-world but to take the world with you, to raise it up: in the Hasidic phrase, which also means to lift it up to its root,[13] to leave nothing outside, to say Yes to everything without exception—everything being not a finite or infinite number of things or events but everything in the universal Thou. The aim, moreover, is not to abandon the particular Thou-relations, not to renounce them or push them into the background, but to let them all stream into the absolute relation, into the relation that arises neither from the aggregate of other relations, nor still less from the elimination of them, but from their becoming All.

And I ask you to grasp this as concretely as you are able to grasp it, each one from his own life, from what he himself knows in an unmediated way of the Thou-relation. All this is not to be left outside.

---

11. Cf. ibid., pp. 125–126: "Can one say what is needed? Not by way of a prescription. All the prescriptions that have been excogitated and invented in the ages of the human spirit, all the preparations, exercises, and meditations that have been suggested have nothing to do with the primally simple fact of encounter. All the advantages of knowledge or power that one may owe to one or another exercise do not approach that of which we are speaking here. All this has its place in the It-world and does not take us one step—does not take the decisive step—out of it. Going forth is unteachable in the sense of prescriptions. It can only be indicated—by drawing a circle that excludes everything else."

12. A question mark was placed on the word *Wirklichen* (actuality) because the sentence is unclear.

13. Buber's interpretation of his dialogical thinking by the Hasidic term *le-ha'alot le-shorsham* is noteworthy; it means in the root, things are authentic; man is supposed to bring the redemption by lifting things back up to their primordial root.

And, moreover, not to let any means exist in this relation, in this decisive relation, but to take every means, everything that still wants to be mean and mediator, with you into immediacy.

A Legend

There is an Indian legend that can perhaps make this clear to you in pictoric form. It tells of an ascetic, M., who for vast ages (these Indian legends habitually speak of thousands and thousands of years), who for vast ages was gathering his strength. He drew, as it were, all his strength into itself, and this strength radiated outward ever more powerfully, so powerfully that it finally touched the gods. And when the gods sent him temptation after temptation in order to break his strength, in order to dissipate his strength, and he withstood their temptations and his strength only increased, they were finally forced to descend and inquire after his wish.

Indra, the prince of the gods, appears before the ascetic and asks him what his desire is. And he answers, approximately: I would like to behold. I would like to gaze on Being itself.[14] And in that moment his request is granted, and all the solid surroundings in which he was standing, all this well-ordered world of forms and colors, of things and beings, of space and time, all this clear, distinct, orderly, constructed world falls apart. He finds himself standing in a tremendous vortex of infinity, of chaos. He can grasp nothing more; he can perceive nothing more; he is standing in the void; he is no longer standing on anything. He is carried off by the vortex and can no longer hold on to anything, not with any sense, not with any organ. But the moment he believes himself utterly lost, the vortex as it were, splits apart, recedes, and M. sees a newborn child emerging from the vortex. M. gazes at this child, and through this gazing he, as it were, acquires being. He reveres the

---

14. Cf. *I and Thou*, p. 136 (and p. 82, where the early theme of beholding the world order also appears).

child and feels that he loves this child, and in that moment the child opens its mouth and inhales him. He feels himself going into the child, and suddenly he sees once more in the child this whole world of things and beings, of spaces and times, everything in its articulation and its necessity.

And then the child exhales him and all is over. He is standing once more on the threshold of his hermitage, gazing into the familiar world.[15]

Mysticism: A Critique

This simple confrontation is that which in all religions, time and again, is grasped as the actual in its actuality. But this simple act—once again we must draw the circle and eliminate whatever is not this—this very simple act of entering into relation does not mean a so-called mystical act. It means nothing more than the acceptance of immediate presence. Of course, the farther the human being has strayed into the It-world, the more he has gotten lost in it, the greater the stakes, the heavier the risk, the more powerful the turning that this acceptance requires. It is not a renouncing of the I, as mysticism usually assumes. The I is as indispensable for the pure relationship as it is for every relationship because every relationship is simply that which occurs between an I and a Thou. It is a giving up, therefore, not of the I but of that false drive for self-affirmation that makes man flee from relationship into orientation, into the It-world, into the having of things.[16] I remind you

---

15. This story is an indication of Buber's interest in myth, which was very conspicuous in his early period.

16. Buber continues from where he stopped before the legend. Cf. *I and Thou*, p. 126: "It can only be indicated—by drawing a circle that excludes everything else. Then the one thing needed becomes visible: the total acceptance of the present. To be sure, this acceptance involves a heavier risk and more fundamental return, the further man has lost his way in separation. What has to be given up is not the I, as most mystics suppose: the I is indispensable for any relationship, including the highest, which always presupposes an I and You. What has to be given up is not the I but that false drive for self-affirmation which impels man to flee from the unreliable, unsolid, unlasting, unpredictable, dangerous world of relation into the having of things."

of the layers that we can distinguish both in the life of a particular human being and in the life of the human race; the layer of nondifferentiation from which emerges the layer of differentiation, of experience, and—hidden, but always revealing itself at the same time—the layer of actualization, of unification.[17]

If one may use a biblical parable:[18] At first there is the human being who has not yet eaten from the Tree of Knowledge, who stands in nondifferentiation—as the Bible puts it, in the nondifferentiation of good and evil. Second, there is the human being who eats from the Tree of Knowledge without also eating from the Tree of Life, the human being who stands in the sundering of good and evil, in the separation of the world. And third, there is the human being who makes the turning. But there is no turning back to not-having-eaten. Rather, the turning means the way to the Tree of Life, to the overarching union of the world-separated worlds in the absolute I, in the pure relation, and to the world that is constructed from it.

This particular consequence I can only suggest at this spot; we shall have occasion to speak of it again. I say that what is meant is not a mystical act; what is meant is not something reserved for a human being of some particular nature or disposition. But it is something that opens up for every human being who does it.

Thus what is meant is not what one calls ecstasy. And it would probably be well to make present to ourselves for a moment how the act of ecstasy relates to this perfectly simple and universally human matter of which we speak.

When one speaks of the ecstatic act in mysticism, one means a union.[19] This way of speaking implies that there is something beyond relation, beyond I and Thou, a unity that transcends this duality. This is something of which it is difficult to speak, of which I have found it

---

17. This passage resembles *Daniel*. Note the terminology: *Orientierung* (orientation), *Verwirklichung* (actualization/realization), and *Einung* (unification).
18. The creation story was used by Buber in his other writings. See *On Judaism* (New York, 1967), 26; and *Good and Evil Two Interpretations* (New York, 1953), 67–80.
19. *Vereinigung*.

harder and harder to speak with only a few words of indication, insofar as it concerns us.

What mystics usually call union, Unio, means—I should like at first to formulate it conceptually, afterwards I shall explain—a hypostasis of the pure relation. I will explain. A hypostasis is an attribute elevated to an independent substance, to the dignity of independence. Something that in actuality only exists by clinging to a substance is now grasped as an independent substance, as has happened in the history of mysticism with God's word, God's wisdom, and the like. But it is possible to hypostatize, to elevate to such independent substances, not only attributes but also relationships.

I mean by this that what is called unity in mysticism is nothing other than the dynamics of relationship. Thus it is not a unity, which has come into being in this moment, that transcends the relationship, that annuls I and Thou and fuses them together. Rather, it is the dynamic of the relationship itself that so to speak moves in front of the members of the relationship, suppresses them, covers them, whereas the two members of the relationship, in the reality of the relationship, immovably confront each other. Here, too, there is relationship but with a strange danger, with the danger of an exorbitance of the human share, of the human share in the act of relation, an exorbitance that wants to annul the relation and thereby clouds the relation, obscures its outline, its actuality.[20] Because of this exorbitance, it becomes impossible to channel the relation into a continuation of life, to let it flow into the construction of a Thou-world. I should like to say now, by

---

20. The text of the lectures here and Buber's following answer to a person in the audience are the sources for the following paragraph in *I and Thou*, p. 135: "What the ecstatic calls unification is the rapturous dynamics of the relationship; not a unity that has come into being at this moment in world time, fusing I and You, but the dynamics of the relationship itself which can stand before the two carriers of this relationship, although they confront each other immovably, and cover the eyes of the enraptured. What we find here is a marginal exorbitance of the act of relation: the relationship itself in its vital unity is felt so vehemently that its members pale in the process: its life predominates so much that the I and Thou between whom it is established are forgotten."

way of anticipation, that this is a theme that will occupy us again. Just as on the other side of what is historically called religion, so on this side of which we are speaking, it is mysticism that lends itself to the danger of breaking off, that is the obstacle to the formation of a continuity of the Thou-world. This esoteric, privileged mysticism and theological dogma are the two poles that each time attract and annul the Thou-relation.

Response to Questions

Before I go on I would like—since we can now, as it were, mark off another stretch of the way—to urge you once again to ask questions if something in what has been defined so far remains unclear to you. It is perhaps of particular importance now because we must now, as it were, enter a new dimension, namely, the question of the historical, of religion in the narrower sense: the displacement of God into the It-world. In the last part it was necessary to speak of various marginal matters more conceptually than has occurred in the course of these lectures, in order to mark off that of which we speak from the other with all possible sharpness. But the conceptual is also, always and inevitably, that which differentiates; and therefore I would appreciate it if you would now, before we pass from this sphere into another, ask questions if something has remained unclear.

Question: Why is this relation to the Thou not in reality? Why does it then have to enter into relation to the transcendent Thou?

Answer: I definitely do mean the Thou in reality. In what I say there is nothing whatsoever about transcendence. I should like to repeat: Whether God is transcendent or immanent is not God's affair; it is the affair of the human being. What is meant is not at all anything transcendent. Transcendence, after all, refers to something to which we cannot place ourselves in immediate, present relation. Therefore I do not mean anything at all transcendent. As long as you speak of the transcendent Thou, we obviously do not mean the same thing. I mean the simple Thou, which is present in immediate presence, as present as any Thou in a human relation, only that this Thou by its nature (is) not . . .

Question: Can I say instead of Thou "my other I"?

Answer: What you say is not at all what this depends on. It does not depend on what you call the Thou. Only, I don't know any better word in human language than Thou. When I say "I" I mean something quite different from when I say "Thou." So if you disarrange these very clear, meaningful basic words, it seems that what is meant loses something of its immediate clarity.[21] For what it is to say "I" and "Thou" we know from our whole life with a distinctness that we could never gather from another person's words.

Question: I think that when the artist is seized by this artistic thing of which we have spoken, to which he says "Thou," we might just as well, from our standpoint, call it his I.

Answer: Absolutely not. Never would an artist at the actual moment of conception perceive as his I the work that he wants to create, find, bring out, make actual. On the contrary, he would perceive it very much as the other, opposite which he stands in this unique kind of relationship, that is, in this relationship of gazing and wanting to actualize, of this discovery and this compulsion to create—not at all as a mirroring, as a detachment, as a fragment but very much as the work that confronts him, which is of a very different character from himself. He of course cannot say what its character is, just as he cannot say what his own character is when he knows himself as present. Once he knows what its character is, he is no longer in conception. But he knows that it is his work, just as he cannot confront his I at all, unless his I splits in two, so that the I results as its own confronter and the human being then, of course, steps to the edge. For then he no longer stands in continuity with his own life; something that science usually terms the pathological happens to him, but I do not want to give it that name. When the I does not find its natural Thou, then this innate Thou unfolds itself, so to speak, with the unnatural, the impossible object. (With the I, it unfolds itself where it really has no room to unfold.)

---

21. In answering a question Buber uses *Grundwort*, a term of great importance in *I and Thou*. Cf. *I and Thou*, p. 53: "The basic words are not single words, but word-pairs."

There arises the contradiction, the crack, the confrontation within one-self. That is a problem by itself. Much that many people have inter-preted as religious was perhaps nothing more than this, which always comes to grief when the person somehow cannot fulfill the simple de-mand of natural life to confront, actually, an actual Thou. This means basically life. This does not mean the kind of rigidity in which this need takes refuge, where it cannot be rightfully fulfilled.

Question: You spoke of the relation to the absolute I. I can under-stand when one calls Thou-relationships absolute relationships, but is it not perhaps also a hypostatization when I speak of pure relation to the absolute Thou? The Thou-relation I can call absolute relation, but the relation to the absolute . . .

Answer: I did not say "to the absolute"; I said "to the absolute Thou," that is, to the Thou that by its nature can no longer become It—nothing more.[22] And therefore I called every other Thou relative because by its nature it becomes It. This is no hypostatization. Not a word has been said about the relation as such, that is, of an absolute, and certainly not of the Thou as a kind of object that would be absolute in any other way than as the Thou of a relation. We did not speak of all that; we spoke only of the relation to the absolute Thou. In the face of this relation every other relation is of course relative, not absolute but relative, for every other relationship is so constituted that by the nature of the Thou—you can check this by the example—that by the nature of the Thou it must change into an It-relation. It cannot remain present because of the nature of the Thou. But here is the relation that perhaps—we shall speak of this later—because of our nature does not remain a Thou-relation but that because of the nature of the Thou does not need to stop, does not have to become past, to become objective. So in this sense, I am using the word "absolute" like the other words

---

22. It is interesting to note the possibility that a question posed by a student who mistook "absolutes" for a noun rather than an adjective may have helped Buber clarify his term for God. While in the lectures, God is usually called Absolute Thou, this term is not used in *I and Thou*. On the other hand, "Eternal Thou," the term most often used for God in *I and Thou*, had never been used in the lectures.

I use, not in the sense of any conceptual world, any philosophically conceptual world, but in this very specific concrete sense of which we are speaking. I am thus using the world "absolute" in the thoroughly concrete sense that here is a relation that does not have to be deflected according to the nature of the Thou. Therefore I call it a pure relation. This, too, is not meant in an academic philosophical way but in this quite particular sense of life.

Question: If you still use the medium of language, then the relation is not as immediate as when they only need to look at each other . . .

Answer: I did very much emphasize that there is no question of fusion, but of confrontation, from being to being, from a whole I to a whole Thou. That is, not in any way that (would be) a splitting off of the I. Medium, or means, is always differentiation. Means is always a part. When I talk about taking the means over into immediacy, this means nothing other than totality. A means is always something that has been split off. If you, for instance, examine in the religions what a mediator is, you will see that it is always . . .

Question: What does mysticism mean when it speaks of Unio?

Answer: What we are speaking of is not Unio. Unio means that strange, actually marginal exorbitance of the Thou-relation in which the relation itself, its unity, is lived with such tremendous strength and vehemence that its members seem to pale and die away. What comes into being here is something marginal, in a certain sense a new unity. But what one calls by this name is in truth nothing but the relation that is experienced so intensely that the life of this relation causes I and Thou to be forgotten. But as long as you carry over anything of the I into this, it is totally false.

Question: . . . not from the corporeal I but from the essential, in which I would like to behold the Divine.

Answer: I cannot carry this out. I know that I can say "I". Everything else is allegorical. Only from the fact that I myself can say "I" do I know of the I. What I mean is not something derived but something immediate. When I say "Thou," this is not derived. It is not some kind of psychological process starting from the I. Of course, in all this there is a limit to communication. I think I have already indicated this, but

I want to say it clearly once more. The limitation of communication is the life of every single one of you; it is life.

Question: There is then no world of appearances, as you say?

Answer: We are already talking past each other. I don't know what could be more actual, more concrete, more irrefutable and unshakeable than when I say "I." If you, about yourself, feel that the I is an appearance, I cannot. Not even in Buddha's sense. We are speaking here only of the stripping away of a certain rigidification that disturbs the I. The "world of appearances" and all these things are of secondary nature; they are merely the superstructure. I am appealing to nothing other than that which every single one of you knows immediately of himself if only he wants to know it; that is, if he asks himself about all the things that he has experienced, if he reflects in complete honesty on his ultimate actuality of life. Then, of course, we are speaking the same language. This is the boundary beyond which I cannot go.

Question: Does one arrive at this relationship, at this absolute Thou—which I, because I can make it clear to myself better in this way, would like to call God—does one arrive at it by saying Thou to the particular things and thus uniting the world with oneself or by having struggled through to God?

Answer: Both. Of the one thing we spoke already, namely, that one needs the Thou-relations, the pure Thou-relations, which should all flow into the decisive relation.

Question: Does this mean, then, that one brings oneself into relation with God?

Answer: No. We spoke of the one thing, that every actual relation into which we enter is only suited to further, to help the decisive relationship if we let it flow in. That is one side of what you are saying. Concerning the other side, how the relations—the particular relations to the Thou each time, the world-relations, the human relations—are determined, transformed through the absolute, through the pure relation: Of this we shall speak the next time. May I remind you that I spoke of the construction of a Thou-world and said: What hinders this is its discontinuity, its lack of coherence; it is always particular Thou-moments, Thou-relations, that have no continuity from one to the next.

And I said that there is something that is capable of creating this continuity, and that is the pure relation to an absolute Thou.

Question: But then it is only by believing in God, after all, that one comes to be able to say Thou to the other things and to see the Thou in everything.

Answer: No, that is not the way it is. Rather, one comes only then to the continuity of all that to which one can say Thou, to the unity of the Thou and the world. Basically one can always say Thou. Any child can say Thou, Thou-saying is the simplest matter of which we speak, as it is the simplest, most primal thing in human life. The reaching for the Thou, the flowing toward the Thou—this requires nothing personal, not even belief in God, as you say. I would not consider "belief"[23] to be an adequate expression. But that is not what is important here. What is important is the lack of continuity, a continuity that can only arise from this decisive relation: It is the unity of the Thou in the world, not the single Thou-relations but their living continuity, that they not remain separate from each other, not atoms that we cannot fit together but parts of something living.

Question: . . . Then that which (. . .) is the great unification of all the many Thou's, which one gains only when one recognizes the one great Thou that we call God when we enter into relation with it.

Answer: One can express it that way. Basically, what is important is that one feel these things. And if one feels something genuinely, it is not so terribly important how one expresses it.

---

23. *Glauben.* This word is translated by Kaufmann as "faith"; (see *I and Thou*, p. 162); however, "belief" corresponds more closely to the idea of an objective credo that Buber is rejecting.

March 5, 1922

A Difficult Problem

We are standing at a very difficult, perhaps the most difficult, point along the way that we are walking together. Even before this, the real responsibility at every step consisted in resolutely and decidedly going beyond the present individualism and relativism of our time and yet not venturing a step where we did not feel truly genuine, adequate spiritual ground under our feet. The responsibility is to go beyond the view that the religious is limited to the human individual, to reject this view and still, with the modesty that is incumbent upon us, to grasp the human person as the point of departure, as the place of origin, of the decisive religious event. We must also go beyond the view that there are different religious perspectives that have, so to speak, equal rights because they proceed from subjectivities that have equal rights; and yet we must stop at subjectivity and not set foot on the ground of an objective domain that we are not authorized to enter upon.

This particular responsibility, which we may take as a time-bound one—as something that corresponds to this specific time, this moment in which we live, this moment between words, between worlds, this moment of the deepest valley—can perhaps also be grasped as something that goes beyond the time-bound. In any case, this responsibility becomes especially difficult and acute at the point at which we are now standing, where we must place that which we have recognized as the

101

nature of the religious event in confrontation with religion and with such religions as have developed in the history of humanity.

We have seen that in the human person as well as in the human race there are two ways that lead out of the primal layer of nondifferentiation: the It-way, which wants to lead toward pure separation (that is, to so-called knowledge of the world, orientation in the world, and use of the world, which is the way that the world is given to us in order that one may know one's way around in it and use it); and the Thou-way, which wants to lead to pure connection (that is, to love of the world and the unfolding of the world, which is the way that does not take the world for granted, as something thus and thus constituted, which one has only to know and to use, but as something that one has to confront in the Thou-relation, to love and to unfold through this love and with it, only thereby bringing it to its true being). The It-world, as we have seen, has its natural space-time continuity, since all things and events can be set immediately into this world and thus form a continuity without gaps in space and time. This It-world comes into being and maintains itself through our constant orientation in the spatial-temporal world.

A Thou-world, as we have also seen, has not come into being so far, and we must understand this to be the result of the discontinuity, that is, the lack of coherency among the single Thou-relations, the single Thou-moments in space and time. These relations, these moments, do not remain present according to the nature of the respective Thous, which must change again and again from presence to object.

Only the relation to the absolute Thou is by nature of another kind. But even in this, in the pure relation, the human being cannot remain— this time not because of the nature of the Thou but because of his own human nature. And thus it seems that even this Thou-relationship, the pure Thou-relationship, cannot provide continuity.

Out of this overwhelming appearance of nonassurance—to speak of the overcoming of this appearance will be our final task; it is not yet time to speak of it—out of this overpowering appearance of nonassurance by the pure Thou-relation of a continuity of the Thou-world, we must first comprehend the existence of religion and in particular the paradox of religions as a plural. And here is the moment in the context of this way we are traveling together when I cannot avoid, in order to make what I mean as plain as possible, saying "I," in another sense than I have previously said it, in the sense of personal confession. And this is precisely because, as we have seen, it is a necessity, a compulsion that has meaning, to take one's point of departure from the I. Religious actuality never starts from the We; it comes to the We. It always starts from the I, which alone is the carrier of the Thou-relation, of all Thou-relations, and, therefore, also of the pure Thou-relation. We reject the false religious individualism that believes that religious life is limited to the I. We stand with a firm footing on what one could call, if one chooses, a religious individualism that takes the I as the unconditional point of departure, the I that is capable of entering only through its absolute relationship into a true We.

An Answer on the Train[1]

It was shortly after Easter in the year 1914 when an old acquaintance, an elderly English clergyman whom I had known for many years, visited me in a suburb of Berlin where I lived at that time. This old man was a very simple believing Christian who, for that reason, precisely for that reason, had done much to assist the return of the Jews to Palestine. When Theodor Herzl's diaries are published you will read a lot about him in them.[2] This man, whom I had not seen for years,

---

1. Buber first prepared this story for publication in 1959. See Paul A. Schilpp and Maurice S. Friedman, eds., "Question and Answer," in *The Philosophy of Martin Buber* (LaSalle, Ill., 1967), 23–25. According to Margot Cohn, Buber's secretary in 1959, Buber dictated the story to her from memory without looking at any source. For a detailed analysis of the story see Part Two, chap. 2.

2. The name of the visitor was William Hechler (Schilpp and Friedman, "Question and Answer," in *The Philosophy of Martin Buber*, p. 23.) Herzl, in his diary entry of March 16, 1896 (*Tagebücher*, vol. 1, 2nd ed. [Tel Aviv, 1934], 357), describes Hechler as a "naïve enthusiast" who has numerous copies of the Bible, maps of Palestine, and a plan for the building of the temple at Beth-El.

announced himself to me unexpectedly one morning and asked if he could visit me immediately. I said he was more than welcome. He arrived about an hour later. I tell you this in order to give you a feeling for the atmosphere of the encounter. What I have to say first is not the reason why I am telling you this story.

After greeting me, he said, "My dear friend, I have come to tell you that in this year the world war will break out." And he unfolded a graphic presentation of the prophecies of Daniel and demonstrated to me that the event would have to take place precisely in this year.

Well, that is not the important part. For no one need know from what sources a premonition flows to him. But as I accompanied this childlike old man, who had quite touched my heart with the way he presented all this to me—it took several hours—as I accompanied him to the railroad station, he suddenly grasped my arm, it was at a street corner, and said: "Dear friend, we are living in a great time"—that meant for him the pre-paracletic, the pre-messianic time—"we are living in a great time. Tell me: Do you believe in God?"[3]

It was said with such a human weightiness, in all his childlikeness and naïveté, that I felt quite heavy hearted about answering him. For in the way he asked the question I could say neither yes nor no. I tried to reassure him in his language, in a language he could understand, for he was quite uneasy.[4] But that is not the decisive thing, for I did not give him a real answer, at least not at that time.

A few months ago now,[5] it is about six months since I was traveling by train to a meeting with some friends, it suddenly came to me, with-

---

3. Buber also relates this question in "Question and Answer," which was dictated in 1959. In certain instances, he described the incident in terms identical with those he had used in the lecture of 1922 even though he did not have any notes in front of him; this shows the importance of this incident for him.

4. Cf. Schilpp and Friedman, "Question and Answer," in *The Philosophy of Martin Buber*, p. 24: "It was a while before I answered, then I reassured the old man as best I could: He need have no concern about me in this matter."

5. The stenographer typed *einen Monat* (one month); however, it was corrected by Buber (himself!) to *einigen Monaten* (a few months). Thus Buber himself specified that the date of "the answer" in the train was the fall of 1921.

out my cogitating on it beforehand (I do not cogitate on such things), without my cogitating on it, the answer came to me all of a sudden in these exact words, that is, not put together from words that I had pondered on earlier but in a sequence of words already joined. (Most of you probably know how that sometimes happens, when suddenly a whole sentence, not just a single word, comes to mind ready-made.) The answer came to me, not as I perhaps could or would have wanted to tell it to the old man, but as I might have given it if I had just been asked in the right way and with these words. This answer was: If believing in God means being able to speak of Him in the third person, then I probably do not believe in God; or at least, I do not know if it is permissible for me to say that I believe in God. For I know, when I speak of him in the third person, whenever it happens, and it has to happen again and again, there is no other way, then my tongue cleaves to the roof of my mouth[6] so quickly that one cannot even call it speech.

But this answer, if I have understood it rightly, is not a negative one. In the moment when I knew these words I did not feel it as a negative answer, not at all.

"The Trojan Women": A Prayer

What I mean I can perhaps demonstrate to you by an example from classical literature. In a fragment by Euripides, *The Trojan Women*,[7] someone—it doesn't matter who—a human being in distress calls on the divinity, or whatever this person considers worthy to be called upon, approximately as follows: "Whoever you may be, unfathomable to knowledge, Zeus, or necessity of nature, or spirit of mortals, 'nous broton,' to you I lift up my voice."[8] That is not what I mean. For we, who stand in the poverty of the naked Thou-relation and have nothing

---

6. An allusion to Psalms 137:6.

7. The quotation from Euripides was interpreted by Buber again in "Religion and Philosophy," in *Eclipse of God* (New York, 1952), 28–31.

8. *Nous broton* was corrected by Buber; it means "spirit of mortals."

in which to wrap it, we know that it is not Zeus, a name, a name of a god among many names of gods, a He out of an assembly of immortal beings. But we also know that it is not the necessity of nature; for in the pure relation we feel all that we feel in the pressure of the It-world as an enchainment of causes and effects in which we are exiled and entangled. We feel how all this falls away from us; that we take this whole world as we find ourselves in it and feel it as something that forces us to live with it; that we take this whole world with us into the relation and take it as a free world, as free as we are who enter into confrontation.

And we know that it is not the human spirit to which we say Thou, for the human spirit is precisely this, whose carriers and living vessels we are.

I am the I when I confront the Thou. So we know, as Euripides did not know, and so it is permissible for us to say that this poverty, this limitedness of our relation, this negativity of our answer is not simply time-bound, not simply the product of a time in which, as in that of Euripides, the heritage, the great heritage, had begun to disintegrate.

We do not call into blind, confused space, whose name we do not know and which never takes form for us. Rather, we speak, when we truly speak, out of presence, in presence.[9]

The Presence of God

Religion, hedged in, withdrawn here onto this narrow bridge, onto this narrow divide between the abysses and yet standing upon it, gazing, speaking—religion in this last sense is presence, is a present that by its nature does not and cannot become past. And when we comprehend

---

9. Buber developed this theme in *I and Thou*, trans. Walter Kaufmann (New York, 1970), 123, in a different way: "Men have addressed their eternal You by many names." This idea was developed later by Buber in an essay; see "Report on Two Talks," in *Eclipse of God*, pp. 7–8.

this correctly, when we feel that here is something that is no longer time-bound, that perhaps does not confess itself at all times as so unreservedly poor, so unreservedly solitary, that perhaps does not in all times reflect so upon itself and its abyss but that is the common element, the eternal in all times—when we feel this we also feel that this present of which we speak is the presence of God.

Religions

And in the face of this quite simple and unimpeachable, this last and substantial point, the immense variety of religions in history: What do they mean? They mean first and foremost, as you probably already know if you have come along on this way step-by-step, the displacement of God into the It-world.[10] We see, in every Thou-relation—recall the examples I have given—how, when the relation breaks off, the nature of the Thou of the relation becomes an It. The beloved person who even now fills the horizon becomes a being among beings; this piece of nature that unfolded itself to us in a maner that was not spatial-temporal or causal becomes a specific little spot, limited and determined in such and such a way. The work, which even now confronts us in conception with immense creative exclusivity, becomes a work in the great continuity of the spiritual, the cultural world. The deed, which even now concentrates our entire being on itself, on this focus of what had to be done, becomes something that can be regarded, not only by other humans but even by ourselves, as something that has occurred by cause and effect, that is a link in the chain of causality. And, as we say, it could not be otherwise. We, who even now stand in freedom, know that what happens depends entirely on our decision. No longer by the nature of the Thou but by our own human nature is God, the absolute Thou, displaced into the It-world.

---

10. Cf. the different version in *I and Thou*, p. 123: ". . . the first myths were hymns of praise. Then the names entered into the It-language; men felt impelled more and more to think of and to talk about their eternal You as an It."

Religions speak of God in the third person, mostly as a He. People seldom realize the extent to which this pronoun is already an anthropomorphism or, more correctly, to what extent this pronoun means a displacement of God into the world of things and essences, how much this is already implied by the gender of the pronoun. God is displaced into the It-world, that is, into the creation that has run away from God. In other words, in history God is a thing. That this is so is the cause of the multiplicity of the subjectivity of religions, their exclusion of one another, their contention with one another—about what exactly? About the nature of the He, about the way He wants to be served. This rivalry among the religions for the universal recognition of the content of each, this contending and everything that goes with it, such as the way humans have tortured and murdered one another throughout history over these things, is not done out of caprice. He would understand me wrongly who would think that I mean caprice or happenstance, or anything not really necessary and easily overcome by good will.[11]

I mean the subline tragedy of the human spirit, nothing less; and any of you who have occupied yourselves seriously with the question of what tragedy is know that tragedy does not mean, as many have supposed, avoidable guilt that brings its own punishment. Rather, tragedy means that the event ineluctably follows from man's being what he is. Out of this fact that Antigone, for example, has certain qualities and a law above her, a necessary and insuperable law, and that Creon has other qualities and another law above him, a law just as necessary and insuperable and that he obeys—from these differences tragedy arises.

In a tragedy there is no being in the right. In this sense I see the history of the religions, the history of the displacement of God into the It-world, as the tragedy—not *a* tragedy but *the* tragedy—of the

---

11. Cf. ibid., p. 161: "And yet we reduce the eternal You ever again to an It, to something, turning God into a thing, in accordance with our nature. Not capriciously. The history of God as a thing, . . . the metamorphoses of the present, of embedment in forms, of objectification, of conceptualization, of dissolution, and renewal . . . are *the way*."

human spirit. Therefore, I repeat, I do not view this tragedy as caprice but as necessity, a necessity decreed by fate, not human fate but world fate, a historical necessity not just of human history, but a cosmic-historical, truly world-historical necessity. It is a creation that has run away from God, a falling away, but the falling away that all the religions in their different ways place somewhere in primal time and that is probably the archetype of all falling away: All true falling away means becoming human. That falling away of which the religions tell means becoming human, and so the religions themselves, every one of them, mean a new way of becoming human by falling away, that is, through part of God's limitation in the world. In some way it is permissible for us to represent the limitation of the world-process as an inhaling and exhaling, as a rhythm of the Divine itself in the world. The way into form is at the same time a way into a prison, into a new prison, but also the way into that which always and alone is given to the human being, visibly, as an image corporeally—the form. The way out of this prison leads into naked, free relation, into the freedom and solitude of formlessness, that is, wordlessness, silence, waiting, readiness. And through all this there is a way. All this is not a circle that returns upon itself. This coming into being and going out of being is not a wandering that is eternally new and the same, essentially the same. But through all this there is a way, a true way into somewhere. Insofar as we can grasp it, we will say in the language that we have been using here that the way out of the prison leads into the construction of a Thou-world. But we are standing at the point along the way at which we are standing; and we do not wish, nor are we permitted, to anticipate. We are permitted only to confess what we are and what we have, but this we must do with complete honesty, neither more nor less.

What do religions mean? What do they contain? From a very much simplified perspective, they contain two things: asserted knowledge and posited action.[12] And here one might ask: Does not some knowledge

---

12. Cf. ibid.: "The asserted knowledge and posited action of the religion—whence do they come?" The word *gesetztes*, which Kaufmann translates as "posited," contains the word *Gesetz* (law).

and some action follow from the pure relation too? Does not man emerge even from the relation to the absolute Thou, from every religious act, from every event of pure relation, with a knowledge and a commandment? But it is important to comprehend correctly what kind of knowledge and action this is and how it differs from the knowledge and the action that the religions teach, so that we may understand how the one can emerge from the other or instead of the other. The knowledge that comes out of pure relation is the knowledge of meaning, which quite simply amounts to this: Whoever knows the pure Thou-relation, to him the question of the meaning of life no longer even exists; and if it existed, it could not be answered. Do you understand me rightly? He cannot say what the meaning is; he cannot point it out; he cannot define it; he cannot find any formulas for it. But he could sooner doubt his body and his bodily perceptions than the meaning. The knowledge of the meaning that cannot be defined is the knowledge that emerges from the pure relation.

And the action—perhaps one can also say the Ought, although the word Ought seems to me somehow too weak for this—the Must, the Being-able that emerges from the pure relation is the action that puts the meaning to the proof, the proof that cannot be prescribed, that is not valid for everybody, that cannot be written down as a law to be set up over everybody's head. Each one must put the meaning to the proof with his own strength, in his own way, within his own limits, in his language, his life, at the place where he stands and in the moment in which he stands, in the uniqueness of his life. And yet there is commandment; the human being does emerge from the pure relation with the unmistakable, unambiguous call to put the meaning to the proof. That in which we humans stand, the mystery, is not overcome in knowledge and will not be overcome by commandment; the mystery remains. We have not broken through it; we have not deciphered it; we have no solution; we have no formula; and we do not know how to apply it, so that one could go to the other and say: Brother, or to several brothers and sisters, thus you ought to do. One can do nothing except truly want to receive the call, be ready for it, go out to meet it, and enter, whole, concentrated, unbroken, undistracted, into that from which one receives the call. The knowledge and action of the religions stand opposed to this.

The knowledge of the religions is knowledge about God, knowledge in the third person, knowledge of qualities; and it is not important that particular religions at some point content themselves with stating negative qualities. In other words, instead of taking up, one after another, all sorts of qualities known to us from our human life and declaring that each of these ways of being limited and confined does not apply to God, they state that God does not have all these relativities, that God is rather what is unconditioned by all this. But this is not the case either. And it is also not important whether they are early religions, religions of a human world that gazes in dreams, sensually, with dream-senses. These religions simply relate: In such and such a way the gods live, this and this happens to them. Knowledge does not depend on whether one relates the Divine as incident, as myth, at the one end, or whether one grasps the Divine and binds it in the word of dogma that is valid for all times and events. Whether knowledge calls us more toward the dynamic or toward the static, it is basically the same thing in the face of the Ultimate.

The action that the religions know is action according to law, that is, an action that in its particulars is not normalized by convention but that is known in all its particulars as something instituted and ordained by the God that one knows, by that He. And again it is not important whether this law is merely ritual law, whether it concerns mainly the forms of worship, or whether it is primarily ethical law, whether it concerns mainly the manner in which this God, this religion, wants His commandments to be fulfilled in the human world. In the ultimate analysis, all this is not what it depends on.

The basic question is a question that we of course cannot answer for ourselves in the way we have answered other questions. Rather we have to appeal to history for an answer, and even then we can only point in the direction of an answer. The question is: How does this knowledge and this action come into being in religions: out of what knowledge and action or in place of what knowledge and action? This question concerns the primal phenomenon, the question of the primal phenomenon of religions, of the historical religions. From this point

one cannot know but, I believe, only intuitively surmise, why the way
to form until now and for the stretch of time known to us has necessarily
been a way to prison. We are standing here on the threshold of the
basic problem of religions: the problem of revelation. And we want to
consider this in the same way we have considered everything until now,
contenting ourselves with that for which we have authorization, unconditional authorization; that is, with the aspect from the human point
of view, from our narrow but unimpeachable truth. And understand
one thing clearly: Revelation in the sense of which we are speaking of
it here is not the prerogative of particular religions. For in the sense
in which we are speaking, there are only religions of revelation.[13]
Whether[14] the revelation from which the religions derive their right
emerges from the self-awareness of human beings or from the world-
awareness of human beings, or (in the religions which in a more specific
sense are called religions) from revelation in the Word; for these are
the three forms of revelation that have confronted us in history. With
this we should conclude for the time being. We shall speak of it next
time.

---

13. Cf. ibid.: "The presence and strength of revelation (for all of them
necessarily invoke some sort of revelation, whether verbal, natural, or
psychic—there are, strictly speaking, only revealed religions), the presence and
strength that man received through revelation—how do they become a
"content"?
14. Syntax unclear in the original.

March 12, 1922

Revelation

At the end of the last lecture we were approaching the problem of revelation, and I had pointed out to you that basically there are only religions of revelation. But now let us ask ourselves, just as simply and as much in the direction of actuality as we have always tried to do along this way, in the direction of the wholly actual, let us ask ourselves what revelation is.

You have certainly understood that for me everything religiously actual is fundamentally a matter of the here and now, not of some historical event that is by its nature unique and incomparable, a concern with the eternal and all-present process that takes on manifold forms only in the manifoldness of history.

And in this sense we now ask what revelation is. We necessarily reject every attempt to symbolize revelation, every attempt to interpret that which appears as the result of revelation merely as symbolic indication of some knowledge of a different character. In that case as we spoke of it at the beginning, religion would be nothing but a compartment of art, and a superfluous secondary compartment at that.

What is the primal phenomenon, the eternal, omnipresent primal phenomenon present in the here and now, of what we call revelation?[1] It is this: that the human being does not emerge from the moment of pure relation as the same person who entered into it.[2]

No doubt you still remember what I said of the pure relation, of the relation to the absolute Thou. This moment of relation to the absolute Thou is not a passageway, not a portal from which the human being emerges as the same person who entered into it. Rather, it is a real event, in which something happens to the human being and with the human being. Each time the human being steps out of the pure relation he has in his nature, in his life, in his person something more, something added, which he did not have before, of which he did not know before and whose origin he cannot designate.[3] Of course, world orientation has drawn even this event into its contemplation, and various scientific and unscientific attempts have been made to demonstrate somehow an empirical origin. And as you know, I have always acknowledged the relative justification of world orientation and am of the opinion that science, the scientific world system, can by no means tolerate any gap and therefore must demonstrate an empirical origin for this. But for this actual contemplation of the actual that we are attempting here, it will not do to content ourselves with a subconsciousness out of which this new thing arises or with any apparatuses that are, so to speak, manufactured for this purpose.[4]

The truth and importance of the event is that something happens

---

1. Cf. *I and Thou*, trans. Walter Kaufmann (New York, 1970), 157: "What is it that is eternal: the primal phenomenon, present in the here and now, of what we call revelation?"

2. Cf. ibid.: "It is man's emerging from the moment of the supreme encounter, being no longer the same as he was when entering into it."

3. Cf. ibid., p. 158: ". . . something happens. The man who steps out of the essential act of pure relation as something More in his being, something new has grown here of which he did not know before and for whose origin he lacks any suitable words."

4. Cf. ibid.: "Wherever the scientific world orientation in its legitimate desire for a causal chain without gaps may place the origin of what is new here: for us, being concerned with the actual contemplation of the actual, no subconscious and no other psychic apparatus will do."

to us; we receive something we did not have before, and we receive it in such a way that we know with our innermost being that something has been given to us. All attempts at interpretation are infinitely weaker, are infinitely vain, in the face of this immensely important event. That is the character of revelation that is inherent in the pure relation. Biblical language phrases it thus: "Those who wait for God *yaḥlifu koaḥ*," that is, they shall receive in exchange a new strength. Or in the language of the modern philosopher Friedrich Nietzsche, who once described this event with the fidelity to actuality of the religious person and without psychologizing it—Nietzsche closes his description with the words: "One accepts, one does not ask who gives."[5]

The human being receives, but what he receives is not a content, but a presence, a presence as strength. And this presence, this strength that enters into the human being, includes three elements in one, not three things one beside the other. First it includes the whole abundance of actual reciprocity, a state in which one is no longer cut off, no longer thrown back on oneself, no longer abandoned, although one cannot tell what it is to which one is linked, with which one is associated, or what its character is. Second, it includes—it is really the same thing, only contemplated from another angle—the confirmation of the meaning. There is undeniably a meaning, not a meaning that can be pointed out and asserted but a meaning that is thus confirmed and guaranteed to oneself, a meaning that one cannot translate. And third, this presence and this strength includes a call to the human being to put this meaning to the proof in his life through his deeds. This meaning, whose guarantee he has received, is not something that remains shut up in the human being, locked inside him, but is something that now steps out

---

5. Cf. ibid.: "Actually, we receive what we did not have before, in such a manner that we know: it has been given to us. In the language of the Bible: 'Those who wait for God will receive strength in exchange.'"

In the lectures, Buber quoted this verse from Isaiah 40:31 in Hebrew and then translated it freely. Buber later translated this verse in *Bücher der Kündigung* (Cologne, 1966), 128: "aber die SEIN harren tauschen Kraft ein" ("They who wait for Him shall renew their strength"). The quote from Nietzsche is from *Ecce Homo*, in section 3 of the discussion of Zarathustra.

of him into the world as actuality and that is put to the proof in the world, by the world. The meaning can be received, but it cannot be known. It cannot be known, but it can be done, can be received and put into action; it cannot be known, pointed out, or stated in words.[6] These triune qualities are inherent in the strength that the human being receives.

These three things in unison act as actual strength upon the life of this human being.

God as an It

How, then, does that which the human being receives change from a strength into a content?[7] For again and again, as we have seen, man, human beings, treat this as a content, as something that can be pointed out, asserted, treated—as an object, as something experienced, experienceable. How does what is not an object become an object? How does that which is present but not objective[8] become an object? How does it become a content that asserts something about the nature, the deeds, and the will of God, that asserts something about the origin, the destiny, and the future—a future that reaches beyond death—of the soul, that asserts something about the coming into being, the mode

---

6. Cf. *I and Thou*, pp. 158–159: "Man receives, and what he receives is not a 'content' but a presence, a presence as strength. This presence and strength includes three elements that are not separate but may nevertheless be contemplated as three. First, the whole abundance of actual reciprocity, of being admitted, of being associated while one is altogehter unable to indicate what that is like with which one is associated. . . . And this is second: the inexpressible confirmation of meaning. It is guaranteed. Nothing, nothing henceforth can be meaningless. . . . This comes third: . . . The meaning can be received but not experienced; it cannot be experienced, but it can be done." *Sinn* (meaning) is a concept of major importance in *Daniel* (New York, 1965), for example, 93–94. To understand the comparison of the lecture with *I and Thou*, it would be helpful to read the entire end section in *I and Thou*.
7. Cf. *I and Thou*, p. 161: "The asserted knowledge and the posited action of the religions—whence do they come? The presence . . . and strength that man received through revelation: how do they become a 'content'?"
8. "Das Gegenwärtige, aber nicht Gegenstehende."

116

of existence,[9] the perfection of the world? I said that the meaning is not known, but perhaps this expression is, after all, not quite adequate, for "to know" is usually used in the sense of knowledge of some experience, even if it be intellectual. To this the stricture does apply that the meaning cannot be known. But "to know" does have, originally, a more living, actual meaning, the sense of a real relation.

In the primal language, to know means immediate relation,[10] and in this sense, to be sure, one can speak of knowing but not of knowledge. How does this living, actual knowing—this entering-into-immediate-relation with a Thou, which is not an It among Its, not a He but only living, giving, revealing Thou—become the knowledge of an It or a He? I have already indicated that there reigns in the human being, immediately and necessarily, a tendency to objectification. The human being longs to have the absolute Thou and to have it continuously in space and time. He longs for a continuity of having God in time and space. He does not want to content himself with the guarantee; rather, he wants to see it spread out as something that has no gap in space and time, that forms a continuum and insures his life at every point and moment.[11]

The act of the pure relation consists, so to speak, in the moment; it has no continuity in time. The human being longs to give it duration, to spread it out in time. Thus God becomes an object of belief.[12] For

---

9. *Bestand*.

10. An allusion to the Hebrew verb *yode'a*, which means both to know and to experience sexual intercourse. Buber elaborated on this term in an essay, "Philosophical and Religious World View," in *A Believing Humanism*, trans. Maurice S. Friedman (New York, 1967), 130–135.

11. Cf. *I and Thou*, pp. 161–162: "Man desires to have God; he desires to have God continually in space and time. He is loath to be satisfied with the inexpressible confirmation of the meaning; he wants to see it spread out as something that one can take out and handle again and again . . . a continuum unbroken in space and time that insures life for him at every point and moment."

12. Cf. ibid., p. 162: "Life's rhythm of pure relation . . . does not suffice man's thirst for continuity. He thirsts for something spread out in time, for duration. Thus God becomes an object of faith." Note the change in content in the two versions: In *I and Thou* pure relations have "rhythm"; in the lectures, "no continuity."

though there is no continuity of the pure relation, there is a continuity of belief. The act of relation consists in solitude, in the person's solitude of the I with the Thou. It is always the I of the human being that confronts the Thou. That is, as we said before, the point of departure. The human being now longs for community. As he longs for duration, he longs for community, for a commonality of relation. And thus God becomes a cult object.[13] Faith provides the continuity in time; cult provides the continuity in space.

The pure relation cannot be held fast. It can only become object; it can only be actualized with everything that makes up life. It cannot be held fast as pure relation, preserved, so to speak; it can only be put to the proof, fulfilled, actualized, confirmed. It cannot be expressed; it can only be done, injected into life. The human being who emerges from the pure relation—if he wants to do it justice, if he wants to fulfill its commandment—can do nothing other than actualize God in the world. Whoever understands this correctly sees that therein lies the true, the only true guarantee of continuity, the only true guarantee of duration in time and space in the face of which all attempts to create continuity in time and space are and must remain merely apparent attempts. The true guarantee of duration is that the pure relation can be fulfilled universally in the world, that the relation to the absolute Thou can be put to the proof by every It becoming Thou, by every thing and every being being lifted up to the Thou, so that the great capability of saying Thou affects all beings.[14] Through this operation

---

13. Cf. ibid.: "The life-structure of the pure relation, the 'lonesomeness' of the I before the You. . . . He [the human being] thirsts for something spread out in space, for the representation in which the community of the faithful is united with its God. Thus God becomes a cult object."

14. Cf. ibid., p. 163: "In truth, however, the pure relation . . . cannot be preserved but only put to the proof in action; it can only be done. . . . Man can do justice to the relation to God that has been given him only by actualizing God in the world in accordance with his ability and the measure of each day, daily. . . . The genuine guarantee of duration is that the pure relation can be fulfilled as the beings become You, . . . so that the holy basic word sounds through all of them. Thus the time of human life is formed into an abundance of actuality."

of the relation in the world, in the community, in the whole abundance of actual life, a continuity of relation in time can and must arise, through which the pure relation, the relation to the absolute Thou, can necessarily shine forth again and again. You remember what I said at the beginning about the task of constructing a Thou-world, a continuous Thou-world, out of the Thou-moments.

I pointed out that a Thou-world cannot be built up out of relations to particular things and beings, that those always remain isolated Thou-moments from which no world builds itself up. And I also pointed out that in the pure relation, the relation to the absolute Thou, the way is given to unite these moments in a continuum. We now see what that means: By putting it to the test, the one who steps forth from the pure relation elevates every It to a Thou, so that this absolute Thou radiates into every relationship, into all of life. And as the guarantee, the true guarantee of continuity in time, is given, so the true guarantee of continuity in the space of community, the guarantee of true community, is given not by the establishment among humans of a commonality of consciousness, a commonality of action, or a commonality of belief and cult—all this is not decisive. Rather, if I may use the image, the lines of the pure Thou-relations of human beings meet in God: Every human steps out of himself into the pure relation, and these pure relations flow together in the one absolute Thou. The true human community is possible only in God, only through this: that the true relations of humans to the absolute Thou, to the center, all these radii that lead from the Is of human beings to the center, form a circle. What comes first is not the circle but the radii that lead to the center. This is what makes

---

The term *Erhebung* (lifting up) bears for Buber a Hasidic motif, as he explicitly states in Lecture Six. Buber's early concept of *Verwirklichung* (actualization) appears three times in this paragraph and only once in the parallel in *I and Thou*. In the following pages one can again see the more common use of *Verwirklichung* in the lectures in contrast to its more restrained use in *I and Thou*. See infra, Part Two, chap. 5.

the circle actual. This is no doubt what is meant by the saying that the Shekhinah is between the beings.[15]

So we have confronting each other the apparent guarantee, which insures the human being in an experience that can be asserted and practiced, which gives the human being a content, a content of faith and a content of action, something graspable, held in common, prescribed, written down, and in that sense revealed, contentually revealed. And the other true guarantee, which gives the human being nothing except the meaning and the strength to actualize it,[16] which does not solve the riddle for the human being, does not unlock what is closed. But it places the human being in the life of the present. Every other, every apparent guarantee means basically a bending back. I shall try to explain this.

God, Prayer, and Presence

The basic meaning of revelation (consists) first of all in this quite personal meaning as we have now grasped it, that is, as something that

---

15. Cf. ibid.: "The genuine guarantee of duration is that the pure relation can be fulfilled as the beings become You, as they are elevated to the You, so that the holy basic word sounds through all of them. Thus the time of human life is formed into an abundance of actuality; and although human life cannot and ought not to overcome the It-relation, it then becomes so permeated by relation that this gains a radiant and penetrating constancy in it. The moments of supreme encounter are no mere flashes of lightning in the dark but like a rising moon on a clear starry night. And thus the genuine guarantee of spatial constancy consists in this that men's relations to their true You, being radii that lead from all I-points to the center, create a circle. Not the periphery, not the community comes first, but the radii, the common relation to the center. That alone assures the genuine existence of a community."

In this case one can see how an idea in the lectures, "the Shekhinah is between the beings," led to the development of an important passage in the book. In the lectures one can still see the Mishnaic origin of this thought from Avot (3:2), which reads in Hebrew, *shekhinah beinehem*.

16. The word *Verwirklichung* (actualization) was corrected to *Wirkung* (action, effect) by a reader.

happens everywhere and all the time, that can happen to every human being, every human being who opens himself up completely, being completely collected and unified in himself. The basic meaning, therefore, of this revelation and of all revelation is a sending forth of the human being. The human being is grasped in this sense and is sent forth to put him to the proof. This calling, this sending forth to the test, to the deed, to humanity, into the world, into the We, to the place of actualization—that is the strength, that is what revelation gives.[17] It can happen, however, and it happens again and again, that the human being, instead of continuing in the right direction, instead of going to where he has been sent, for the reasons I explained previously, out of this natural longing that wants to satisfy itself quickly and easily, bends back toward the sending forth, toward the one who sends him out. Again and again the human being, instead of putting revelation to the proof with the world, wants to occupy himself with the revelation, with the one who reveals, and he can only do that by placing it as an It into the world of things and believing that he knows and can speak of it as an It.

Perhaps this can be understood by analogy with a simple event that you all know. The human being perceives something, some piece of the world, he feels something, senses something, wants something, and now simply strives to follow this event completely, to let this sensation, this feeling, this will work itself out completely. The human being reflects on himself; he occupies himself with his own sensation, his own feeling, his own will; he makes the sensation, the will, the feeling into an object. He bends back on his I and misses the truth of the event in a wrong direction. The event now does not work itself out in its truth.

---

17. Cf. *I and Thou*, p. 164: "All revelation is a calling and a mission. But again and again man shuns actualization and bends back toward the revealer: he would rather attend to God than to the world." Cf. *The Star of Redemption*, trans. William W. Hallo (New York, 1970), 204–215. In Buber's copy of *The Star* this passage is underlined.

This is something that precisely in our time is a quite typical occurrence.[18]

This event of a bending back toward that which gives, instead of letting the gift work itself out, is in a certain way analogous to the above.

In the being who has been sent forth, God is a presence; in this bending back God becomes an object.[19] But in one thing, at the very least, I would like not to be misunderstood: True prayer is not a bending back. True prayer is simply nothing other than a standing in reciprocity, the saying of Thou; and thus it is included with perfect right in the pure relation.[20] For the one who is sent forth does not go away from God; rather, the one who is sent forth has God always before him. Thus he cannot truly occupy himself with God.[21] He can only speak to him; he can address him; he can pray to him. But he cannot rightfully make him an object. For this, too, there is a phrase that expresses it perfectly: *shiviti adonai le-negdi tamid.*[22] With the eternal presence, the eternal presentness of God, man is entering-into-relation, over and over, with this eternal presence.

---

18. Cf. *I and Thou*, p. 164: ". . . he [the human being] would rather attend to God than to the world. Now that he has bent back, however, he is no longer confronted by a You; he can do nothing but place a divine It in the realm of things, believe that he knows about God as an It, and talk about him. Even as the egomaniac does not live . . . directly . . . a perception, . . . thus the theomaniac . . . will not let the gift take full effect but reflects instead on that which gives, and misses both."

19. Cf. ibid., pp. 164–165: "When you are sent forth, God remains presence for you; . . . Bending back, on the other hand, turns God into an object."

20. Cf. ibid., p. 167: "That true prayer lives in religions testifies to their true life; as long as it lives in them, they live."

21. Cf. ibid., p. 166: "Whoever is sent forth in a revelation takes with him in his eyes an image of God; however suprasensible it may be, he takes it along in the eyes of his spirit, in the altogether not metaphorical but entirely real visual power of his spirit."

22. The stenographer wrote the first word from Psalms 16:8, *Schiwisi*. In attempting to explain his concept of encounter, Buber at this point uses the Hebrew term *neged*. The translation of the verse is: "I have set Him before me." In Buber's German translation of the Bible (*Die Schriftwerke*, 4th ed. [Heidelberg, 1976]), it reads: "Ich hege IHN mir stets gegenüber."

But this can no longer occur only in solitude but by our also stepping into the world, putting the meaning to the proof in the world. From the world this relation shines forth again and again. Although I indicated this the previous time, I would like to say it simply now: Even though we recognize this duality quite clearly, we are not permitted to comprehend it in the sense that this bending back, this becoming an object, this becoming past of the divine—that this is caprice. I have said it before and I ask you now to understand it correctly: The objectifying tendency is not caprice. Rather, it is a necessity of human history; it beongs necessarily to the way of humankind. It has a primal meaning that is connected with the meaning of creation.[23]

There are two world tendencies that are bound together in the happenings of the world, in the dynamics of world history. The expansion of the world and the turning toward God are both quite real. The turning is not something to which only the human is called; it is something that has been placed as an eternal call in the entire happening of the world.[24] Again and again the world has run away from God into an It that exists in itself, and again and again it still tries to draw even God into this It and thus close off the turning to God. Again and again, too, the call to the turning lives above the world and in it, penetrating and moving it. God's call of "Enough!" which was once spoken to a world expanding beyond measure and bounds into selfhood is spoken and will be spoken eternally: "Stop, turn back!"

That is the call of the Thou, the call to the Thou, the guarantee of the Thou-world, which wants to come into being through the human being. And completely present, completely internal, strong, powerful, alive and so plain, so powerfully plain as nowhere else, so nakedly plain as nowhere else, these two world tendencies confront each other in the way religions come into being.

---

23. Cf. *I and Thou*, p. 165: "Not caprice is at work here, although the movement toward the It may at times go so far."

24. Cf. ibid.: "For the two basic metacosmic movements of the world— its expansion into its own being and returning . . . It is in the return that the word is born on earth; in spreading out it enters the chrysalis of religion." See entire paragraph.

The history of religion and of religions is the history of the eternal battle and accommodation of the movement and countermovement and the being-bound-together of these two tendencies. The flight from God has its place in religion itself, and the turning, the being able to say Thou again and again, has its true place in religion itself. Here occurs the innermost of what we have discussed.

In their fundamental nature, the revelations of religions are nothing more or less than the eternal, all-present revelation, the revelation of the here and now. Never and nowhere has a revelation happened that is not also happening here and now.[25]

But there is a history, there is nonetheless a qualitative difference between historical ages.[26]

I shall try to explain this. There is the revelation, the eternal revelation, and there is the human freedom, the person is placed in freedom. This insoluble paradox in which we stand, in which our life is accomplished, which carries our life—the paradox that God has determined the world and that the human being is free—this contradiction, which is no contradiction but which unfolds as a contradiction, this, too, leads us into the problem of which we are speaking here. Every actual event in the world is an encounter. In every actual event of human life there is not only the human being. History is not confined to the powers of the human being and of nature alone, although one cannot distinguish and say: This is to be ascribed to human and natural forces and this to another force. For in truth there is only the One, from which we create abstractions. But we can grasp the One only in these abstractions. We live in confrontation with abstractions; they

---

25. Cf. *Das verborgene Licht* (Frankfurt a. M., 1924), 17: "For there is no level of being on which one cannot find God's holiness everywhere and at all times."

26. Cf. *I and Thou*, p. 166: "The powerful revelations that stand at the beginnings of great communities . . . are nothing else than the eternal revelation. . . . But there is a qualitative difference between historical ages." Note that in *I and Thou* religion is only *Ausbreitung* (expansion); in the lectures it is both *Umkehr* (turning) and *Ausbreitung*.

determine our concrete life. These are the boundaries of our life: this polarity, this confrontation (of) I and Thou.

I repeat: Every actual event is an event of encounter. History is not only the human being, and yet there is nowhere a limitation of human freedom. This means that there is no contentual revelation; every contentual revelation would be a limitation. There is no limitation to one of the sides on the scale of human decision.

God does not name himself or define himself to the human being. The word of revelation is *ehyeh asher ehyeh*, that is: That which reveals is the revealer. That which has being, is, nothing more. The eternal source of strength flows; the eternal touch is waiting; the eternal voice sounds, nothing more.[27]

As I have already said, there are only religions of revelation. Every religion invokes its own revealed word on which it stands and from which it derives its existence.

But the revelations that the religions invoke, which I might perhaps call the forceful revelations, in contrast to those quiet ones that occur here and now and at all everywhere—at all times the powerful revelations that stand at the beginnings of great communities, the beginnings of peoples, religions, ages are nothing else than the eternal revelation. It is not the voice that is different, but the hearer and the moment.[28]

But there is a qualitative difference between historical times. There are times of ripening; that is, the stuff of the human spirit accumulates

---

27. Cf. ibid., p. 160: "I neither know of nor believe in any revelation that is not the same in its primal phenomenon. I do not believe in God's naming Himself or in God's defining Himself before man. The word revelation is: I am there as whoever I am there. That which reveals is that which reveals. That which has being is there, nothing more. The eternal source of strength flows, the eternal touch is waiting, the eternal voice sounds, nothing more."

28. Cf. ibid., pp. 165–166: "The powerful revelations invoked by the religions are essentially the same as the quiet one that occurs everywhere and at all times. The powerful revelations that stand at the beginnings of great communities, at the turning points of human time, are nothing else than the eternal revelation. But revelation does not pour into the world through its recipient as if he were a funnel; it confers itself on him, it seizes his whole element . . ."

so enormously, again and again, that it needs only one call to be melted down into creation, into the new word.[29]

The forceful revelation lays hold of the entire stuff of the human spirit, melts it down, and creates from it a new form, a new form of God in the world.[30]

The latent tendency to objectification becomes creative through the touch. Perhaps we may say this with an image: We must again and again resort to images that are yet not metaphorical. The voice, the eternal voice, becomes word through contact with the human being, with the surface of the human being that it touches, so to speak, with the skin, the ear, the living person that it touches. Through contact with the human being the voice becomes the Word; it becomes God's word. But only in the human being does the voice become a word of God, a word that speaks of God.[31]

The human being most certainly does not create God. But he creates, again and again, God's form. And since the human being is not a single human being but, rather, all the humans, the many humans, the innumerable dead and living, past and future humans—since the human being is all human beings, he creates God's form as forms. But this, I say it again, is not arbitrary or incidental. Rather, it is through this that in history, in the way of history, ever new regions of the world and of the spirit are lifted up into form, summoned to divine form, to the incarnation, as it were, of God. Ever new spheres are drawn into the theophany.[32]

---

29. Cf. ibid., p. 166: "But there is a qualitative difference between historical ages. There are times of ripening when the true element of the human spirit, held down and buried, grows ready underground with such pressure and such tension that it merely waits to be touched by one who will touch it—and then erupts."

30. Cf. ibid.: "The revelation that then appears . . . recasts it and produces a form, a new form of God in the world."

31. Cf. ibid.: "Even the man who is 'mouth' is precisely that and not a mouthpiece—not an instrument but an organ, an autonomous, sounding organ; and to sound means to modify sound."

32. Cf. ibid.: "Ever new regions of the world and the spirit are thus lifted up into form, called to divine form, in the course of history, in the transformations of the human element. Ever new spheres become the place of a theophany."

This is a mirroring of that paradox of which we spoke, the paradox of coming into form. It is not human autocracy and arbitrariness that is at work here, nor is it God's pure passage through the human being. But it is the mixture, the intermixture of the divine and human, of Thou and It. The voice that reveals and sends forth is not form, deed, that to which the human being is sent forth. His putting truth to the proof is not a form. Only through the bending back upon the revelation, only through the divine presence becoming object, does a form of God come into being, again and again and constantly. Thus God comes into being as form; religions come into being as forms.[33] Here God has become an object, but the essence lives on.

God can become a presence again and again, and this is always occurring in the religions, in true prayer, in which cult and belief unite into the pure relation. That true prayer lives in the religions is a guarantee of their authentic life. As long as it truly lives in them, they truly live. When we speak of religions becoming rigid, the innermost meaning of this is that the true prayer in them rigidifies; that it becomes harder and harder for them to say Thou truly with a whole, undivided being; that the human being, in order to say Thou, begins to flee from religions into the freedom of relation.[34] And—this too we must see clearly—in the fact of form, the rigidification is already inherent. It is the progressive ascendancy of objectification. And again we see the two tendencies: the expansion, the running away from God, and the eternal swing back.

Again and again come times of liberation, of the holding of breath,

---

33. Cf. ibid., p. 167: "Form is a mixture of You and It, too. In faith and cult it can freeze into an object; but from the gist of the relation that survives in it, it turns ever again into presence."

34. Cf. ibid., p. 167: "God is near his forms as long as man does not remove them from him. In true prayer, cult and faith are unified and purified into living relation. That true prayer lives in religions testifies to their true life; as long as it lives in them, they live. Degeneration of religions means the degeneration of prayer in them: the relational power in them is buried more and more by objecthood; they find it ever more difficult to say You with their whole undivided being."

of the silence between word and word, between revelation, between forceful revelation and forceful revelation. And again and again the revelation leads to the form. But this is not a circle, as I have already indicated. Rather, through these forms, through the formations of God in the religions, through them leads the way.[35]

The Kingdom of God

That is the essential difference between religions and the kingdom of God. The way leads through the religions; this way, through the forms into something that is no longer form, is necessary. Until now, community, insofar as we could grasp it, was only possible through form and in form. And yet we can perhaps say the following: Through forms it somehow does not lead merely into that which we can intuitively surmise but also into the next thing and the one after next to a form of community in which human beings are bound together through the purity of their relation.

Here, too, the formal still reigns, will still reign somehow, but it becomes purer and purer. The Thou imposes its will ever more imperiously upon the It. We may well say that history is a mysterious approach to closeness.[36] Somehow, through all that, we humans come closer. This perspective, which I can only indicate here, is what we have been able to arrive at in these few steps that we have taken together. These are steps through the gateway, the steps to the end of the beginning.

For this way that we have traveled together is only the beginning. It is, as it were, the introduction to the way. Now on the main part of the way, it would be appropriate to behold how the two tendencies of which we have spoken have reigned and continue to reign in humanity's religious life. This would be a matter further down the way.

35. Cf. ibid., p. 168: "But the path is not a circle. It is the way."
36. Cf. ibid.: "And the theophany comes ever *closer* . . . to the realm. . . . History is a mysterious approach to closeness."

The stretch that we are now concluding leads us in a certain sense back to a survey of the point of departure, as every further stretch will lead us thither. We stand and remain in the mystery. We cannot go over the surface of it any more than we can become it. But we confront it truly. We stand to it in community. We stand in its reciprocity. We stand in its presence.

PART TWO:

The History and Development of I and Thou

ONE

1918: An Early Outline

Martin Buber had been recognized widely for his diverse achievements prior to the publication of *I and Thou*.[1] For years he had enjoyed fame for his artistic retelling of Hasidic tales, his influential essays on Judaism, his successful editorship of *Der Jude*, his Zionist leadership, and his mystical writings. Yet the appearance of *I and Thou* in late 1922 constituted far more than simply the addition of one more area of inquiry to his broad philosophical interests. *I and Thou* marked both a shift away from a hitherto predominant mysticism and the genesis of his now-famous dialogical thinking. Buber attributed this departue to the shattering impact of the World War and to the influence of Hasidic thought.[2]

In the epilogue to *I and Thou* and elsewhere, Buber stated that the book was planned as early as 1916 and that a draft was composed in

---

1. Margot Cohn and Rafael Buber, *Martin Buber: A Bibliography of His Writings, 1897–1978* (Jerusalem, 1980). The list of Buber's publications prior to *I and Thou* includes some 260 entries.

2. In this context I do not mean Hasidism as such but Hasidism as Buber has conceived it; as is known, there are substantial differences between the two. See Gershom Scholem's criticism "Martin Buber's Interpretation of Hasidism," in *Commentary*, 1961, later republished in Scholem, *The Messianic Idea* (New York, 1971), 227–250, and Buber's reply "Interpreting Hasidism" in *Commentary*, 1963, 218–225. See also Rivka Schatz-Uffenheimer's article and Buber's reply in Paul A. Schilpp and Maurice S. Friedman, eds., *The Philosophy of Martin Buber*, (LaSalle, Ill., 1967), 403ff., 731ff.

1919.[3] In a more detailed statement in his 1954 article "On the History of the Dialogical Principle,"[4] he further emphasized that *I and Thou* was independent of the influence of other contemporary philosophers, specifically Hermann Cohen, Ferdinand Ebner, and Franz Rosenzweig.[5] Given that Buber was known to have kept many valuable documents, scholars have sought to locate early plans and drafts in an attempt to trace the history of *I and Thou*. In the prologue to his new English translation of the book, published in 1970, Walter Kaufmann included an undated plan that he tentatively identified with the 1916 sketch.[6] But a comparison of this outline with recently published correspondence between Buber and Rosenzweig shows that it was, in fact, composed in the summer of 1922, after *I and Thou* had been completed.[7] My research in the Martin Buber Archive has, however, brought to light a short outline, in Buber's own handwriting, which is dated February 5, 1918. This plan, together with correspondence from 1919–1920, in which similar themes are referred to, corroborates to some extent Buber's retrospective discussions of the beginnings of *I and Thou*. They place Buber, spiritually and philosophically, in the essentially religious frame of mind from which his dialogical thinking developed.

The outline of 1918 was preserved because Buber used it for the end of *I and Thou*. It was placed in his handwritten manuscript of the book together with another page on which he noted thoughts "for the end" of the work. It seems evident that this second page is a later addition, as it is written on different paper and contains terms—Thou, He, It, and Thou-relation—that, as we shall see, Buber had not yet adopted in 1918. Among the thoughts "for the end" found on this second page are the following:

---

3. Martin Buber, *I and Thou*, trans. Walter Kaufmann (New York, 1970), 169. All quotations from *I and Thou* appearing in the present study are taken from this translation.

4. *Between Man and Man*, ed. Maurice S. Friedman and trans. Ronald G. Smith, 2nd ed. (New York, 1967), 206–224.

5. Hermann Cohen, *Religion der Vernunft aus den Quellen des Judentums* (Leipzig, 1919); Ferdinand Ebner, *Das Wort und die geistigen Realitäten* (Innsbruck, 1921); Franz Rosenzweig, *Der Stern der Erlösung* (Frankfurt a. M., 1921).

6. "A Plan Martin Buber Abandoned," in *I and Thou*, pp. 49–50.

7. Grete Schaeder, *Martin Buber: Briefwechsel aus sieben Jahrzehnten*, vol. 2 (Heidelberg, 1972–1975), 112–123; and infra, pp. 190, 224.

The gothic towers, to which heaven? To the starry heaven
of Kant, which is "above" us or above our world.
There is no salvation for the world but to pass into the
Kingdom (as Being into "death").
To call God He or It that is allegory.
Religions come into existence when duration replaces
eternity.
The theophany comes.[8]

One must stress from the outset that dialogical terminology is absent
from the outline of 1918 and is rare in the pre-*I and Thou* writings.
Furthermore, in the light of the nondialogical nature of the lectures of
1922, the tendencies inherent in the outline, out of which Buber's
thought developed, only reached their true dialogical character at a later
stage, in the final version of *I and Thou*. The paired expressions I-Thou
and I-it do not appear even once in the lectures, that is, four months
before the completion of the book.

The outline follows:

Line 1. 5.II.18 [February 5, 1918]
Line 2. The Confronted and the Between
Line 3. 60a
Line 4. The Confronted as Kernel and Substance
Line 5. Forms of the Confronted (God, Work, Beloved, etc.)
Line 6. The Relations to the Confronted (to create, to love, to
command, etc.)
Line 7. The Between as an Hypostatization of the *Relation*
Line 8. God-Confronted
Line 9. Demon-Between
Line 10. The Tendency to the Redemption of the Between/
Dionysus. Christ
Lines 11
and   12. To show the Dualism of the Confronted and Between in
Myth, Magic, and Mystery

---

8. "Die Türme der Gotik—zu welchem Himmel? Kants Sternhimmel
'über' uns und unserer Welt?
Es gibt für die Welt keine Rettung als dass sie ins Reich vergeht (wie das
Wesen in den 'Tod').
Von Gott Er oder Es sagen: das ist Allegorie.
Die Religionen entstehen, wenn die Dauer an Stelle der Ewigkeit tritt.
Die kommende Theophanie."

Buber attempted to construct a view from two major concepts, the Confronted and the Between, in other words, the Substance that man encounters and the satanic obstacles, or mediators, in between. One can clearly see that in 1918 Buber's thought did not revolve around two types of relationships. Critics have already shown that the concept of orientation in his earlier mystical treatise *Daniel* (1913) resembles the I-It of *I and Thou* (1923) and that these expressions of experience and knowledge are subordinate in value to "realization" in *Daniel* and to I-Thou in his later works. In 1918, however, Buber attempted to construct a system without using I-It or any similar term. He built his system solely in relation to the Confronted Substance, which can probably be identified with what he calls being in *I and Thou*; and he opposes it with the obstacles, or the Demon-Between. This is nonsubstance, a kind of hypostatization of hindrances in which one treats that which really does not exist as if it were substance.[9] In other words, Buber was attempting to build a philosophical system solely on the basis of I-Thou.

"The Confronted and the Between" of line 2 of the outline is apparently the title for the proposed work. The Confronted is a synonym for the Encountered, which Buber later also calls Thou. Confronting or encountering, a recurring theme in *I and Thou*, is the source and foundation of Buber's concept of dialogue: "I confront a human being as my Thou and speak the basic word I-Thou to him."[10] The Confronted is nevertheless described in 1918 in classical philosophical language as Substance. For obvious reasons Buber later abandoned the latter term as inappropriate to dialogical thinking; it does not appear at all in *I and Thou*.

It is noteworthy that the very same examples of the Confronted—God, work, beloved—that Buber notes in this early plan recur in the lectures and in *I and Thou*. The double and even triple repetition of the selfsame examples undoubtedly indicates a primary interest in them as such. The beloved is later called Thou. Work apparently refers to the work of art. In the lectures Buber says, "To the artist his work does

---

9. In May 1922, Buber had the following motto for *I and Thou*, which he later abandoned: "Die Götter und die Dämonen stritten miteinander, da sprachen die Dämonen in Hochmut" ("The Gods and the Demons argued, since the Demons spoke haughtily.")

10. *I and Thou*, pp. 59–60; also lecture.

not appear as an It in the world of object . . . but as a Thou."[11] The third and most significant example, that of God as the Confronted, later became the basis for Buber's development of a concept of God as Eternal Thou.

The outline of 1918 represents a clear departure from Buber's earlier mysticism. Line 8 explicitly links God and the Confronted; that is, the encounter with God replaces mystical union. In "The Holy Way" (1918),[12] God is both present and transcendent, as in many Hasidic sources. In that work, Buber calls God *gegenwärtige Substanz* (present substance), whereas in the outline of 1918, God is both Substance and the Confronted. Even at this initial stage of the development toward *I and Thou*, the terms present and presence play an important role in Buber's formulation of his concept of God. In "The Holy Way," Buber criticizes the mystical approach of those who turn their backs to the world and enjoy only the sun. God must be found in their lives, in their community—*between* them. While this concept of between is in fact much closer to that developed in the dialogical context, one does not find in this essay an explicit conceptualization of the encounter, which is partially present in the outline of 1918.

The theme of relations also appears in the outline (line 6). It is clear that simultaneous with the development of the Confronted, Buber attempted to formulate the means and methods of relating to this confronting substance. The importance of relation, a term also drawn from classical philosophy, grew in proportion to Buber's gradual discarding of mystical unity in favor of encounter. In *I and Thou* the concept of relation became of paramount importance: "In the beginning is relation."[13] In the outline of 1918, language or speech, which is the bridge between the I and the Thou in *I and Thou*, is not mentioned.

The short outline of 1918 can be considered as an embryonic stage of *I and Thou*. A positive element, confrontation, was crystallizing in his mind, whereas the nature of what one must overcome to reach encounter was not yet clearly defined. The between of 1918 differs significantly from the later concept of I-It; the between here is a non-

---

11. In the lectures Buber says that by work of art he actually means creative conception. This idea is clearer in the lectures than in *I and Thou*, p. 60, where he says, "This is the eternal origin of art that a human being confronts."

12. Martin Buber, "The Holy Way," in *On Judaism* (New York, 1967), 108ff.

13. *I and Thou*, p. 69.

substance, an obstacle, a demon. Buber expresses a far more negative attitude to this between than to the I-It. A similarly negative attitude toward the It-world relation prevails in the lectures of 1922, where it is called "lie" and "treason." Such emphatic negation is not apparent anywhere in *I and Thou.*

It is to be noted, however, that the concept of between in the final passage of *I and Thou* does approximate that of the outline of 1918. It appears that, when writing his final paragraph, Buber combined elements from the outline of 1918 and from the page of thoughts "for the end" of the book—between from the one and theophany from the other: "And the theophany comes ever closer, it comes ever closer to the sphere *between beings*—comes closer to the realm that hides in our midst, in the between."[14] This between is not the same that Buber developed to express the interhuman I-Thou relationship, but rather it is a concept rooted in the outline of 1918.

Buber concludes *I and Thou* by giving universal and almost redemptive significance to the I-Thou relation, which man raises above the I-It. "The relation to the Thou is unmediated. Nothing conceptual intervenes between I and Thou, no prior knowledge and no imagination."[15]

Although in *I and Thou* the I-It is nowhere called Demon or treason and is a more neutral concept—"without It a human being cannot live"[16]—it nevertheless maintains some of the negative connotations that prevail in his earlier writings. In 1914 Buber wrote an essay entitled "The Demon in the Dream," in which he showed that the Demon is but a temptation and not a being in itself.[17] Similarly in the outline of 1918, the Demon-Between is a nonsubstance, a hypostatization that hinders man's meeting with his Confronted. These views may stem from several sources, but there is room for the hypothesis that they were significantly influenced by Buber's understanding of Hasidic thought. The notion that obstacles or powers of evil assume various forms and hinder man from reaching his goal is a theme that can be found in certain Hasidic stories, for example, those of Rabbi Nachman

---

14. Ibid., p. 168.

15. Kaufmann explains "unmediated" as the "absence of any intermediaries," ibid., p. 62.

16. Ibid., p. 85.

17. Martin Buber, *Pointing the Way: Collected Essays*, trans. by Maurice S. Friedman (New York, 1957), 11ff.

and some of those of the Baal Shem Tov. It is known that in the years preceding the writing of *I and Thou*, Buber was immersed in his work on Hasidic literature. At the end of 1921 he explained the dialogical principle to Rosenzweig by using Hasidic examples, speaking of "a truth beyond Hasidism." Also, in addition to his Frankfurt lectures, "Religion as Presence," on the themes of *I and Thou*, he also taught a seminar on Hasidism.

The meaning of the between as a hypostatization of the relation in the outline of 1918 (line 7) can be more precisely interpreted by its parallel in the lectures of 1922,[18] where, in discussing the difference between his present theory and mystical unity, Buber said: "What the mystics usually call union, Unio, means—I should like at first to formulate it conceptually . . .—a hypostasis of the pure relation." Evidently, there are two kinds of hypostatization, that of the attribute and that of the relation.

As Buber explained in his lectures, an attribute has no independent existence; it exists only in relation to something else. The mystic raises it to the position of an independent entity, and that is his error. The examples cited by Buber in this regard included the word of God and His wisdom, examples that can be viewed from the vantage point of Christian and Jewish mysticism alike. Buber rejected the positing of mystical and, to a lesser extent, mythical intermediaries between God and the world. And, for the most part, he excluded them from his Hasidic interpretations, despite the fact that they play a significant part in that literature.

His attack, however, was directed more specifically against those who make a hypostatization of relations. Perhaps as an expression of personal disillusionment with his previous ecstatic experiences, he insisted that the mystic does not achieve real mystical union. In 1922, he stressed that "the duality always remains." In *I and Thou*, he wrote that "the members become pale in the process and all that grows is relation."[19] The mystic is drunk not with union but with relation. The relation grows to such an extent that the Confronted Thou is finally obscured, and thus relation, which is meant to be a bridge and a con-

---

18. See Lecture Six, supra, p. 93.
19. *I and Thou*, p. 135: "What we find here is a marginal exorbitance of the act of relation: the relationship itself in its vital unity is felt so vehemently that its members pale in the process: its life predominates so much that the I and the You between whom it is established are forgotten."

nection between beings, becomes an obstacle and a hindrance: The mystic achieves neither union nor confrontation.

The tendency to redeem the world by Christ and by Dionysus is noted in line 10 of the outline. Here Buber considers contemporary concepts of redemption, clearly without identifying himself with them. Dionysus apparently refers to Nietzsche's Dionysian type. The hubris inherent in the mystic's claim to have united with God is also the tragedy of Nietzsche's deified superman. Buber rejected Nietzsche's attempt to replace God with man. Redemption knows no between, neither a deified man nor a human God. Christ, too, is viewed as a between, an obstacle to the direct relationship between God and man. Jesus the teacher, and not Christ the Redeemer, was admired by Buber, and only with the former did Buber feel a kinship. He opposed the Christian principle of a mediator between God and man, as well as the claim that the Father can be reached only by way of the Son.[20] For Buber the Jew, there can be only the direct relation with God.

The outline of 1918 proves that the original conception of *I and Thou* precedes its publication by at least five years. Recently published letters offer further evidence. On January 21, 1919, Buber wrote to his friend Hugo Bergman: "I am now working on the foundation of a philosophical system (social and religious). To the construction of this sytem, the future years will be devoted."[21] This statement corroborates Buber's testimony, on several occasions, that he wrote a "rough draft" of *I and Thou* in 1919. However, no papers in the archive have yet been identified with this draft. We know neither its length nor details of its themes, although the plan of 1918 suggests it contents and point of departure. In letters of 1919 and 1920, Buber called his work a "Prolegomena to a Philosophy of Religion," a title that clearly indicates

---

20. Martin Buber, "Spinoza, Shabbtai Zvi, and the Baal Shem," in *The Origin and Meaning of Hasidism* (New York, 1960), 92.

21. Schaeder, *Briefwechsel*, vol. 2, pp. 27–28. In this letter Buber also expresses his personal hope to live in Palestine. He wrote: "What you say about Palestine agrees basically with my own feeling. However, I can hardly think of going there before 1922. (In the coming winter, 1919/1920, we think of going there for a few months and seeking a lot upon which to build.) . . . I hope when the university opens in about 5–6 years, to be able to lecture there in Hebrew. . . . Whether I'll be ready for it much earlier appears to me doubtful."

Kant's influence.[22] This title occurs first in the letter of 1919 to Hugo Bergman and then later on in a letter to him of May 1922, indicating that Buber referred throughout to the very same work, namely, *I and Thou*.[23]

The dates of the letters that describe his work on the prolegomena testify to his having struggled intermittently with it during the years 1918–1920. On March 3, 1920, Buber wrote that he had recently been preoccupied with his prolegomena and was therefore *not* inclined to interrupt his work in order to attend a Zionist meeting in Prague at the end of the month: "I am deeply engrossed in my prolegomena on religious philosophy and am presently at its most difficult part. This work has lain dormant for five years;[24] I returned to it only recently, after overcoming great spiritual and corporeal inhibitions."[25] In the end Buber did interrupt his work and atttended the Zionist conference.[26]

In addition to the outline of 1918 and the letters, we also have Buber's retrospective testimony that "the clarification occurred first of all, here too, in relation to my interpretation of Hasidism. In the Preface, written in September 1919, to my Book *Der Grosse Maggid und*

---

22. In the proposed table of contents for *I and Thou*, Buber called a section "The Religious Antinomy," which illustrates, again, the impact of Kant. *The Critique of Pure Reason* was similar to his own point of departure, but in "Religion as Presence" he was critical of Kant's attitude to religion in general.

23. See Buber's letter to Bergman, dated May 13, 1922 (Schaeder, *Briefwechsel*, vol. 2, p. 99). He wrote: "The prolegomena to my work on religion, *I and Thou*, which treats the original phenomenon, will appear soon." The prolegomena is also mentioned by Buber in a letter to Richard Beer-Hofmann dated January 3, 1922 (in MBA, MS Var. 350/83).

24. Which alludes to a beginning as early as 1915!

25. Schaeder, *Briefwechsel*, vol. 2, p. 66.

26. On this meeting see Hans Kohn, *Martin Buber: sein Werk und seine Zeit: Ein Beitrag zur Geistesgeschichte Mitteleuropas, 1880–1930* (Cologne, 1961), 177, as well as Samuel Hugo Bergman, *Faith and Reason* (New York, 1972), 98. This occasion was the only time Buber and A. D. Gordon met. The call of the aged Tolstoy-like advocate of manual labor for the group to come to settle in Palestine made a deep impression on those who attended the conference. Buber, who was in many philosophical points close to Gordon, wrote several short pieces on him: "Der wahre Lehrer" (The True Teacher), "Der Acker und die Sterne" (The Field and the Stars), "Ein Träger der Verwirklichung" (A Bearer of Realization), in *Israel und Palästina* (Zurich, 1950); and "Gordon and the Land" (in Hebrew), in a memorial volume dedicated to A. D. Gordon (Tel Aviv, 1942).

seine Nachfolge [1921], Jewish teaching was described as 'wholly based on the two-directional relation of the human I and the Divine Thou, on reciprocity, on the *meeting*.' Soon after, in the autumn of 1919, followed the first yet rough draft [*unbeholfene Niederschrift*] of *I and Thou*."[27]

Traces of this clarification can be detected in his essay of 1919, "*Herut*: On Youth and Religion." At one point in this essay he refers to God as "the Thou in itself,"[28] a term that later recurs in the lectures. In *I and Thou*, it is connected to "the infinite Thou." Hugo Bergman has shown that "*Herut*" already represents a significant departure from Buber's early thinking.[29] In it Buber summarized his argument that religion, which is dogma and rules, is merely the result of the human attempt to make the encounter with God comprehensible through a symbolic ordering of the knowable and doable. Significantly, there are clear similarities, both in content and language, between the first few pages of "*Herut*" and the last pages of *I and Thou*, again showing that the third part of *I and Thou* was central at the work's inception and that it was the first part to reach its final form.

After the winter of 1920, Buber's work on the prolegomena was interrupted. It is possible that many of the basic elements had not yet reached the degree of clarity that would permit him to push ahead. Buber spoke retrospectively in 1954 of a "two-year interruption," during which time he did not read any works in philosophy that could have helped him to clarify his thoughts. Historical evidence now available shortens that two-year period and suggests a more complex picture of Buber's development involving hitherto unverified influences.

---

27. "The History of the Dialogical Principle" in *Between Man and Man*, p. 215; and in *Werke*, vol. 1 (Munich/Heidelberg, 1962–1964), 297–298.

28. "Das Du an sich," in "Cheruth" (1919), in *Der Jude und sein Judentum: Gesammelte Aufsätze und Reden* (Cologne, 1963), 123. "Religion als Gegenwart," in Rivka Horwitz, *Buber's Way to I and Thou* (Heidelberg, 1978), p. 109, and n. 32. Buber retained the paragraph from "Religion als Gegenwart" in *Ich und Du, Werke*, vol. 1, p. 132, but altered the expression from "das Du an sich" ("the Thou in itself") to "das unendliche Du" ("the infinite Thou").

29. Hugo Bergman, "Martin Buber and Mysticism," in Schilpp and Friedman, *The Philosophy of Martin Buber*, p. 302.

T W O

1919–1921: "I . . . began with Ebner's Fragments"

The outline of 1918 reveals that a marked shift had already taken place in Buber's thought during the last year of the World War, prior to any possible contact with the respective books on dialogical thinking published by Hermann Cohen, Ferdinand Ebner, and Franz Rosenzweig after the war. By February 1918, Buber no longer saw God as exclusively immanent and had begun to develop the Confronted as a theme of metaphysical import. This rudimentary shift gained momentum during subsequent years until, in 1922, Buber arrived at the conclusion that one can only address God as Thou. That year, in a burst of creativity, he adopted the terms It and Thou; and in the final stages of his work on *I and Thou*, he introduced notions of dialogue and speech into his thinking.

It must still be asked, on the basis of philological and historical evidence, whether any other contemporary thinkers might have significantly influenced the development of Buber's thought during the period 1920–1921, that is, whether an external influence, perhaps previously absent, now aided him in crystallizing the fragmentary thoughts of 1918. The evidence of parallel lines of thought in the writings of Cohen, Ebner, and Rosenzweig suggests these thinkers for consideration in this context. From the outset, however, any influence on the part of Rosenzweig at this stage must be ruled out; Buber's contact with him and his writings began in December 1921, at a time when Buber had already formulated many of the ideas of his book. Rosenzweig's influence can be related only to the revision of "Religion as Presence," a theme that will be treated extensively later.

The influence of Hermann Cohen, the liberal, rationalist philosopher, interpreter of Kant, and founder of the Marburg school, appears, at first glance, quite plausible. Having developed a philosophy centering on nature and ethics in his earlier writings, Cohen realized in the last years of his life that the individual can be fully discovered only in his relation with God. In his last book, *Religion of Reason from the Sources of Judaism* (1919), he treated the themes of I, Thou, the individual and his suffering, revelation, and redemption, while emphasizing also the social aspect of life, that is, the demand to aid one's suffering fellowman. Of this book, Buber wrote: "It may be regarded as a continuation of the line of Jacobi when it is recognized here that only the Thou . . . brings me to consciousness of my I, and that it is 'the personality' that is raised by the Thou to the light of the day. But something formerly unexpressed in philosophy becomes explicit when it says of . . . their 'correlation' that it could not enter into completion if it were not preceded by the inclusive correlation of man and man."[1]

Despite Buber's use of similar language, he explicitly denied having been influenced by Cohen. It is, in fact, difficult to conceive of Cohen, whose philosophy differed so radically from Buber's and for whom Buber had little personal liking, as a source of influence and inspiration in the years under discussion.[2] The entire growth of Buber's thought is based on foundations completely opposed to those of Cohen. Buber in his early mystical stage admired Spinoza; Cohen, for most of his life, rejected Spinoza vociferously. Buber sought the myth in Judaism and, at one time, embraced mysticism; Cohen rejected both mythology and mysticism. Buber, alienated from Judaism as a youth, returned by way of Zionism, which always remained for him an ideal; Cohen stood firm in his opposition to Zionism and saw in it merely the desire to be a "nation like all nations."

Cohen represented a type of liberal Judaism—stressing ethical monotheism and viewing Judaism as a religion, specifically, a religion of reason—that Buber attacked decisively. Such rational interpretation of Judaism is, according to him, hardly closer to authentic "religiosity" than is rabbinic Judaism. In his essay "Jewish Religiosity," Buber clearly rejected the post-Kantian description of Judaism as ethical mon-

---

1. *Werke*, vol. 1 (Munich/Heidelberg, 1962–1964), 295; *Between Man and Man*, ed. Maurice S. Friedman and trans. Ronald G. Smith, 2nd ed. (New York, 1967), 212.

2. Rosenzweig, in his article "Hermann Cohens jüdische Schriften," in *Kleinere Schriften* (Berlin 1937), 346, states that the meeting between Cohen and Buber could have been fruitful, "but neither saw the other."

otheism: "The meaning of the act of decision in Judaism is falsified if it is viewed as merely an ethical act."[3] In Lecture Two of "Religion as Presence" he criticized the recurrent attempt to consider religion as a function of the ethical, both in its crude forms and as presented by Kant's postulate of practical reason.[4] Such attempts rob religion of its independence and authentic existence. Kant's ethics and his categorical imperative played no particular role in Buber's understanding of Judaism. Seeking the individual and national dark sources of our existence, Buber asserted: "I am a Jew, therefore nothing Jewish should be alien to me," and "my soul is my people"; what we define as "good," he later said, is the *direction* of the unified soul toward God.[5]

A comparison of correlation in Cohen's *Religion of Reason* with I and Thou in Buber's work illustrates how their thinking differs in structure, as well as in content. For Cohen, religion is dependent on ethics, which deal with man as part of the whole. But ethics are impersonal, rational, and universal—remotely comparable to the realm of I-It in Buber's work—and, as such, are insufficient to deal with *all* aspects of human life. It cannot, most particularly, encompass the realms of the individual, the relation between God and man, and the relation between man and man. These are uncovered only by correlation: by suffering, pity, and compassion. The individual is discovered in his sins; when man stands before God he may be forgiven and purified. It is, Cohen tried to show, in the realm of religion, not ethics, that the individual emerges. This realm of religion is, to a degree, comparable to the realm of I-Thou in Buber's writings.

Whereas for Buber the I-It is to be overcome, for Cohen ethics are not secondary, let alone negative. Pure religion depends on ethics, and thus Cohen's I-Thou—if we may so call it—remains within the realm of I-It and in the end unites with it. In marked contrast, Buber's I-It, although part of human fate, is that which man wishes to, and must, overcome.

These contrasting foundations set Buber and Cohen worlds apart. The philosophical chasm between the two was exposed when the aging

---

3. Martin Buber, *Der Jude und sein Judentum* (Cologne, 1963), 69; English in *On Judaism* (New York, 1967), 83.

4. Lecture Two, supra, p. 34; on Kant, see supra, p. 34.

5. *Werke*, vol. 1, pp. 648ff.; "Evil and Good," in *Good and Evil*, trans. Ronald G. Smith (New York, 1953), 140ff. Author's emphasis.

Cohen's anti-Zionist article, "Religion and Zionism,"[6] was attacked openly by Buber in his "Peoples, States, and Zion," which appeared in *Der Jude.*[7]

In marked contrast to Buber, Rosenzweig expressed admiration for the older Cohen and his final work, considering it "a very great book— yet really easily written," with a promising future.[8] Although Rosenzweig never accepted Cohen's neo-Kantian philosophy (and perhaps therefore discerned the gap between the younger and older Cohen),[9] he shared with him to a certain degree both his liberalism and his low opinion of the Zionist option.[10] Rosenzweig clearly admired this dynamic personality and philosopher of Judaism. He found tremendous support and comfort in Cohen's courses on Maimonides and on the philosophy of religion, given in Berlin at a time when Rosenzweig was still struggling to establish himself in his new Jewish position.

When Buber and Rosenzweig met in January 1922, they discussed Cohen. Rosenzweig related that Buber "tried in vain to hide his lack of sympathy" for Cohen, and the two remained opposed in their opinions of him.[11] Through the subsequent years of friendship with Ro-

---

6. Hermann Cohen, "Religion und Zionismus," and "Antwort," in *Jüdische Schriften*, vol. 2 (Berlin, 1924), 319–327, 328–340.

7. Martin Buber, "Völker, Staaten und Zion," in *Judentum*, pp. 280–308; letter to Hermann Cohen (July 1916); "Zion, der Staat und die Menschheit: Bemerkungen zu Hermann Cohens 'Antwort,'" *Der Jude*, September 1916, 425ff. See also Rosenzweig, *Kleinere Schriften*, p. 345.

8. Franz Rosenzweig, *Briefe* (Berlin, 1935), 393. See also Rosenzweig's review, "Hermann Cohens Nachlasswerk," in *Kleinere Schriften*, pp. 294–298, where he writes that he foresees commentaries and interpretations of the book to be written in the coming centuries, in places such as Siberia, Tierra del Fuego, New Guinea, and Cameroon. Rosenzweig himself gave a course on the book at the Lehrhaus in 1921; see Richard Koch, "Das Freie Jüdische Lehrhaus in Frankfurt am-Main," *Der Jude*, vol. VII (1923), 116–125.

9. It was Rosenzweig who first posited a clear philosophical distinction between the young Cohen and the old. This line of thought was carried on by Julius Guttmann and Samuel Hugo Bergman, in opposition to Alexander Altmann. See Rosenzweig, "Hermann Cohens jüdische Schriften," pp. 305ff.; Julius Guttmann, *The Philosophies of Judaism* (New York/London, 1964), 366; Samuel Hugo Bergman, *Faith and Reason* (Washington, D.C., 1964 and New York, 1972), 46; Alexander Altmann, "Hermann Cohens Begriffe der Korrelation," in *In zwei Welten*, ed. Hans Tramer (Tel Aviv, 1962), 377–399.

10. Rosenzweig considered himself a follower of Cohen rather than a Zionist (*Briefe*, p. 235).

11. Ibid., p. 414.

senzweig, Buber's attitude may have mellowed. He became more sympathetic and wrote several short articles on Cohen.[12] But in 1922 and the preceding years he certainly did not share his friend's admiration for, or interest in, Cohen.

The spiritual remoteness that marked this relationship—that effectively nullified Cohen as a source of influence for Buber—is absent from the relation between Buber and Ferdinand Ebner. Although the two never actually met or corresponded, certain basic elements of Buber's philosophy parallel the very foundation of Ebner's fragments, entitled *Das Wort und die geistigen Realitäten* (The Word and the Spiritual Realities).[13] Buber himself, responding in 1932 to one of his admirers, Hermann Gerson, suggested that if he wanted to write something about *I and Thou*, he might consider beginning with a comparison between the book and Ebner's fragments, which, he notes, he was not yet aware of when writing his book.[14] Several critics have, in fact, noted parallel lines of thought, but they have consistently attempted to maintain the respective independence of the discoveries and thinking of the two. Emil Brunner, for example, in his evaluation of *I and Thou*, quotes Karl Heim's contention that Buber's discovery of dialogical thinking is nothing less than a Copernican revolution in the thinking of mankind. Brunner adds that this evaluation is, however, applicable "not so much to

---

12. Martin Buber, "The Love of God and the Idea of Deity," in *Eclipse of God* (New York, 1952), where he criticizes Cohen's contention that "the love of God is the love of the moral idea," while pointing out that although Cohen thought of God as an idea, he loved him as God (p. 58); idem, "Die Tränen" and "Philon und Cohen," in *Judentum*, pp. 800–814 (the latter article is a fragment from 1928).

13. Ferdinand Ebner, *Das Wort und die geistigen Realitäten* (Innsbruck, 1921 and Vienna, 1952); included in *Schriften* 3 vols. (Munich, 1963–1965). All quotations are from the last edition.

14. In a letter of December 23, 1932, to Herman Gerson, Buber writes: "In the work on me it would be best to proceed from the I-Thou category. It would then be possible to make a fruitful comparison with Ebner (whom I did not know at the time I wrote the first version) and several other contemporaries who were working independently." He suggested that *I and Thou* should be compared with the works of the Protestant theologians Karl Heim, Friedrich Gogarten, and Emil Brunner (Grete Schaeder, ed., *Martin Buber: Briefwechsel aus sieben Jahrzehnten*, vol. 2 [Heidelberg, 1972–1975], 455). Ebner is also mentioned in Buber's letter to Ronald G. Smith (ibid., p. 628). On first reading *Ich und Du*, Rosenzweig also noted the similarity between Buber and Ebner (ibid., p. 126).

Martin Buber as to a then unknown Austrian thinker, Ferdinand Ebner, who, in his book *Das Wort und die geistigen Realitäten,* had published the identical discovery a year before Buber, *without either one knowing of the other.* However, shortly after the publication of his book, Ferdinand Ebner was struck by tuberculosis and fell victim to it within a few years. Buber, on the other hand, had the opportunity to make public and explain his discovery in a large number of publications."[15]

Likewise, Hugo Bergman[16] and Harold Stahmer,[17] in their respective discussions of the parallels between Buber's and Ebner's thought, have tended to view the two events as disconnected, as a rare coincidence in the history of ideas, when two thinkers have independently reached strikingly similar conclusions. No critic has raised doubts as to their having worked in complete isolation from one another.

And yet, according to Buber's own published testimony in "On the History of the Dialogical Principle," he did have knowledge of Ebner's writings when he was working on *I and Thou,* although he insisted that he read Ebner's work "too late" to affect his own thought. He wrote: "Ferdinand Ebner, a Catholic schoolteacher in the Austrian province, [at a time when he was] heavily afflicted by sickness and depression, wrote his 'pneumatological fragments,' which he collected in the book *Das Wort und die geistigen Realitaten* [The Word and the Spiritual Realities, 1921]. Ebner proceeds from the experience of the 'solitude of the I' [*Icheinsamkeit*], in that existential sense that it has won in our time." Ebner finds salvation, Buber wrote, in the thought that "there is only one single Thou and that is God alone." To be sure, he also postulated that man should also love man; but in the last analysis, for Ebner only love for God is authentic.[18]

Buber then made the following statement: "As I wrote the third and last part [of *I and Thou*], I . . . began with Ebner's fragments." In a footnote he explained: "I happened to see some of them that were published in an issue of *Brenner,* and then sent for the book." Contin-

---

15. Emil Brunner, "Judaism and Christianity in Buber," in Paul A. Schilpp and Maurice S. Friedman, eds., *The Philosophy of Martin Buber* (LaSalle, Ill., 1967), 309. Author's emphasis.

16. *Dialogical Philosophy from Kierkegaard to Buber* (in Hebrew) (Jerusalem, 1974), 180.

17. *Speak That I May See Thee!* (New York, 1968), 217.

18. *Werke,* vol. 1, p. 296; *Between Man and Man,* p. 213.

uing, he wrote that "Ebner's book showed me, as no other since then, here and there in an almost uncanny nearness, that in this one time men of different kinds of traditions had devoted themselves to the search for the buried treasure."[19] It is thus evident that Buber was not unaware of Ebner's writings during a period crucial to the development of his own philosophy. One must now examine the evidence, historical and philological, to determine whether Buber was not only aware of Ebner's thought but also influenced by it.

Buber notes several encounters with Ebner's work. He first came across chapters of the book in 1920 in the Austrian periodical *Der Brenner*, to which he subscribed regularly. He was personally acquainted with Carl Dallago, one of the frequent contributors; and the journal treated themes—religions of the Far East, Kierkegaard, Dostoevsky, Pascal—of extreme interest to Buber.[20] It is most likely, therefore, that he would have read Ebner's fragments in 1920 when they appeared in *Der Brenner*.

Ludwig von Ficker, the editor of *Der Brenner*, received Ebner's book from the theologian Theodor Haecker for publication in 1919.[21] Financially unable to publish it immediately, he printed parts of it in his periodical. These "fragments," as Ebner calls his chapters, comprise nearly one-third of the complete book, including chapters 1, 2, 3, 16 and 18.[22] Numerous recurring themes of Ebner's basic existential philosophy come to the fore, providing a clear impression of the work as a whole. The following excerpts are some examples of his thinking, which Buber may have encountered in *Der Brenner* in 1920:

---

19. *Werke*, vol. 1, p. 298; *Between Man and Man*, p. 215.

20. For Buber's acquaintance with *Der Brenner*, see also his letter of December 9, 1922, to Gogarten, which includes a plan for ecumenical relations. Several names are mentioned, and he adds, "It would be pleasing to me if someone from the Brenner circle could be there, but I have an—almost instinctive—objection to Haecker (Schaeder, *Briefwechsel*, vol. 2, p. 144). Buber's library was said to contain numerous issues of *Der Brenner*. See also Ebner, *Schriften*, vol. 2, p. 1096; and p. 156. Ebner too had reasons to believe that Buber knew *Der Brenner*.

21. Theodor Haecker (1879–1945), philosopher and critic, translator of Kierkegaard into German, converted to Catholicism in 1921.

22. See von Ficker's letter of September 17, 1919, to Ebner, in *Schriften*, vol. 3, p. 281. Five of the book's eighteen chapters were published in *Der Brenner*; see also *Schriften*, vol. 2, p. 1085.

From Fragment 1:

The "I" is a later discovery . . . I-solitude is not original in the I, but the event of a spiritual act in it, a deed of the I, namely, its shutting itself up from the Thou. The I and the Thou are the spiritual realities of life. Consequently, the I exists only in its relation to the Thou and not outside it. . . . The insight into the spiritual realities of life means nothing less than the end of idealism. . . . Language is something which on the one hand presupposes the I and Thou, and on the other hand forms it.

The most important and impressive (which throws light on the final essence of the word) is that man's relation to God takes the form of this I-Thou relationship. It is the basic and primal form [*Grund und Urform*] of the relation to God, that just because it is and shall be a "personal" one it can be no other than the relation of the I to the Thou. In the last ground of our spiritual life, God is the true Thou of the true I in man.

From Fragment 2:

The spiritual life of man is bound up with speech in the closest and most indissoluble manner and rests like the latter on the relation of the I to the Thou.

Since I and Thou exist only in relation to each other, there is neither an I that has no absolute existence without a Thou, nor a Thou which is without an I.

Because the relationship of God is and must be a personal one, it can only be conceived as a relationship of the I to the Thou, the "first" to the "second person," as one says in grammar, and where one certainly does not express a hierarchy.

From Fragment 3:

To believe in the name of God means to believe in God as the addressed being, as the "addressed person," as precisely the Thou of the I in man; in other words: in his personal existence. . . .

God has either a personal existence or none at all. Because God exists personally, his relation to man is also a personal one, and we mean nothing else than this when we speak of the Grace of God which corresponds to man's humble trust in him, the trust of the I in the Thou that comes to meet it. . . .

The personality of God could have existed even without any relations: this is, however, not the case, because the personal existence of man is in its relation to God and could not have been otherwise.

From Fragment 18:

The man who has found the true Thou of his I, the meaning of his existence in God, no longer asks about the meaning of life. He knows

his existence as laid in the hand of God and, despite all need, all suffering and misfortune, all the breaking up of his life in the world, he
demands no other meaning for it than he clearly and simply grasps in
his relationship with God.

A man who inwardly grasps the problem of life as wholly his
problem . . . must be able to believe in God, in the "Thou coming to
meet him." [From M. Friedman, ed. *The Worlds of Existentialism: A
Critical Reader* (New York, 1964).]

In light of the outline of 1918, these fragments take on a potentially
decisive role in the further clarification of Buber's new thinking. What
is certain is that Buber was sufficiently impressed by them to order
the book, which he received no earlier than September 1921.[23] Most
important, he returned to a more intensive study of Ebner's work when
writing the third part of *I and Thou* in 1922.

Of central importance is Ebner's concept of God as Thou, repeatedly emphasized in the fragments in 1920. In *"Herut"* (1919), with its
several parallels to *I and Thou*, Buber, too, on a single occasion, referred
to God as "the Thou in itself." But this is but an isolated instant: In
1919 he still spoke of God primarily in the third person, as the Unconditioned and the Absolute. It is evident that he had not yet arrived
at the concept of God that would become the basis of his dialogical
philosophy: God as Absolute, or Eternal, Thou. His consistent use of
Thou as a name of God is not apparent before winter 1921/1922 in
"Religion as Presence."

We are left with the question of what occurred in Buber's life between 1919 and 1922 that led him to reject his earlier notion of God
as Absolute or He. Buber himself credited his discovery of a new name
for God to an extraordinary experience, which he recounted in the
course of Lecture Seven on March 5, 1922—a story that begins with
a frustrating, unanswered question in 1914 and concludes with a pivotal
answer in the fall of 1921.

From his other writings, we know that Buber experienced more
than one creative moment of illumination and inspiration. In a letter
to Rosenzweig, for example, Buber indicates that it was in such a moment that he had a breakthrough in his plan for a volume to follow *I
and Thou*. Rosenzweig, for his part, related to Buber that he, too, had

---

23. Ebner himself received his book only on September 9, 1921; see his
letter to Luise Karpischek, in ibid., vol. 3, p. 421.

known this phenomenon. In 1917, while serving at the Macedonian front, he had stepped on an ugly thorn; thus, *The Star* was conceived.[24]

Buber's account in Lecture Seven of the moment in which he first perceived that God must always be addressed as "Thou" bears, in the present context, a historical significance that demands it be quoted in full. For his moment of discovery represents the turning point in his way to *I and Thou*, after which the final obstacles to the drafting of the book were removed.

> It was shortly after Easter in the year 1914 when an old acquaintance, an elderly English clergyman whom I had known for many years, visited me in a suburb of Berlin where I lived at that time. This old man, was a very simple believing Christian who for that reason had done much to assist the return of the Jews to Palestine. This man, whom I had not seen for a few years, anounced himself to me unexpectedly one morning and asked if he could visit me immediately. I invited him. He arrived about an hour later. I tell you this to give you a feeling of the atmosphere of the encounter. What I have to say first is not the reason why I am telling you this story.
>
> After greeting me, he said, "My dear friend, I have come to tell you that in this year a world war will break out." And he unfolded a graphic presentation of the prophecy of Daniel, and demonstrated to me that the event would have to take place precisely in this year.
>
> Well, that is not the important part. For no one need know from

---

24. See infra, p. 190. On the conception of *The Star*, see Appendix B, p. 225.

The phenomenon of creative moments is not necessarily limited to religious thinkers or artists; it may also occur to scientists. It is interesting to note the close parallels between Buber's story and Henri Poincare's description of creative experience. Poincaire concludes that the creative experience has four stages: (1) The subject is chosen, either through personal initiative or in response to a question asked by another. (2) An attempt is made to solve the problem through regular rational means. If the rational attempt at a solution is unsuccessful, then (3) the question is "pushed" into the subconscious, which works on the problem while the person is not aware of it. If the appropriate concept for dealing with the problem is found, then there is a moment of "discovery." Then the problem, with its solution, is returned to the consciousness of the person. (4) In the fourth and final stage, the person translates his "discovery" into symbols which can be communicated to others. Poincare's explanation of the discovery process seems to fit well the manner in which Buber, as he himself relates, solved one of his most difficult problems. See Ahron Katchalsy, *In the Crucible of Scientific Revolution* [Hebrew] (Tel Aviv, 1972), 103ff.

what sources the premonition flows to him. But as I accompanied this childlike old man, who had quite touched my heart with the way he presented all this to me—it took several hours—as I accompanied him to the railroad station, he suddenly grasped my arm, it was at a street corner, and said: "Dear friend, we are living in a great time"—that meant for him the pre-paraclectic, the pre-messianic time—"we are living in a great time—tell me: Do you believe in God?"

It was said with such a human weightiness, in all his childlikeness and naïvité, that I felt quite heavy hearted about answering him. For in the way he asked the question I could say neither yes nor no. I tried to reassure him in his language, in a language he could understand, for he was quite uneasy. But that is not the decisive thing, for I did not give him a real answer, at least not at that time.

A few months ago now, it is about six months since I was traveling by train to a meeting with some friends, it came to me, without my cogitating on it beforehand (I do not cogitate on such things), without my cogitating on it the answer came to me all of a sudden in these exact words, that is, not put together from words that I had pondered on earlier but in a sequence of words already joined. (Most of you probably know how that sometimes happens, when suddenly a whole sentence, not just a single word, comes to mind ready-made.) The answer came to me, not as I perhaps could or would have wanted to tell it to the old man, but as I might have given it if I had just been asked in the right way and with these words. This answer was: 'If believing in God means to speak of Him in the third person, then I probably do not believe in God; or at least, I do not know if it is permissible for me to say that I believe in God. For I know, when I speak of Him in the third person whenever it happens, and it has to happen again and again, there is no other way, then my tongue cleaves to the roof of my mouth so quickly that one cannot even call it speech.'

But this answer, if I had understood it rightly, is not a negative one. In the moment when I knew these words I did not feel it as a negative answer, not at all. This answer, however, when correctly understood, is not negative. At the moment when I knew these words I had no negative feelings, none at all.

The pastor mentioned in the story was the Reverend William H. Hechler.[25] Buber's inability to satisfy this concerned Englishman must

---

25. A detailed article on Hechler, including a bibliography and photo-graph, can be found in *Encyclopaedia Judaica*, (1972), S. V. "Hechler, William Henry." Hechler was the chaplain of the British legation in Vienna, an English enthusiast whose life was saturated with biblical imagery, and to whom the restoration of Israel and Zion as prophesied in Scripture was a vital concern. He had been a friend of Theodor Herzl and helped him make contacts with European nobility.

have been repressed for seven years until the moment of inspiration on the train. For Buber, the answer was a sudden awareness that *God must always be addressed in the second person, as the Confronted—as Thou.* The force and the vitality of his future book and philosophy rest on his discovery of the new name for God.

Buber did not publish this story until 1960 in his *Begegnung: Au-tobiographische Fragmente*, under the title "Question and Answer."[26] Both in this printed version and in the lectures of 1922, the answer is strikingly similar and is related to the question posed by the Englishman in 1914. However, in his "Autobiographical Fragments," Buber shifted the date of his inspiration from 1921 to 1914, claiming to have found the answer immediately after the departure of the chaplain, whereas in Lecture Seven he refers to an event that had occurred only half a year earlier, namely, in the fall of 1921. The proximity of the lectures to the events related would seem to make that version more reliable. It could well be that Buber, in 1960 over eighty years old, did not remember all the details of this episode from 1921. Furthermore, Buber entered a handwritten correction in the stenographer's manuscript in order to fix the date accurately.[27] Most importantly, the impact of such an answer cannot be seen in either his thought or his vocabulary in 1914. The 1921 date is most significant in terms of his spiritual development. The answer was very likely a sudden resonance in response to the spiritual chord struck by Ebner's fragments. They provided Buber with the solution to one of the most difficult problems of his new philosophy, namely, the question of a new concept of God. It appears that Buber felt inspired by Ebner because the content of the answer is reminiscent of Ebner's fragments.

Buber's admission to having returned to Ebner's fragments when working on the last part of *I and Thou* is given substance by a comparative analysis of Lecture Seven of "Religion as Presence"—in content the last part of *I and Thou*—and the fragments. From such analysis, clear indications of the return to, that is, the influence of, Ebner emerge. Significantly, this lecture, which not only includes the story "Question and Answer" but also bears, both in content and in language, similar-

26. The story first appeared in *Begegnung: Autobiographische Fragmente* (Stuttgart, 1960), 33–35. It was reprinted as "Question and Answer" in "Autobiographical Fragments," in Schilpp and Friedman, *The Philosophy of Martin Buber*, pp. 23–25.
27. For the change, see Lecture Seven, supra, p. 104 n. 5.

ities to Ebner's writings, was excluded from the printed book.[28] In it Buber stated, for example, the following:

> Religions speak of God in the third person, mostly as a He. People seldom realize the extent to which this pronoun is already an anthropomorphism or, more correctly, to what extent this pronoun means a displacement of God into the world of things and essences, how much this is already implied by the gender of the pronoun. God is displaced into the It-world, that is, into the creation that has run away from God. In other words, in history God is a thing.[29]

Buber's use of the term anthropomorphism to mean the reference to God as He is especially noteworthy, since it is hardly a common usage. However, it is employed repeatedly by Ebner, for example:

> The spiritual idleness of the question how God created the world out of nothing, how He governs and rules it, aims at God in the "third person," that is, at God outside the personal relation to us and ours to Him. . . . "God in the third person," this is a creation of human phantasy, this divine child, that feeds itself by terrestrial experiences and forms in man's image. In it lies anthropomorphism, whether it turn to a visible concrete picture of God and an idol, or whether it escape into a non-sensual abstraction.[30]

In Lecture Seven, Buber bemoaned the multiplicity of religions, their subjectivity, and their subsequent mutual exclusion of one another.[31] He argued that this tragic situation originates in the attempt to form God as a He and to establish His laws. Strikingly similar thoughts are found in Ebner's fragment 16: "There is only one religion which is divine and has nothing human . . . in it; only thus can man gain a real relation to God. All others are religions only in name; they are only human attempts to form a religion—human, and therefore attempts which are failures in themselves."[32]

---

28. It is possible that when Buber stated, "As I wrote the third and last part, I . . . began with Ebner's fragments," he may, in fact, have been referring to Lecture Seven.

29. Lecture Seven, supra, p. 108. But cf. Hans Kohn, *Martin Buber, sein Werk und seine Zeit: Ein Beitrag zur Geistesgeschichte Mittelenropas, 1880–1930* (Cologne, 1961), 159.

30. *Schriften*, vol. 1, pp. 281–282.

31. Lecture Seven, supra, p. 107.

32. *Schriften*, vol. 1, p. 304.

Ebner died in 1931. His posthumously published works appeared in 1963–1965 and included many previously unpublished articles in which he expressed a measure of surprise at the parallels between his own work and that of Buber. In the unfinished article, "Nachwort zur Mitarbeit am Brenner," begun August 20, 1927, he wrote: "It is to be assumed that Buber, when publishing his work, did not know the fragments; he may one day be surprised when he comes across them, not less than the author of those fragments was surprised when an accident led him to read Buber's book."[33] Ebner noted the thematic similarities between the two works and made special reference to the short epilogue to *I and Thou* (dropped from later editions), which reads: "Conception of the work whose beginning is represented by this book, May 1916; first draft of this book, summer 1919; final version, spring 1922." Ebner was intrigued and observed:

> In the history of literature it has occurred several times that two minds, quite independent of each other, and at the same time, have conceived the same thoughts and accepted them for publication. This is what occurred with the fragments and Buber's book; because the line of thought which this book develops, in a lyrical-mystical order which may be characteristic of Buber, is nothing else than the basic thought of the Fragments; the essential relation of the I to the Thou, and the roots of this being in the Word. . . . The problem of the shift in relationship to God from the "You are" to the "He is" . . . by which the foundation of all "theology" as well as all intellectual denial of God was formed, . . . Buber knows. He does not merely know it but solves it in his mystical character.[34]

In a second, regrettably undated article, "The History of the Frag-

---

33. Ibid., p. 584.
34. "Precisely this problem, which was not noticed by any of the critics of the fragments—he [Buber] might have felt very much philosophically superior to them—concerns a particular and until now unknown spiritual act. By means of it, the affirmation of being of the second person was transformed into that of the third person; the sense of the ancient words 'Thou art' was transformed into the substantially different 'He (God) is.' This transformation formed the basis of all 'theology,' as well as all intellectual denial of God. It is precisely this deeply meaningful problem that Martin Buber knows. Not only does he know the problem; rather, he has, in his mystical way, solved it. Yet, he has failed to draw two consequences: the 'loneliness of the I' and 'the dream of the spirit, which is dreamed in it'" (ibid., vol. 1, pp. 583–584).

ments," Ebner expressed doubt, however, as to whether Buber was in fact unacquainted with his work:

> Buber was apparently familiar with *Der Brenner*; at any rate, he sent a copy of his book [*I and Thou*] to Carl Dallago, most likely because he admired his imitation of Tao-te-king. Perhaps he also read my fragments, and for their sake set the dates on the development of his work at the end, dates which are otherwise superfluous. It is really noteworthy, and in this case wonderful, how close the thoughts of the fragments are to the more mystical-lyrical book of Buber.[35]

It has already become clear that on a cardinal point—the idea of God as the true Thou of the human I—Buber follows Ebner closely. Ebner objects to those who maintain that God can be considered other than in the second person. For him, *God in the third person does not exist.*[36] To consider God in the third person is merely a human convention, an anthropomorphism. In Buber's words, "Whoever pronounces the word God . . . really means Thou. . . . By its very nature the Eternal Thou cannot become an It. . . . 'He' is still a metaphor."[37]

In their respective expansions of this primary affirmation, Ebner and Buber exhibit a certain congruence in which pronounced similarities abound. Ebner's attacks on psychological, theological, metaphysical, mathematical, and scientific attempts to reach God are all evident in *I and Thou*, no less than is his opposition to the approach of the mystic. Ebner objected to those who wish to prove the existence of God in the third person before establishing a personal relationship with Him; Buber spoke against those who objectify God, for God can neither be conceived nor experienced. For him, proofs cannot lead man to God. "It is not as if God is inferred from nature as its cause, or from history as its helmsman."[38] In a vein similar to Ebner's contention that "to believe in God is to believe in His name," Buber developed an entire section of his book dealing with God's infinite being as addressed by many names.

A number of critics have argued that the Thou, particularly in Ebner's writings, evidences the Neoplatonic colorings of an infinite.

---

35. Ibid., vol. 2, p. 1096, also p. 1179.
36. Ibid., vol. 1, p. 255.
37. *Werke*, vol. 1, p. 154; *I and Thou*, trans. Walter Kaufmann (New York, 1970), 161.
38. *Werke*, vol. 1, p. 132; *I and Thou*, p. 129.

Buber, too, repeatedly argued that God does not border on anything; nor is He limited by anything: He remains always Thou and always present. For both, God, not theology, is most important; Ebner, a nonpracticing Catholic, and Buber, a nonpracticing Jew, had little admiration for religious forms. In a series of articles in *Der Brenner* in 1921–1922, Ebner opposed Christ to the forms of Christianity, separating, somewhat like Buber, the early origins of faith from historically developed forms and dogma. Buber repeatedly attacked religious forms as the relegation of God to the It-world.

Beyond the crucial, fundamental concurrence on the nature of the Eternal Thou, however, Buber and Ebner followed strikingly divergent paths. Both Ebner and Buber viewed the Thou-less, objectified world of It as clearly negative. But Ebner's objection and opposition to the It-world was vehement to the point of denying the world altogether. Hans Ehrenberg once wrote to him: "Don't you live in loneliness . . . and have a bitter relation to the world? You have not come beyond the statement of Ivan Karamazov, 'I believe in God but I do not recognize His world.'"[39] Buber himself noted this extreme pessimism: "[Ebner] acknowledges himself in a more direct fashion than Kierkegaard, as one who is not able to find the Thou in man. . . . He finds salvation in the thought that 'there is only one single Thou and that is God.'"[40]

Buber was far more community-minded than Ebner, who showed little interest in the social aspects of life. Buber consistently offered the possibility of an I-Thou relation between man and man, turning again and again to the theme of an ideal community of believers. He even held out the possibility of an I-Thou relation between man and nature. Ebner, like many existential thinkers, drew a clear distinction between

---

39. *Schriften*, vol. 3, p. 465. Hans Ehrenberg, who was in the process of publishing Ludwig Feuerbach's *Philosophie der Zukunft* (Stuttgart, 1922), pointed out to Ebner that Feuerbach was, in effect, his forerunner (*Schriften*, vol. 3, p. 490). Ehrenberg was planning to review Ebner's book (see Ebner's letter, p. 446). In a letter of October 15, 1923, to Ludwig von Ficker, Ebner reacted to Ehrenberg's review: "The entire article seems noteworthy to me. Does it only appear to be the case, or is it really so, that he already knew the essence of my basic idea, before he even read my book?" Ehrenberg seems to have been instrumental in bringing together Ebner and Rosenzweig in the winter of 1921. His relationship with Ebner, coupled with the fact that he was Rosenzweig's cousin, as well as one of his closest friends and correspondents, facilitated his role as "go-between."

40. *Werke*, vol. 1, p. 296; *Between Man and Man*, p. 123.

man and nature. For him an animal may possess self-consciousness but not language; it is therefore always and ever an It.

Indeed, the importance of linguistic capability is far more central and developed in Ebner's writings than in *I and Thou*. Etymologies and discussions of the philosophy of language, following and moving beyond the thought of Johann Georg Hamann, formed a major portion of Ebner's work; they are minimal in *I and Thou*. Elementary similarities do exist, such as Ebner's fundamental identification of spirit and Word, which is present also in *I and Thou*. Ebner's philosophy, however, is founded on the Gospel of John—the Word derives from God and, in the end, returns to Him—and, according to Harold Stahmer's evaluation, is inseparably linked to Ebner's understanding of Christianity.[41] Hugo Bergman, on the other hand, argued that Ebner's dialogical thinking can be divorced from the christological emphasis. It may be that in this case there occurred a cross-fertilization of ideas between these two philosophers of different religious convictions. Thus Buber's statement in Book Two of *I and Thou*, "Spirit is the Word," and his comparison of Spirit not with the "blood that circulates within us" but, rather, with "the air that we breath"[42] may very well be derived from his earlier reading of Ebner. This influence may have remained partially dormant as it matured, later taking on the stamp of originality within the framework of Buber's thinking.

The central importance of language seems to have occurred to Buber only *after* that stage in his development represented by the lectures and after his meeting Rosenzweig. Several of the statements on language found in *I and Thou* showing a proximity to Ebner's work were written only after March 1922. It remains an open and puzzling question why at the stage represented by "Religion as Presence," Buber concentrated only on the ideas of I and Thou and of love and disregarded the importance of language, given that the two were inseparably intertwined in Ebner's writings. What seems probable is that his development was gradual and that his treatment of language in *I and Thou* is, at least in part, a result of later thoughts or of the combined influence of Ebner's writings and the close personal friendship with Franz Rosenzweig, which deepened his thoughts on dialogue. The similarities between Ebner's writings and Rosenzweig's *The Star of Redemption* are consid-

---

41. Stahmer, *Speak That I May See Thee!* pp. 234ff.
42. *Werke*, vol. 1, p. 103; *I and Thou*, p. 89.

erable,[43] especially regarding the philosophy of language. In this case, it indeed was a historical coincidence that two thinkers wrote about similar ideas at the same time without knowing one another. Their ideas of man in the here and now, standing before God, represent a return to biblical thinking, as opposed to Greek or idealistic thought. Rosenzweig considered his philosophy an attack on the tradition of Greek monism, from "Ionia to Jena." Dialogical thinking is not necessarily Jewish, but in this sense it is anti-idealistic. In any case, one may safely assume that the notion of dialogical thinking occupied Buber and Rosenzweig from the time of their first meeting in December 1921, that is, months after the publication of *The Star*. One may safely assume that this work was discussed by Buber and Rosenzweig in the winter of 1921–1922.

43. See *Schriften*, vol. 3, p. 477. Ebner was at first suspicious of *The Star of Redemption*, calling it the work of a "Zionist religious philosopher" and somehow related to Ehrenberg (see *Schriften*, vol. 2, p. 1093). Later, however, he showed greater interest in the book (see *Schriften*, vol. 1, pp. 582, 780ff.).

THREE

Winter 1921/1922

The dialogical theory expressed in *I and Thou* was itself formulated not in the solitude of a monologue but, at least in its last stages of development, in a living dialogue between Buber and Rosenzweig. Their fruitful relationship reassures us that Buber's theory in fact lies within the realm of human possibilities.

The collaborative translation of the Bible by Buber and Rosenzweig is well known.[1] Their work started in 1925 when Rosenzweig was already almost totally paralyzed, and it continued until his death in 1929. The patient effort demanded of Buber in this enterprise was immeasurable. The weekly meetings were held in Rosenzweig's home; immobile and unable to speak, he could express himself only with one finger on a specially constructed typewriter. Yet despite this overwhelming handicap, the two progressed at a rapid pace.[2]

The joint effort, a painstaking labor indeed, produced one of the

---

1. See Buber's memoirs, "Aus den Anfangen unserer Schriftubertragung," in *Die Schrift und ihre Verdeutschung*, trans. Martin Buber and Franz Rosenzweig (Berlin, 1936), 316–329. Together they translated the books of Genesis through Isaiah 53. The rest of the Bible was translated by Buber alone, after the Holocaust.

2. After Rosenzweig's death, Buber wrote several essays about him: "Für die Sache der Treue," "Franz Rosenzweig," and "Rosenzweig und die Existenz" in *Der Jude und sein Judentum* (Cologne, 1963), 815–830. The most revealing of Buber's articles on Rosenzweig is found in a Hebrew literary magazine: "The Translation of the Bible: Its Intent and Methods," *Moznayim*, 1940, 26–33, 247–250.

best Bible translations in our century. The two men were prompted by a shared commitment to Jewish education and revival in Germany following the First World War and also by the thought of drawing the Christian world back to its Jewish sources.[3] The philosophy of language behind their work intended to elicit from the reader an active response: to feel the immediacy of the Hebrew text, the Hebrew rhythm, and the sound of each work. In their Hebraized German translation they also tried to incorporate traditional rabbinic interpretation.

The productivity and the creative cooperation that this friendship engendered are indeed rare. In the previous decade, Buber had been a close friend of the socialist Gustav Landauer.[4] They did not, however, produce any common work. Nor did Buber and the great Hebrew writer S. Y. Agnon[5] complete the projected work on Hasidism, which they undertook together in the 1920s. Only in Rosenzweig did Buber find a friend and collaborator whose concerns and very being so matched those of his own that the two were able to extend their friendship into mutual creativity. Although their opinions often differed, they were able to work together in harmony, complementing one another's knowledge and experience. Rosenzweig drew upon Buber's experience and erudition in the fields of Jewish learning, biblical interpretation,

---

3. See Reinhold Mayer, *Franz Rosenzweig: Eine Philosophie der dialogischen Erfahrung* (Munich, 1973), 108. In 1925 in a letter to Buber, Rosenzweig expressed his concern over the fact that under the influence of Adolf von Harnack, the Christians are turning to Marcionites. He wrote (*Briefe* [Berlin, 1935], 544): "Is it really clear to you that the situation which the new Marcionites are theoretically striving toward is already practically there? Today's Christian understands the Bible to be only the New Testament, maybe just the Psalms, which he mostly thinks belongs to the New Testament"; and he continues: "Thus we are becoming missionaries." This may be an answer to Gershom Scholem's question "At the Completion of Buber's Bible translation": "for whom is the translation now intended" "now"—meaning after the Holocaust. See Scholem, *The Messianic Idea in Judaism* (New York, 1971), 318.
4. On Gustav Landauer, see Grete Schaeder, ed., *Martin Buber: Briefwechsel aus Sieben Jahrzehnten*, vol. 1 (Heidelberg, 1972–1975), 61ff., and the correspondence between Buber and Landauer in vols. 1 and 2. Buber published Landauer's *Die Revolution* (Frankfurt a. M., 1907); *Shakespeare: Dargestellt in Vorträgen*, 2 vols. (Frankfurt a. M., 1920); *Der Werdende Mensch* (Potsdam, 1921); *Beginnen: Aufsätze über Sozialismus* (Cologne, 1924). With the help of Ina Britschgi-Schimmer he also published *Gustav Landauer: Sein Lebensgang in Briefen*, 2 vols. (Frankfurt a. M., 1929).
5. On Agnon, see infra, pp. 175, 180.

and Hasidic thought. Buber, in turn, was stimulated by Rosenzweig's previous interest in Christian theology and in ecumenism.

Scholars have long been aware of the close friendship that existed between Buber and Rosenzweig at the time they were working on their translation; they have not, however, realized that the depth and significance of this relationship dated back to as early as December 1921. The following letter, written by Rosenzweig to Eugen Mayer on January 23, 1923, provides a useful introduction to the study of the friendship at its inception.

> I can well understand the mistrust which you held against Buber when you were a young student, because I held it too. It weakened in the first years of *Der Jude*; remarks which appeared in the editorial there suggested a Buber quite different from the author of the bloated Ba'al Shem. This impression became a certainty when I got to know him in December 1921. I would never have invited him to come to the Lehrhaus had I not recognized with certainty at that visit his absolute authenticity, or, more precisely, his having become authentic. . . . In spiritual matters he is the one to whom one can speak best, in human matters the most responsible person I know. I do not use superlatives easily. Mystical eccentricity is hateful to me; I liked Nobel not because of his inclination to mysticism but despite it. In this rejection of mysticism I am in complete agreement with Buber. There can be no harsher critic of the former "famous" Buber than he himself, not only privately but also publicly. . . .
>
> Buber is for me an impressive sage. . . . Knowledge does not easily impress me; however, in comparison with Buber's sagacity, I feel myself a dwarf.[6]

Buber and Rosenzweig had lived near one another since 1920, when the latter moved to Frankfurt to head the Freies Jüdisches Lehrhaus.[7] The meeting that started their friendship took place as a consequence of the relationship which they developed with Rabbi Nehemiah Nobel, a prominent figure in Frankfurt Jewry, and with Ernest Simon, later to become an outstanding Jewish educator. Buber and Nobel were active in Zionist affairs; both attended the Twelfth Zionist Congress

---

6. In Franz Rosenzweig, *Briefe und Tagebücher*, vol. 2 (Haag, 1979), 882–883.

7. Buber moved to Heppenheim, thirty-five minutes from Frankfurt by train, during World War I.

in September 1921. Rosenzweig was drawn to Nobel to learn Talmud
and halakhah. Under his influence Rosenzweig started to observe more
of the Jewish law. As the director of the Lehrhaus in which Nobel was
a leading figure, Rosenzweig was again in close contact with him. In
the fall of 1921, a group of Nobel's admirers decided to prepare a
Festschrift for his fiftieth birthday, which Rosenzweig and Ernst Simon
edited and to which Buber, following Simon's suggestion, contributed.[8]
Buber sent his contribution—three Hasidic tales—and a letter to Rosenzweig. The letter is lost, and we have only Rosenzweig's reply of
October 16, 1921, in which he sincerely thanked Buber for his letter
and contribution to the volume. He then wrote, "I would very much
like to help out with *Der Jude*. Perhaps in the 'education column,' but
I do not yet rightly know. I shall write you again on this subject after
the holidays, or, more preferably, I shall visit you once on a Sunday
for a few hours, if that is all right with you. . . . If your respected wife
might still remember my visit to you in March 1914, together with
Hermann Badt and Bertha Strauss, please give her my humblest
regards."[9]

It is quite clear that they had not seen each other since March 1914,
when Rosenzweig joined friends who were on their way to visit
Buber.[10] Buber's answer to the above letter from Rosenzweig bears no
indication of any meeting since 1914. His reply in a postcard sent eleven
days later showed interest, yet no urgency; he postponed the meeting
for a month, saying, "We would be very happy to see you and your

---

8. See Rosenzweig, *Briefe*, pp. 459ff. The Festschrift was entitled *Gabe,
Herrn Rabbiner Dr. Nobel zum 50. Geburstag* (Frankfurt a. M., 1921); Rabbi Nobel's fiftieth birthday was November 30, 1921. Rosenzweig related that a quotation from Rabbi Nobel's writings had been chosen as a dedication for the
book; each contributor was asked to sign his name in appreciation and agreement with Rabbi Nobel's thoughts on the task of the rabbi. A sudden telegram
from Buber expressing his protest roused Rosenzweig's interest in Buber. The
latter's sincere protest had galvanized the compilers of the volume, for they
too could not wholeheartedly agree with the dedication (Rosenzweig, *Briefe*,
p. 461). It was subsequently changed (see *Gabe*, p. 6) so that it would express
only Nobel's thoughts. Buber then agreed to sign.

9. Unpublished letter in MBA, MS Var. 350/59.

10. Hermann Badt and his sister, Bertha Badt-Strauss, had set a date to
visit Buber and were at the railroad station on their way to his home when
they met Rosenzweig by chance. He insisted on accompanying them. See Bertha Badt-Strauss, "I Knew Buber," *The National Jewish Monthly*, December
1951.

wife (we both remember well your visit). . . . I would be glad to discuss several things with you."[11] And in another postcard sent on November 25, 1921, Buber wrote, "Prepare yourself for a lengthy visit so that we can discuss several things."[12]

Buber's seemingly new interest in Rosenzweig seven years after their last meeting may, in fact, have resulted from a new, and now positive, interest in the thoughts expressed by Rosenzweig in an article of 1914, which has generally been cited as a lasting source of estrangement between the two. In that year Rosenzweig wrote "Atheistische Theologie," ("Atheistic Theology") for *Vom Judentum*, an annual published by Buber's disciples in Prague. In the article, which attacked Buber without once mentioning his name, Rosenzweig took a stand against the new theology, which held that self-awareness and ultimate truth originate not outside man but within the national consciousness and personality of the people itself. In marked contrast to such views, he posited the polarity of God and man as the basis for an understanding of revelation; and he rejected the notion of God as a mere human projection. The article, openly critical of mystical thinking, was rejected, with Buber's knowledge, by the editor of *Vom Judentum*.[13] Scholars have assumed that this incident left the two effectively estranged for years, including those years in which Buber developed and gave final form to *I and Thou*.

The alienation between the two, particularly on Buber's part, may not have been so total as has been thought. Buber appreciated criticism and was not personally offended by it. Only a year after the 1914 incident, when he became editor of *Der Jude*, he personally invited Rosenzweig to contribute to the journal, knowing that any such contribution might well differ substantially from his own thinking. On November 22, 1915, outlining the plan of the journal, he wrote to Rosenzweig, "I would be glad to count you among my co-workers." And he expressed the hope that he would soon receive Rosenzweig's

---

11. Unpublished letter in the MBA, MS Var 350/59.
12. Unpublished letter in the MBA, MS Var. 350/59.
13. The editor who refused the article was Leo Herrmann. The intended second volume of *Vom Judentum* was ultimately never published because of the war. The article was later published in Rosenzweig's *Kleinere Schriften*, (Berlin, 1937) 278–290, 540. An English translation appeared in the *Canadian Journal of Theology*, April 1968. On the Prague circle and their attitude to Zionism, see Samuel Hugo Bergman, "The Spirit and Destiny of Western Zionism" (in Hebrew), in *Prague and Jerusalem*, ed. Felix Weltsch (Jerusalem, 1950).

acceptance and plans regarding his contribution,[14] thus revealing his continued openness to Rosenzweig. For his part, Rosenzweig held *Der Jude* in high esteem[15] and sent Buber a preprint of his 1917 article "It's Time,"[16] which Buber, in turn, passed on to Hugo Bergman for review in *Der Jude*.[17] Furthermore, Rosenzweig sided with Buber in the latter's debate with Hermann Cohen on Zionism.[18]

But obviously even more effective than Buber's general openness was the shift in his thinking evidenced by the outline of 1918 and the lecture series "Religion as Presence." By 1921, the central points of Rosenzweig's "Atheistic Theology" no longer constituted a barrier between the two, and perhaps the ideas even attracted Buber.

Moreover, Buber must have had some knowledge of Rosenzweig's *The Star of Redemption*, which appeared in March 1921.[19] Margarete

---

14. Schaeder, *Briefwechsel*, vol. 1, p. 404.
15. Rosenzweig, *Briefe*, p. 125.
16. Ibid., p. 370.
17. The review appeared in *Der Jude*, 1918–1919, 42–43. Samuel Hugo Bergman has related to me that Buber sent the article to him at the front. The article appears in Rosenzweig, *Kleinere Schriften*, pp. 56–78, and in English translation in *On Jewish Learning*, ed. Nahum N. Glatzer (New York, 1955), 27–54.
18. Rosenzweig considered Buber's article "Zion, der Staat und die Menschheit" ("Peoples, States, and Zion," supra, p. 146) Buber's best work and perhaps the best on the theme since Judah Halevi (*Briefe*, p. 134).
19. A letter published in *Briefe* (p. 370) together with a comment by the editor of that volume (found as an outline among his posthumous writings) was reprinted by Grete Schaeder (*Briefwechsel*, vol. 2, pp. 54–56), who has suggested this as proof of Rosenzweig's having sent Buber the manuscript of *The Star of Redemption* in 1919. In the letter Rosenzweig asked for assistance in securing a Jewish publisher for his manuscript, which he enclosed. She suggested, as further corroboration, Buber's letter of June 1, 1952, to Maurice Friedman, in which Buber wrote that he had "not read *Der Stern* in 1919, only looked at it; the real reading came much later." The Rosenzweig family, however, has indicated that a publisher was secured *without* Buber's assistance and that neither the letter nor the manuscript was ever mailed to him. Moreover, Rosenzweig's letter of December 1921 describing his momentous meeting with Buber states clearly that Buber had not yet read the book (*Briefe*, p 462); only on January 4, 1922, does Rosenzweig state that Buber had finished reading *The Star* (*Briefe*, p. 414). Had Buber been in possession of the manuscript in 1919, he would have read it if he were planning to present it to a publisher. Rosenzweig's own statements indicate that Buber no doubt read it between December 4, 1921, and January 4, 1922. Note also that the Rosenzweig's letter to Buber of October 16, 1921 (supra, p. 164), gives the impression that they had not seen each other since 1914.

Susman, writing to Buber on April 30, 1921, noted that "Rosenzweig would like me to write something about his book for *Der Jude*. I, too, would like to do this, if you agree. I was greatly impressed by it."[20] Her review was published in *Der Jude* in February 1922.[21] Other mutual acquaintances, such as Ernst Simon or Rabbi Nobel—who preached on *The Star* in his synagogue in the fall of 1921—may have shared with Buber some of their impressions of Rosenzweig, the man and the teacher, and of his book.

Buber and Rosenzweig finally met on December 4, 1921, when Rosenzweig and his wife visited Buber's residence in Heppenheim, not far from Frankfurt. Impressions of that extraordinary meeting, which influenced Buber's life and brought him into contact with someone who was to become one of his closest friends, are found in their letters. Buber wrote to Rosenzweig, "I am sure you realized after the first half-hour of your visit to my home in Heppenheim that I talked to you in a way I wished I could talk to all human beings—a messianic wish indeed."[22] From that afternoon a definite urgency was felt in their relationship, which lasted until Rosenzweig's death in 1929.

Rosenzweig, in a letter to a friend, also described the meeting:

> . . . in the course of the conversation . . . I suddenly realized that Buber was not even spiritually any longer the mystical subjectivist for which he was revered by people; rather, even in the realm of the spirit, he was becoming a sound and reasonable man. I was completely taken by the sincerity with which he dealt with all matters. When he came to speak about Hasidic books, he remarked that he was astonished that only once in all those years had somebody inquired about their sources. . . . He thought he might on some occasion, be interested in presenting the sources to a few people.[23]

Rosenzweig quickly took advantage of the offer and asked Buber to consider him as a pupil and teach him some Hasidic sources on the spot. In this context Rosenzweig commented that Buber "attempted to teach me, together with the text and in a very detailed manner, the

20. Schaeder, *Briefwechsel*, vol. 2, p. 75.
21. *Der Jude*, pp. 259–264.
22. Schaeder, *Briefwechsel*, vol. 2, p. 138; Rosenzweig, *On Jewish Learning*, p. 109.
23. Letter to Rudolf Hallo, Rosenzweig, *Briefe*, p. 462. The one person who inquired was the young Gershom Scholem.

importance and the reality of the word, which was hardly alien to me; at that time [December 1921] he did not yet know *The Star*."

"The importance and the reality of the word" (a phrase that indicates an awareness of Ebner) was, in Buber's language, an allusion to that which is now known as dialogical thinking and for which no term had at that time been coined. The situation was noteworthy and not without irony. Rosenzweig knew Buber's work on Hasidism and admired his skillful elaboration of the Hasidic tales—which constituted virtually the sum of Western European Jewry's knowledge of Hasidism. Rosenzweig, interested in learning more about Hasidism and its sources, turned the conversation in this direction; Buber, at that time immersed in formulating his thoughts toward *I and Thou*, turned the conversation in that direction. Buber took a Hasidic text and used it as a basis for elaborating his dialogical thinking. Thus, on their first meeting Buber tried to teach Rosenzweig the dialogical principle, unaware that his guest had formulated his own thoughts on the matter in a book that appeared a year earlier. In the course of the conversation, Rosenzweig no doubt told his host about his work, which Buber then read before their second meeting.[24]

Buber's course at the Lehrhaus, the basis of his future book, grew out of the sudden friendship that began on this afternoon in December 1921. On December 6, Rosenzweig wrote to Buber asking him to accept a teaching position.[25] Having considered Buber's plan to teach Hasidic sources, he presented Buber with the possibility of delivering a series of lectures at the Lehrhaus "on a number of successive Sundays in January and February[26] . . . [to] begin with a public lecture, the title of which would perhaps already indicate that not 'Hasidism,' but the truth itself is at stake." Rosenzweig suggested that, in accordance with what Buber had told him during "the lovely hour in [his] study," the theme of the lectures could be "God and the World" and that in addition Buber could perhaps offer "an hour and a half or two hours of source study, for which a small circle would then be established and which would certainly always be related to what had been brought out before in the public lecture."

24. Rosenzweig, *Briefe*, p. 414.
25. Unpublished letter in the MBA, MS Var. 350/59.
26. Rosenzweig was concerned that Buber's course be accessible to as large an audience as possible. Thus he suggested Frankfurt instead of Heppenheim and Sunday mornings instead of weekdays.

"I think of this combination," Rosenzweig wrote, "because I myself have always experienced that the simultaneity of breadth and depth is pedagogically most efficient. One must have a teacher who is always alternately distant and near, never solely the one or the other." Rosenzweig wanted this situation to materialize because of "simple selfish interest, because I personally would like it for myself." He asked Buber to consider the proposition favorably so that if the conditions put forward were unsuitable, Buber himself might devise an alternative. In conclusion, he asked Buber to check Rashi on the birth of Cain, in which "he quotes the Talmud in a courageous and yet quite simple interpretation—and not at all apologetic."[27]

Two days later, on December 8, Buber replied:

> Dear Dr. Rosenzweig,
>   . . . To your lecture proposal I have, to my own astonishment (since having to reject [offers] has by now become a custom with me), from the first moment a positive feeling that I must attribute primarily to your visit and to a feeling of contact that remained from it. The concerns start only with the details. In this trimester I could teach only a very narrow and limited subject, perhaps to be called "Religion as Presence" (the prolegomena of a corresponding work in which I am engaged [*befasst*]); but then the appropriate supplement to this lecture would be a discussion of selected religious texts (certainly including Hasidic as well)—that [a course on Hasidic sources] would have to be postponed to a later period. After all, the present undertaking could be considered as a preparation for a closer circle. This is my pro and con. Regarding your suggestion for time (weekly, yet starting only from January 15) . . . I am agreeable. Please let me know your opinion.
>   Rashi's interpretation [on Cain] is nice but not convincing to me; why, I would like to explain to you in our next meeting. . . .
>   With best regards to both of you, also from my wife.[28]

Buber's decision to entitle his course "Religion as Presence" shows

---

27. The question involves a problem of a christological Bible interpretation of Luther. The difficult verse of Genesis 4:1 on the birth of Cain was translated by Luther in a way that is close to Targum Jonathan, as if God or an angel of God were the father of Cain. This comment was rejected by Rashi, who suggests that Eve might have said: "When He created me and my husband, He created us by Himself, but in the case of this one [Cain] we are copartners with Him."

28. Schaeder, *Briefwechsel*, vol. 2, p. 92.

that religion was indeed his point of departure in the development of his dialogical thinking. The religious themes treated in the lectures stand near the end of a long line of development running through his earlier essay "Jewish Religiosity" (1914) through "*Herut*" and other speeches on Judaism, and culminating in *I and Thou*. Having become quite aware that Buber had radically changed his philosophical orientation, Rosenzweig, in a letter of Friday, December 9,[29] expressed his satisfaction with the course theme as formulated by Buber. He indicated, however, his personal dislike for the word "religion,"[30] which had become

> . . . too much like a foxhole, from which the idealistic escapes lead out the back when one thinks that he already has the fox and it can no longer escape. But the public prefers to venture into the foxhole of his word—precisely because of the security of the numerous exits— rather than into the exitless lion's den (where the tracks lead not outside, only inside) of the word God. And so it will still be best to call it "Religion as Presence," even though it will afterwards in truth deal with "God's Presence." And that this is the case I saw, to my happy surprise, when I visited you on Sunday. I really had to think of Goethe's famous expression: "When people think I am still in Ossmanstedt, then I am already in Jena."

In addition to suggesting that the course comprise eight lectures from January 15 to March 5, Rosenzweig inquired how the seminar accompanying the lectures should be announced in terms of the selection of religious texts, asking parenthetically whether "including Hasidic ones" should be added. In the end Buber offered a seminar on Hasidic sources alone;[31] thus the lectures that formed the basis of *I and Thou* were illustrated through Hasidic tales. Moreover, Rosenzweig

---

29. Ibid., p. 93.

30. In "Das neue Denken," in *Kleinere Schriften*, p. 374, Rosenzweig states that the word "religion" does not appear even once in *The Star of Redemption*.

31. See Richard Koch, "Das Freie Jüdische Lehrhaus in Frankfurt am Main" *Der Jude*, vol. VII, (1923), 123. It seems likely that these stories were incorporated in *Das verborgene Licht* (Frankfurt a. M., 1924), a collection of Hasidic tales. Several of them are compatible with the philosophy of *I and Thou*; for example, compare "Uberall" (p. 17), which resembles some of the stories in *The Ten Rungs* (New York, 1970), with "there is nothing where one could not find God" (*I and Thou*, p. 129). The titles of the stories used in the seminar itself remain unknown.

raised the issue of whether the course announcement should state that knowledge of Hebrew was a prerequisite. He had the impression that, on the one hand, so broad a treatment would be valuable even for those who knew no Hebrew but that, on the other hand, such a prerequisite might entice someone to learn Hebrew.[32] Thus, he suggested a compromise, as follows: "Hebrew knowledge desired." This would not directly frighten the public away, and yet it would attract, by way of suggestion, the required exclusive circle. "This would better prepare the ground," he wrote, "for the narrower circle than if one were to require Hebrew, which, especially under the circumstances (here in Frankfurt), would gain for one the wrong people as participants."

Rosenzweig concluded the letter by returning to the Rashi interpretation, amplifying it with thoughts on translation. The nature of Rosenzweig's comments are indicative of the intellectual relation in which the two stood at this early date. He pointed out that Rashi's interpretation is not "convincing" for him either. For Rosenzweig there are two kinds of interpretation: One arrests the growth of the text until it somehow appears as the interpreter would like, whereas the other grows as a natural shoot out of the old stem.[33] It was the latter interpretations that Rosenzweig sought and could enjoy, although he admitted that the roof of the text-free remained hidden from him in the subterranean darkness. "Yes, do not all *these* (and, of course, *only* these) interpretations together finally constitute the tree for *us*, the tree, which gives shade in summer and fruits in the prosperous autumns, and which, of course, stands barren in the winter, but even then is still recognizable in its form and beautiful in its being recognizable [*Erkennbarkeit*]—and who knows whether the spring will not soon return and it will blossom again?"

---

32. From the MBA, MS Var. 350/59. Hebrew was of paramount importance to Rosenzweig, both as a language of prayer and as a means whereby Jewish learning could be intensified (see Nahum N. Glatzer, *Franz Rosenzweig: His Life and Thought* [New York, 1961], 102). Rosenzweig himself taught Hebrew language courses at the Lehrhaus and noted that "in the elementary Hebrew course you have to fight for every student" (p. 93). See also p. 297 on the holy language; and see the school plan in "It's Time," in Rosenzweig, *On Jewish Learning*, pp. 27–54.

33. The same line of thought is apparent in Rosenzweig's "Nachwort zu Jehuda Halevi," in *Kleinere Schriften*, pp. 200–219. This epilogue to the translation of Judah Halevi's poems appears in English in Glatzer, *Franz Rosenzweig*, pp. 252–261.

Their subsequent correspondence treats the technical arrangements for the course; both show serious interest in all details. On December 13, Rosenzweig explained to Buber that he planned to secure for the lectures a centrally located hall, the Fochs Conservatory. He also inquired whether Buber was interested in giving subtitles to the lectures. Buber replied on December 18[34] that he had attempted to give a title to each lecture but in the end found this to be an impossible task. In the same letter he asked Rosenzweig to provide a good stenographer to take notes of the course.

Rosenzweig knew that Buber's prestige would add considerably to the stature of the institute and thus tried to be as helpful as possible. In his letter of December 21,[35] he detailed for Buber the attempts being made at the Lehrhaus to encourage audience participation. This aim, clarified by Rosenzweig in his article "Towards a Renaissance of Jewish Learning,"[36] was realized at the Lehrhaus as part of the procedure of learning not for the sake of objective information but for the purpose of molding minds. Buber, who envisaged the fulfillment of a similar goal in folk schools, welcomed, as Rosenzweig noted, the opportunity to engage in a dialogue with an audience capable of raising questions and challenging him for answers—something rather rare in the universities at that time. Buber esteemed the Lehrhaus and once said that he considered it to be the best Jewish institute in Western Europe. He drew on this experience when reviving the education of the Jews in Germany in 1933.

In preparing his lectures in December 1921, Buber read *The Star of Redemption*. Ironically, in his initial reading he expressed greater interest in Rosenzweig's positive attitude toward Christianity—of which Buber previously may have been little aware—than in his treatment of dialogical thinking.[37] Also in the course of his preparations—this was Buber's first lecture series, as previously he had given only single lectures—he requested another meeting with Rosenzweig. Frankfurt was inconvenient since Rosenzweig had left to spend the winter vacation in Cassel, his hometown. Buber therefore decided to accept a longstanding invitation to lecture in Cassel, so that they could meet there.

---

34. Unpublished letter in the MBA, MS Var. 350/59.
35. Unpublished letter in the MBA, MS Var. 350/59.
36. *On Jewish Learning*, pp. 55–71. Cf. also Buber, "Universität und Volks-hochschule" (1924), in *Der Jude und sein Judentum*, pp. 685–688.
37. Rosenzweig, *Briefe*, p. 414.

On Tuesday, January 3, the energetic Buber arrived in Cassel and delivered his lecture on "Nationalism,"[38] very likely an elaboration of the address that he had delivered at the Twelfth Zionist Congress in Karlsbad on September 5, 1921, and that he would later present in several other communities.[39] Its main point comprised an attack on that unfettered nationalism that easily becomes a striving for power and makes an idol of peoplehood.

Dr. Joseph Prager, then a leading figure in the community of Cassel, has related privately that Buber, Rosenzweig, and about ten devoted Blau-Weiss youths joined him in his home for further conversation after the lecture. The Blau-Weiss Zionist Youth Organization was much influenced by Buber and welcomed the opportunity to meet privately with him. Yet Buber did not come out to meet with them; he left the public behind and sat in an antechamber, where he discussed matters of common interest with Rosenzweig. After the meeting, Buber left Cassel, continuing by midnight train to Berlin. The following day Rosenzweig wrote to his wife, "With Buber it was wonderful, . . . even more remarkable than in Heppenheim because in the meantime he had read *The Star*." Analyzing Buber's reaction to *The Star*, he commented, "Where he ought to have agreed, that is, Book II [the part on the dialogical thinking], he did not see it quite right. . . . Speech I shall properly teach him in Frankfurt.[40]

In tracing the development of his dialogical thinking in his 1954 article, "On the History of the Dialogical Principle," Buber emphasized a plan of 1916 and a draft of 1919 and explicitly stated that the works of Cohen, Rosenzweig, and Ebner had not influenced his. Buber even quoted a letter from Rosenzweig's *Briefe*: "therefore Rosenzweig states in one of his letters [*Briefe*, p. 462] that in December, 1921 I did not yet know his book."[41] Rosenzweig, in his 1925 article, "The New Thinking,"[42] seems to corroborate Buber's testimony when he states

---

38. Related to me by Dr. Joseph Prager.

39. Later published in Martin Buber, *Kampf um Israel* (Berlin, 1933), 225–242; idem, *Israel and the World* (New York, 1965), 214–226.

40. *Briefe*, p. 414. That night, Rosenzweig also discussed with Buber the Jewish attitude to sacrifice. See Rosenzweig's letter to Eduard Strauss, *Briefe*, p. 416.

41. Buber, *Werke*, vol. 1 (Munich/Heidelberg, 1962–1964), 298; idem, *Between Man and Man*, ed. Maurice S. Friedman and trans. Ronald G. Smith, 2nd ed. (New York, 1967), 215.

42. *Kleinere Schriften*, p. 388; Glatzer, *Franz Rosenzweig*, p. 200.

that the works of Ebner and Buber, which were "written at exactly the same time as my book, approached the heart of the new thinking . . . independently of the aforementioned books, and of each other."

These statements, made by Buber and Rosenzweig alike, have led scholars to believe that no contact existed between the two at the time of the writing of *I and Thou*. Although there is now ample proof of such a living contact, for some reason Buber felt the need to deny that he had been familiar with the work of his contemporaries at the time he was writing the book. Thus, for example, his aforementioned use of Rosenzweig's letter to prove that he had not read *The Star* in December 1921 appears disingenuous, especially when one learns from another letter (*Briefe*, p. 414, January 4, 1922) that Buber had read the book only a few weeks later.

FOUR

Summer 1922

Buber's course, consisting of eight Sunday morning lectures, began on January 15, 1922.[1] "The audience," as Nahum Glatzer recalls, "of about one hundred and fifty men and women, Jews and Gentiles, witnessed a unique phenomenon; here religious thought was no longer a recapitulation of the past but a present-day event of startling immediacy."[2] Among those who attended at least one was the famous Hebrew writer S. Y. Agnon,[3] who shared Buber's great interest in Hasidism.[4] Rosenzweig, to the extent his health permitted, frequented the lectures, as he said, out of "simple selfish interest." The young Rahel Sislé (later

---

1. The lectures were delivered on only eight of the nine Sundays between January 15 and March 12. See Rosenzweig, *Briefe* (Berlin, 1935), 465–466.

2. Nahum Glatzer, "The Frankfort Lehrhaus," (in *Leo Baeck Institute Yearbook*, vol. 1, 1956), p. 112. At that time the Jewish population of Frankfurt numbered approximately 30,000. Some 600 persons were registered for courses at the Lehrhaus that year (ibid., pp. 109–112).

3. Unpublished correspondence between Buber and Agnon in the MBA, MS Var. 350/65.

4. In July 1923, Buber and Agnon signed a contract for a joint project, *Sefer Ha-Hasiduth*, which was to be an anthology of Hasidic tales and philosophy. The contract with Moriyah-Devir Publishing House—on whose behalf Haim Nahman Bialik signed—is in the MBA, MS Var. 350/A. 86. The undertaking was never completed, in part because of the fire that destroyed Agnon's library, including some 4,000 books and manuscripts and part of his Hasidic collection. Agnon referred to the contemplated work with Buber, and to the fire, in his acceptance address upon receiving the Nobel Prize for literature in 1966.

Mrs. Arthur Schwarzschild) was present and even preserved her notes of the lectures. In addition to Glatzer, other disciples of Buber and Rosenzweig were present, including Ernst Simon. Scores of less well known personalities—Jews as well as Christians—were attracted by Buber's fame and their interest in him. Yet Rosenzweig commented that Sunday morning was an ill-chosen hour because students arrived with their skis and sweaters en route to the Taunus Mountains for winter sport.

On the very afternoon of the first lecture, Rosenzweig wrote to Buber that he had forgotten that morning to tell him about the stenographer's letter, which he now enclosed. Rosenzweig commented that her rate was not too high. "In any case, hired labor cannot be gotten much cheaper nowadays. And you will see that she does a good job." Turning to Buber's lecture, he added: "It was wonderful this morning, and when the people become even more accustomed to refraining from parading their multi-faceted knowledge before you, and the air is purified of worldly reason and Platonic ideas, it will be even more beautiful."[5]

On Saturday evening, January 21, Rabbi Nobel, the greatest preacher of German Jewry at that time and the most prominent teacher at the Lehrhaus, delivered a public lecture on Goethe, despite his failing health. The following Tuesday, January 24, he died at the age of fifty. The loss of Rabbi Nobel affected Rosenzweig deeply and made his new friendship with Buber even more central. On January 25, he wrote to Buber:

Dear Doctor,
You have already seen in the newspaper the terrible thing that has befallen us here. For me, a part of life's basis has been pulled from under my feet. One never knows his future; yet one can usually see before him the beginning of the road that leads into the future. At least one considers him a happy man who sees before him the beginning of the road. And until yesterday morning I would have called myself that.

I have the feeling that I must write you this. It can be no accident that in the last hour of that happiness, which I have lost, I had with you that talk—bleak and filled with despair—yet compelling one to forge onward, albeit in the darkness.

Stay with us; be preserved for me![6]

---

5. Unpublished letter in the MBA, MS Var. 350/59.

It is very probable that the talk mentioned by Rosenzweig took place on the previous Sunday, January 22, when Buber delivered his second lecture at the Lehrhaus.

The darkness to which he refers is most likely his tragic paralysis, which was becoming increasingly noticeable at the time[7] and about which he held no illusions. Glatzer writes that in November or December 1921, Rosenzweig noticed the symptoms of a disturbance of the motor system. Dr. Richard Koch, a friend, examined him and informed him of the gravity of his ailment, which he recognized as incipient paralysis. At that time Rosenzweig remarked, "I do not ask my physicians for advice because I do not want them to lie."[8] In the beginning he kept his condition a secret from his immediate family, but the letter seems to indicate that he discussed it with Buber at an early date.

Rosenzweig did indeed forge onward; in that trimester, January–March 1922, he still played a very active role in the Lehrhaus, despite his growing physical disability. In the middle of February his lectures were transferred to large rooms which his landlord provided for this purpose in his own home, and seminar groups met in his study. He maintained his commitment to establishing Hebrew as a basis for Jewish revival in Germany, teaching three Hebrew courses in addition to one in philosophy.[9] The Hebrew courses were "Biblical and Prayerbook Hebrew," "Readings in Exodus," and "Maimonides' *Mishneh Torah, Hilkhot Teshuvah* (Laws of Repentance)." The course in philosophy, entitled "The Science of Man," presented Rosenzweig's treat-

---

6. Grete Schaeder, ed., *Martin Buber: Briefwechsel aus sieben Jahrzehnten*, vol. 2 (Heidelberg, 1972–1975), 97.

7. Eyewitnesses related that Rosenzweig was limping perceptibly at Rabbi Nobel's funeral.

8. Nahum N. Glatzer, *Franz Rosenzweig: His Life and Thought* (New York, 1961), 106.

9. For a list of Rosenzweig's courses at the Lehrhaus see Koch, "Das Freie Jüdische Lehrhaus in Frankfurt-am-Main," *Der Jude*, 1923, 116–125; a description of courses can be found in Glatzer, "The Frankfort Lehrhaus." For the content of Rosenzweig's courses see Rivka Horwitz, "The Unpublished Writings of Franz Rosenzweig," *Journal of Jewish Studies*, 20 (1969): 57–80. The notes of Rosenzweig's courses at the Lehrhaus in 1920–1922, including "The Science of Man," are now available: Franz Rosenzweig, *Gesammelte Schriften*, vol. 3 (Dordrecht, 1984), 577–655.

ment of dialogical thinking, which amplified themes developed earlier in the *The Star of Redemption*.

In the book he made use of a very delicate and complicated dialectical system. Ingenious as this complex system is, it nonetheless represents a grave shortcoming for one who argued that truth is not a system but God. As would be expected, and as borne out by Hugo Bergman's testimony, Buber was critical of the extreme systematizing, which runs completely against the grain of his own thought, and which, in Buber's words, "fits too well."[10] The system led Rosenzweig, in his treatment of dialogical thinking in the second book of *The Star of Redemption*, to conclude that dialogue initially exists only between God and man: God calls and man answers; God is active and man passive. Only afterward does the possibility of dialogue between man and man arise. Perhaps he was attempting to address the shortcomings of this system in his Lehrhaus lectures in 1922. There his thoughts were presented in a far less rigid fashion.

The two philosophers differed considerably in the way they approached their courses. Buber began with a much broader question: What is "religion" in its true sense. Rosenzweig, on the other hand, discussed the narrow and paradoxical problem of the meaning of "my freedom," which, briefly, he developed as an issue of "being and having." He reasoned that in employing the genitive, or possessive, form, one usually describes something that one has, for example, my coat, my shoe, my ring—objects that are not essential to my being. They are things that one possesses that may be compared with those of other human beings. But does this then mean that "my freedom," like "my coat," is a possession and nonessential to my being? Yet how can man be himself without it? For it is, Rosenzweig insisted, the most individual and essential element of man's being. As such, is it then the divine element in man? Or must it be viewed merely as a necessity of terrestrial existence? Rosenzweig concluded, finally, that man's freedom is neither solely divine nor solely wordly, thus making man the bridge between the Creator and the creation.

Furthermore, whereas Buber spoke of Thou-relation, Rosenzweig disliked the term "relation," taken from the discipline of philosophy. When reading a partial draft of Hermann Cohen's *Religion of Reason*

---

10. Cf. Ernst Simon's saying: "God has one truth, *the* truth, but he has no system." See *Brücken* (Heidelberg, 1965), 314.

From the Sources of Judaism in 1918, he wrote to Cohen, "I do not know what I would give if I could erase the unfortunate word 'correlation' from the work."[11] He suggested that it be replaced by "bond," "mutuality," or some other term. In describing the bond between God and man, or between man and man, Rosenzweig tried to avoid language loaded with philosophical associations, preferring instead the terminology "used by women and children." Buber faced a similar problem and coined the term "between," giving it a special meaning to express the relation between the I and the Thou. Rosenzweig, using no special term in his lectures, developed his thought through the use of examples, such as: "What is the meaning of 'I am yours'?"

Buber and Rosenzweig agreed that man is molded in a relation and that the I becomes I when the I confronts Thou. Rosenzweig argued that "I am I" only when "I am yours," and he attacked the idealism of Fichte, which asserts that "the I is." This is, as Rosenzweig says in "The Science of Man," "factually fantastic and linguistically impossible." Although Buber employed similar locutions, such as "the Thou meets," Rosenzweig did not raise this point against his friend's work.

Despite these differences, the affinity they felt was great, especially in comparison with their former alienation. They were now pacing in the same general direction. Thus, in that trimester students could attend two courses on dialogical thinking given by authorities. Surprisingly, there is little to suggest that the public was aware of, or initially influenced by, the new direction that the two had taken.

Because of Rosenzweig's paralysis, this was one of the last courses he would teach. "Buber could still have been an important epoch in my life," he wrote to a friend in June, "if there were still an opportunity. The intellectual proximity in the lectures is very great; did you notice it? But more than this, for me, is the enormous veracity . . . of his being."[12] And again in August 1922, he wrote to the same friend:

> Buber? Yes, he might have marked an important epoch in my life; the day after Nobel's death I wrote him to this effect. Now it has turned out not to be an epoch, since epochs imply long perspectives; an epoch can only be such when we feel that it is still the penultimate one. . . . But it's marvelous for me, and a great blessing.[13]

---

11. Rosenzweig, *Briefe*, p. 288.

12. Letter to Gertrud Oppenheim, written in Königsberg during the second half of 1922 (in ibid., p. 437).

13. Ibid., p. 441; Glatzer, *Franz Rosenzweig*, p. 116.

While teaching his course and continuing his work on Hasidism, Buber aided Rosenzweig both by securing for the Lehrhaus one of the greatest Hebrew writers of our era, S. Y. Agnon, and by helping Rosenzweig with his work on Judah Halevi. Buber was acquainted with the Hebrew writers Bialik and Agnon, then temporarily residing in Homburg (a town near Frankfurt) before their departure for Palestine.[14] At Buber's initiative in 1916, Leo Herrmann published two of Agnon's stories in a German anthology. The writer was only twenty-eight years old, but, already then, Buber sensed that it was Agnon's calling to describe ardently and firmly these two great loves, the Hasid and the halutz. Eastern Europe and Palestine—Jewish life both in its wane and in its rebirth.[15] In 1922, Buber brought together Agnon and Rosenzweig; Agnon then taught at the Lehrhaus from April 24 to June 15, 1922. With the audience he read some of his own writings in Hebrew, including, as Rosenzweig relates, "The Legend of the Scribe," and attempted a discussion of them in Hebrew.[16] When it became clear that no one spoke Hebrew—although everyone pretended to—the course was canceled. But the attempt itself must have added stature to the institute, and Agnon's appearance on the German scene proved to be an outstanding event for German Jewish youth.

Buber also assisted Rosenzweig in his endeavor to translate Judah

---

14. Glatzer, *Franz Rosenzweig*, p. 111. On Bialik and the Lehrhaus, see Rosenzweig, *Briefe*, p. 488.

15. From Buber's introduction "Über Agnon," to the German translation of Agnon's stories "Autstieg" and "Totentanz," in *Treue, Eine Jüdische Sammelschrift*, ed. Leo Hermann (Berlin, 1916), 59ff. Buber and Agnon began corresponding in 1909. In 1913 Buber sent him a copy of *Daniel*, in which Agnon showed little interest. Buber recognized Agnon's talent very early. They shared a deep affection for Hasidic literature. In a short Hebrew piece, written in honor of Buber's fiftieth birthday, which appeared in a Palestinian literary supplement in 1928, Agnon compared Buber with the "precious Jews" who open inns somewhere far from Jewish settlements on the off chance that a Jew will pass by seeking kosher food. Buber "writes in a foreign language" and would satisfy thirsty souls with pure ideas. "His 'new' Hasidism is not a new creation, but one that is beloved anew by him from day to day." He often comprehends the mystery of an idea far better than he who first expressed it and sometimes elevates small matters to lofty heights, as he "raised Hasidic tales to the level of universal legend" (*Davar* Literary Supplement, February 2, 1928).

16. Rosenzweig, *Briefe*, p. 467.

Halevi's poems into German.[17] Rosenzweig had a great interest in Halevi, one of the greatest medieval Hebrew poets, whose philosophy is, in some respects, a forerunner of modern religious existentialism. Yet the idea of translating his poetry occurred only after the appearance of Emil B. Cohn's translation (1921), "which annoyed [him] so much that verse came out of it."[18] During 1922, Rosenzweig worked on an anthology entitled *Sixty Hymns and Poems of Jehuda Halevi in German*, and, as he admits, in critical moments Buber's encouragement saved the work: "Without him the book would never have been written."[19]

By the end of January 1922, deep spiritual contacts between Buber and Rosenzweig were firmly established. Rosenzweig attended Buber's lectures regularly until he was confined to his home, thereafter relying on a stenographic copy. No long, significant letters are found in the Archive from the period February to June 1922, although there are a number of short postcards in which Buber, at a time when he had no telephone, attempts to set dates for meeting with Rosenzweig. Buber's trips to Frankfurt, for lectures or for business meetings with his publisher, Rütten and Loening, became occasions for visits to Rosenzweig at his home. One postcard in particular clearly proves that in the course of these visits Buber discussed *I and Thou* with Rosenzweig. The date is significant since it is from the very period in which he wrote *I and Thou*.

Heppenheim, 19.IV.22 [April 19, 1922]

Dear Doctor:

If it is convenient for you, I'll come to you on Friday at three for a short while. May nothing interfere! If the time does not suit you, please leave me a note at Rütten and Loening. I will inform Ernst Simon, who would like to talk with me about the subject of my last lecture, that I am coming to you. I assume that you would not mind his visiting at the same time; and the subject is, to be sure, our common and eternal one.[20]

---

17. See Buber's memoirs, "Aus den Anfängen unserer Schriftübertragung," in Martin Buber and Franz Rosenzweig, *Die Schrift und ihre Verdeutschung* Berlin, 1936), p. 317. They also discussed problems of translation and interpretation through translation; their undertaking of the translation of the Bible into German has its roots in discussions of this nature (ibid.).

18. Rosenzweig, *Briefe*, p. 472; Glatzer, *Franz Rosenzweig*, p. 122.

19. Rosenzweig, *Briefe*, p. 513; Glatzer, *Franz Rosenzweig*, p. 123. Rosenzweig dedicated his translation to Buber: "Martin Buber zugeeignet."

20. From an unpublished letter in the MBA, MS Var. 350/59.

The "last lecture," which Ernst Simon wished to discuss with Buber, constitutes the last part of *I and Thou*, as one can now easily see from Lecture Eight and its parallels in the book.[21] Buber's postcard to Rosenzweig was prompted by a letter that Simon had sent to him the day before. During the recent Passover holiday, Simon had read Buber's 1919 essay *"Herut"* for the first time. Writing to Buber on April 18, he pointed out that he agreed with the first two-thirds of the article "almost word for word," but he had significant objections to the third part. "Hence I read, with Rosenzweig, the stenograph of your present lectures, wherein the problem also appears, sometimes in similar fashion and sometimes otherwise. How much can I rely on unpublished ideas?"[22]

Undoubtedly, it was discussions such as these that led Buber to make a careful study of Rosenzweig's *The Star of Redemption*; Buber's statement that no page in the *The Star* was alien to him could hardly have been made by many other religious thinkers of the early 1920s.[23] It is reasonable to assume that *The Star* itself then became a subject of the give-and-take between the two.

In the early summer of 1922 Rosenzweig considered revising the book as soon as possible, since the progress of his paralysis was so rapid that he did not expect to live more than another few months. In June he wrote in his diary, "I am asking my wife to remember that I fervently wish to have *The Star of Redemption* translated into Hebrew."[24] And he himself prepared a second German edition of his book,[25] with subtitles to be printed alongside the paragraphs and revisions of misprints that appeared in the first edition. The publication of this second edition was realized only in 1930. Buber's copy of *Der Stern der Erlösung* contains these subtitles, in his own handwriting, as well as corrections of the

---

21. See supra, p. 116ff.

22. Schaeder, *Briefwechsel*, vol. 2, p. 98.

23. In a letter of August 21, 1922, Buber wrote, "in contrast to *The Star*, in which there is no page which is alien to me no matter how far removed many are in terms of their views" (ibid., p. 115). Rosenstock-Huessy wrote in 1924 to Buber that since Dante the greatest work he knows is *The Star* (Schaeder, *Briefwechsel*, vol. 2, p. 215). Scholem, Walter Benjamin, and Isaac Breuer were also among the early readers of that work.

24. Glatzer, *Franz Rosenzweig*, p. 116. *Der Stern der Erlösung* was translated into Hebrew by Yehoshua Amir in 1970. The work received the Tschernichowsky Prize as the best translation of the year.

25. Glatzer, *Franz Rosenzweig*, p. 115.

misprints.[26] He may have assisted Rosenzweig in preparing the book for print just as he later asked his colleague to comment on the galley proofs of *I and Thou*. Alternatively, he may have copied these subtitles from Rosenzweig's edition in order to facilitate the reading of the text.

The question must be raised whether Buber and Rosenzweig were, in 1922, part of a wider circle that shared their interest in religious existentialism—in Kierkegaard, the Bible, and the consideration of God in terms of a Confronter and of man as a sinner who may be purified by God. The search for details does not reveal any trend toward religious existentialism among other teachers at the Lehrhaus nor among other Jewish friends with whom Buber or Rosenzweig then corresponded. Hermann Cohen, the only other Jew who had written a work along such lines, had died in 1918. They were indeed isolated in the Jewish world of 1922.

Julius Gutmann once wrote that "the Jewish people did not begin to philosophize because of an irresistable urge to do so. They received philosophies from outside . . . and then transformed them and adapted them according to a specific Jewish point of view."[27] His description, in a sense, applies to Buber and Rosenzweig, who, in an effort to influence their own generation, adapted religious existentialism to Judaism and attempted to explain religion in accordance with their understanding of this new school of thought. But in contrast to earlier Jewish philosophers, they wished to confront and influence the general public as well.

Ample information exists on the circle of friends with whom Rosenzweig carried on discussions from 1910. From his letters it is clear that his baptized cousins Hans and Rudolf Ehrenberg shared many of his spiritual interests. Hans Ehrenberg was a philosopher and a pastor; Rudolf was a biologist. Each wrote a number of books. Before and during the First World War, the three of them worked closely with Eugen Rosenstock in clarifying their theological concerns and the basic principles of their new theories.[28]

Very little is known concerning those of Buber's friends who tended toward what was to become known as religious existentialism and who

---

26. In the MBA.

27. Julius Guttmann, *Philosophies of Judaism* (New York/London, 1964) 3; and Rosenzweig, *Briefe*, p. 476.

28. Ample evidence is to be found throughout Rosenzweig's *Briefe*.

may have debated such themes with him in 1921–1922.[29] While the possible influence of Ferdinand Ebner must, I believe, be taken seriously, it was clearly not the result of personal meetings or correspondence between the two. There is, however, one friend with whom Buber seems to have shared his new thinking—Florens Christian Rang. The very fact that in September 1922, Buber also sent Rang the galley sheets of *I and Thou* for criticism leads one to assume that the two debated the themes of the book prior to its publication.[30] However, very little is known about their relationship during this period. Buber's interest in a dialogue between religions represented a turning point and change in his philosophy.

Rang was a man of diverse interests and changing views.[31] He had earned a degree in law but then became a minister; he was well versed in philosophy and theology and wrote in the fields of political theory and literature. He had known Buber as early as 1914, when they shared an interest in uniting the religious with the political sphere of life. In June of that year, the two, together with Gustav Landauer and several others, attempted to form a group that would work toward the unity of mankind and of the nations. The war, however, brought an end to their plans; Rang altered his view and assumed an important position in the occupied territories. But in 1917, while stationed in Berlin, he turned against the war and resigned his post. After the war he wrote *Deutsche Bauhütte*, in which he proposed that relations between Germany and France be restored and that Germany help rebuild France.[32] Hans Kohn, an authority in political philosophy, judged Rang's book "one of the greatest works of its time in political theory."[33]

---

29. An unpublished letter of 1922 (date unclear), in the MBA, MS Var 350/59, indicates that Buber had met Rosenstock through Rosenzweig. Hans Ehrenberg, who had met Ebner in 1921, corresponded with Buber beginning on December 5, 1922, when he submitted a manuscript to him (via Rosenzweig) for criticism.

30. In 1932 Buber dedicated *Königtum Gottes* to both Rosenzweig and Rang. Rosenzweig, too, valued Rang's opinion highly; see his "Das neue Denken," in *Kleinere Schriften* (Berlin, 1937), 388; and *Briefe*, p. 530.

31. A short biography of Rang (1864–1924) can be found in Alfons Paquet's "Florens," *Die Kreatur*, vol. 1, no. 1 (1926–1927), 131–134.

32. Florens Christian Rang, *Deutsche Bauhütte: Philosophische Politik Frankreich gegenüber* (Sannerz, 1924).

33. Hans Kohn, *Martin Buber, sein Werk und seine Zeit: Ein Beitrag zur geistesgeschicte Mitteleuropas, 1880–1930* (Cologne, 1961), 330. See also Schaeder, *Briefwechsel*, vol. 1, introduction and letters 248 and 377.

In 1919 Rang participated in the Frankfurter Bund, a group devoted to education and politics, in which Buber, Hermann Herrigel, Rosenstock, Alfons Pacquet, and Theodor Spira were active. The meetings provided the occasion for Buber and Rang to see each other regularly. Although Rang was then not an influential figure, Buber valued his opinion and friendship highly.

During his lifetime Rang wrote extensively but published very little.[34] However, a number of his articles, together with a biography, were published posthumously in *Die Kreatur*, an ecumenical journal that, in format and content, closely approximated a plan for a journal— to be edited by a Jew, a Catholic, and a Protestant—envisioned by Rang in 1924,[35] the last year of his life. It would appear that *Die Kreatur*, which first appeared in 1926, in fact reflected a trend toward the free debate between Judaism and Christianity to which Rang's circle of friends had been attracted during his lifetime. There is reason to believe that Buber's participation in this endeavor had been significantly influenced by his contact with Rosenzweig, who had pursued such interests for over a decade.[36]

The ecumenism that found expression in *Die Kreatur* was not exactly spiritual continuation of the Patmos Verlag, a publishing house founded toward the end of the First World War by Karl Barth, Hans and Rudolf Ehrenberg, Eugen Rosenstock, and several others but in which Jews

---

34. Some of his letters run twenty pages and more, which may account for his difficulties in securing publishers. A great many of his manuscripts were in Buber's possession. Between 1926 and 1929, the following articles of Rang's were published posthumously in *Die Kreatur*: in vol. 1 (1926–1927), "Das Reich," no. 1; "Freundschaft," no. 2; "Vom Weltbuch der Person," no. 3; "Intuition," no. 4; in vol. 2 (1927–1928), "Glaube, Liebe und Arbeitsamkeit," no. 1; "Historische Psychologie des Karnevals," no. 3; in vol. 3 (1929–1930), "Betrachtung der Zeit," no. 1; "Ein Brief," no. 3. The German Academy for Language and Poetry published his *Shakespeare der Christ: Eine Deutung der Sonette* (Heidelberg, 1954).

35. See the dedication to the first issue of *Die Kreatur*: "Florens Christian Rang was the one who conceived the plan." The initiative to found this journal issued from a conversation between Buber and Rang. Rosenzweig would probably have participated more actively had his health permitted it. The title *Die Kreatur* (The living being, a play on words evoking the creation.), was, in fact, Rosenzweig's idea; the last issue, published in 1930, was dedicated to him.

36. See Samuel Hugo Bergman, "The Spirit and Destiny of Western Zionism" (in Hebrew), in *Prague and Jerusalem*, ed. Felix Weltsch (Jerusalem, 1950), 206.

did not participate. The existential and ecumenical call issued by the Patmos Verlag was little appreciated by the general public, but by 1926 the ground had been prepared and *Die Kreatur* met with greater interest. In retrospect, the journal can be seen as representing the vanguard of a phenomenon that today is considered a sine qua non by many sectors of religious thought and life. Its three editors, Martin Buber, Joseph Wittig, and Viktor von Weizsäcker—Jew, Catholic, and Protestant, although none a classical representative of his faith—worked together in deep sympathy and understanding. All existential thinkers and opponents of Hegelian philosophy, they found Heidegger's "thrown man" to be mute and concluded that we may speak only when there are those who speak *otherwise*. In his memoirs Rosenstock writes of their enterprise: "They all discovered that man does not speak as God. A man does not speak as a woman, nor a Christian as a Jew, nor a child as a professor. Therefore, and only therefore, they can and must speak to each other."[37]

Die Kreatur embodied the belief that men of faith may differ in their interpretation of revelation, of the absolute event, yet agree that all men *are* created by God and share in the hope for redemption at the end of time. In the dedication appearing in the first issue of the journal, the editors stated: "There is going together without a coming together, . . . a mutual influence without a common life. There is a unity of prayer without a unity of worshippers. Parallels that meet in the infinite." Their view stood in sharp contrast to the religious tolerance advocated by Lessing in his well-known story of the three rings, in which an implicit skepticism derives from the impossibility of knowing which ring is the genuine ring, whether one's religion is the "true religion." The circle of thinkers affiliated with *Die Kreatur* included Walter Benjamin, Nikolai Berdyaev, Hugo Bergman, Hans Ehrenberg, Rudolf Ehrenberg, Eugen Rosenstock, Leo Schestow, Ernst Simon, Eduard Strauss, and Ludwig Strauss. As a group, they recognized and affirmed not only the plurality of religions but also the innate truth of each religion; thus they opposed effacing or obscuring the differences inherent in each faith in its particular historical configuration.

Rang's posthumous publications in *Die Kreatur* evidence his particular concern with the social and religious aspects of life and his sym-

---

37. Eugen Rosenstock-Huessy, "Rückblick auf *Die Kreatur*," in *Deutsche Beitrage zur geistigen Überlieferung* (Chicago, 1947), 210; idem, *Ja und Nein: Autobiographische Fragmente* (Heidelberg, 1968), 110.

pathy for human suffering. In "Betrachtung der Zeit," he argues that not only is the relationship between man and man decisive but also the one between man and thing. The techniques of war—the methods of killing and the treatment of man as thing—are but symptoms of the sickness of the age.[38] Philosophy, he observed in "Das Reich," the true science of the spirit, which should provide man's values, had withered; God had become an "idea," an idol.[39] Rang supplemented his objection to the war with an attack on German idealism. Yet he never sank into pessimism and remained constantly ready to work, as he said, "for the kingdom of God."

Rang's comments on the galley sheets of *I and Thou* are indicative of the extent of his spiritual affinity with Buber.[40] It is noteworthy that in his reply he addressed Buber in the intimate *du* form, which few of Buber's friends permitted themselves to employ with him. Rang barely hid his enthusiasm over the little book, stating that the reader, like himself, will be touched by "a breath of holiness."[41] He felt that there was nothing to say regarding the essential points of the book, other than that they must be accepted and verified in life. However, since Buber also mentioned a second volume,[42] he wished openly to express his criticism, which is summarized in one paradoxical sentence: "The little book is too clear and therefore lacks clarity." It exhibited, according to Rang, too little dread of the unspeakable. He agreed with Buber's criticism of theology and psychology and of Rudolf Otto's *mysterium tremendum*, yet he felt that Buber's solution, too, was problematic. Indeed God reveals His presence, but he who fails to meet Him, fails altogether. The light of day deceives, and that which is the essential is easily overlooked. Pointing to human frailty, he argued that, just as one must limit the pagan understanding of tragedy, so must one check the optimism of religion.

In brief, Rang and Buber, despite their philosophical affinity, worked from two distinct points of departure. Guided by Augustine's concept of the Word, Rang argued that "in truth there exists no I-Thou, but only Thou, spoken to God, of which the I is but an echo." In contrast, Buber's metaphysical structure, founded on his statement,

---

38. "Betrachtung, *Die Kreatur*, vol. 3, no. 1, 1929–1930, 92.
39. "Das Reich," ibid., vol. 1, no. 1, 1926–1927, 107.
40. Schaeder, *Briefwechsel*, vol. 2, pp. 131–134.
41. Ibid., p. 132.
42. See Appendix C.

"in the beginning is relation," suggested that he required the duality of two poles: I and Thou.

More of Buber's thoughts on *I and Thou* and the volumes to follow it are revealed in a letter of May 13, 1922, which he wrote to his friend and disciple, the philosopher Hugo Bergman, who was then living in Jerusalem:

> Dear Mr. Bergman,
>
> . . . The prolegomena volume of my work on religion, *I and Thou*, which deals with the primary phenomena, will appear soon. The first part of the work will hopefuly follow in the autumn; if the same grace to work [*Arbeitsgnade*], which has been granted to me for a while, remains, then the whole will be finished in 1924. Would you in principal—reserving a final decision until after the reading—consider translating the book (that is, for the time being, the prolegomena) into Hebrew? It is of great importance to me that this book reach the Hebrew reader. But this can be only if it is, as it were, not merely intellectually but also emotionally well translated. For me, my real work has started only with this volume.
>
> When the whole is completed, I would like, if the external possibility be granted to me, to try to realize in Eretz Israel the adult education center that I have in mind (and that is different from anything known by this name). I will by then know enough Hebrew—with which I presently deal historically [*sprachgeschichtlich*]—and will not yet be too old; my heart has become younger. For the university I have only a moderate interest; for the center in every village, a lively one.[43]

In the summer of 1922, Buber wrote a number of plans for the subsequent volumes of his "work on religion." For example, on page 100 of the notebook into which he copied *I and Thou*, at the end of the manuscript, three separate outlines appear:

---

43. Schaeder, *Briefwechsel*, vol. 2, p. 99. Buber did hope to realize his dreams and visions in Eretz Isreal, but one hindrance led to another, and he came to Israel only in 1938. *I and Thou* was not translated by Bergman, who, as he wrote to Buber, was not proficient enough to undertake the task. Later, Woislavsky translated the work, and it appeared in 1959. Buber did not succeed in feeling the pulse of the people in the land and at times felt bitter and alienated. Although his fame increased and his philosophy met with a growing, receptive audience in the United States and Germany, he did not succeed in sharing his views with a wide public in Israel.

BOOK SERIES
Religion as Presence
  I. I and Thou
  II. The primary forms of the religious life
  III. The religious person
  IV. The religions
  V. The religious power and our time

The Religious Life
  1. The revelation
  2. The consecration (mystery)
  3. The service (sacrifice and prayer)
  4. The knowledge (myth-dogma)
  5. The teaching
  6. The community
  7. The kingdom

The Primary Forms and Magic
  I. I and Thou
  II. Primary forms of religious life: 1. magic 2. The sacrifice 3. The
      mystery 4. The prayer
  III. Knowledge of God and Law of God: 1. myth 2. dogma 3. law
      4. teaching
  IV. The person and the community: 1. The originator 2. The priest
      3. The prophet 4. The reformer 5. The lonely man
  V. The religious power and our time (The power and the kingdom)

The proposed five-volume masterpiece occupied Buber during the coming year; he still mentions it on January 14, 1923,[44] in an unpublished letter to Elijahu Rappeport. However, shortly thereafter he encountered difficulties, and the project was abandoned.

An examination of the proposal for future volumes indicates that Buber's concerns remained essentially those pertaining to religious life. Most of the historical evidence available, both correspondence with Rosenzweig and a handwritten manuscript, concerns the volume to follow *I and Thou*. The correspondence shows that Buber again intended to teach a course that would serve as a preparatory stage in the crystallization of the themes of the next volume.

Rosenzweig, increasingly aware that death was not distant, felt an urgency about guaranteeing Buber's future participation in the Lehr-

---

44. MBA, MS Var. 350/59.

haus. He seems to have considered that the presence of Buber, and Buber alone, could assure the successful fulfillment of the goals of Jewish education exemplified by the Lehrhaus. It was thus catastrophic for him when, in the summer of 1922, Buber, not realizing the impact his decision would have, suddenly informed Rosenzweig that he had chosen to cancel the course. In his undated reply Rosenzweig besought him to reconsider: to deliver three lectures or, if not, then two—or at the worst, to have his name appear on the program and then withdraw at the last minute.[45] Deeply sensitive to Rosenzweig's situation, Buber immediately grasped the gravity of his decision and, in a letter of July 28, 1922, agreed—"if I can by this do you a personal favor"—to deliver three lectures, which he tentatively entitled "Das wahre Leben" ("The True Life"). He closed his letter with Psalm 22,[46] which expressed the hope of the suffering man.

In his reply of July 30, Rosenzweig discussed the technicalities of the course, exhibiting the same concern for detail that he had shown in the planning of "Religion as Presence." He asked whether each lecture should be given a title or whether they should be called "three addresses" to distinguish them from "the former series." Perhaps in response to Buber's having sent the psalm, he suggested that each lecture conclude with a reading from the Book of Psalms or a passage from aggadic literature. He noted that "the former would be more to your liking" and recalled that Hermann Cohen had similarly concluded his course on Maimonides with a reading of psalms. He added that prior to his illness, Psalm 22 had been his companion but that he now preferred the tranquility of Psalm 23.[47]

Then, in a letter of August 15, Buber wrote that he now wished to return to the original plan of four lectures.[48] He revealed to Rosenzweig how, in a moment of inspiration while walking in the meadows of Staffelberg, he suddenly discovered the element that had eluded him in the conception of the second volume, which was to be his philosophy of history. He now proposed a series of four lectures on "The Primary Forms of Religious Life": (1) The Religious Life—Magic and Religion; (2) Sacrifice; (3) Mysterium; (4) Prayer.

The contents of the correspondence and the two-page manuscript

---

45. Schaeder, *Briefwechsel*, vol. 2, pp. 108–109.
46. Ibid., p. 109.
47. Ibid., p. 110.
48. Ibid., pp. 112–113.

preserved in the Martin Buber Archive[49] indicate two seemingly contradictory directions in Buber's treatment of the sphere of magic and paganism. On one hand, a definite attempt is made to characterize magic and paganism as illegitimate religious forms, which have no place in true religious life. On the other hand, magic and paganism are presented as primary forms—albeit the lowest—in the configuration of religious life. In an attempt to counter prevailing evolutionary theories, which held that primitive stages are superseded by higher and more developed forms of religion, Buber suggested that all four forms are present simultaneously. In a manuscript he says that the primary forms are "eternal forms." In a letter of August 22, 1922, Rosenzweig compared Buber's structuring of world history to music, in which magic, "the paganism of all nations," and prayer, "Judaism in all religion," form the decrescendo and crescendo, respectively, of a unified musical whole.[50]

Although speaking of the primal forms as "eternal," Buber nonetheless associated each primal form with a particular historical period: magic with the religions of ancient Egypt and Babylonia, sacrifice with those of India and Persia, mysterium with those of Assyria and Greece, and, finally, prayer with Judaism and Christianity. He chose to exclude Chinese religions from his overly simplified scheme. It is significant that, like Rosenzweig in *The Star of Redemption*, Buber places *both* Judaism and Christianity on the highest rung.

Rosenzweig's suggestion that Buber might conclude his lectures with a reading of psalms seems to have been well received. Concurrently with his four lectures in the following trimester (January–March 1923), Buber offered a course on prayer and conducted a seminar in Hebrew on selected psalms.[51]

49. MBA, MS Var. 350/59.
50. Schaeder, *Briefwechsel*, vol. 2, p. 118.
51. See Koch, "Das Freie Jüdische Lehrhaus in Frankfurt-am-Main," pp. 116–125.

F I V E

Franz Rosenzweig and I and Thou

In comparing "Religion as Presence" with *I and Thou*, certain similarities in two areas seem to indicate Rosenzweig's influence. The first, and by far the more consequential issue, concerns Buber's concept of dialogue, which is central to *I and Thou* but which is almost completely absent from the manuscript of "Religion as Presence." The second concerns the gradual elimination of the terms "realization" and "orientation." Realization especially, which is tied to the mystical notion of unification propounded by Buber in 1913, was freely employed in the lectures but abandoned as an important philosophical term after 1923.

One must clearly distinguish between the stage of confrontation and that of dialogue in the development of Buber's philosophy. Both in the outline of 1918 and in "Religion as Presence" in 1922, he devised a philosophy of confrontation, which marks a movement away from his earlier inherently mystical striving for unity. Whereas in *Daniel* he advocated unity between a man and a tree,[1] in the years after 1918 he came to reject mystical solutions, arguing that unity can never be attained and that man is left only with confrontation. The idea was first outlined briefly in 1918, and, perhaps under the influence of Ebner, it was called Thou-relation in 1922.

Yet what does Buber mean in January–March 1922 by Thou-relation or confrontation? Clearly it is not experience or unity. It is sig-

---

1. *Daniel* (New York, 1965), 54.

nificant that the elements of speech, language, and dialogue are absent from Buber's conception of the Thou-relation or of confrontation at that time. While there is a reference to man conversing with nature, this thought is certainly not developed. *The dialogical basis of the I-Thou was, in fact, one of the very last additions to an already existing structure.* This fact goes far, I believe, in explaining many of the problematical formulations and inconsistencies present in the published version of *I and Thou.*

Without the benefit of having seen the manuscript of "Religion as Presence," Gershom Scholem concluded that one can detect a mystical point of departure in *I and Thou.* It still remains unclear in what manner the Thou-relation found in the lectures from which *I and Thou* was written differs from that which Buber earlier called realization. Thus, for example, in Lecture Four, turning his attention to the content of confrontation, Buber stated, "The Thou that encounters me is not something I must experience—it is something I must *realize.*"[2]

This problem can be more fully clarified through a consideration of the examples that Buber presented in "Religion as Presence" in order to explain the Thou-relation. The four cardinal examples are: man's relation to his beloved, to a tree (that is, to nature), to a work of art, and to a potential act that he has decided to realize. Buber contended that he employs the examples in order to avoid rigid systematization. They are central to the study of his concept of the Thou-relation, since after having explained them in Lecture Four, he returns to them in all of the subsequent lectures, without developing others. Moreover, a number of passages in *I and Thou* are directly developed from these same examples.

The examples have their source *not* in dialogical thinking but in the philosophy expressed in *Daniel.* Three of the four do not lend themselves to real dialogue; one of them cannot even be adapted to dialogical thinking. They can be explained only in the framework of a concept of confrontation that does not include dialogue or speech. Their contents thus clash with much of Ebner's discussion of the Thou in his fragments, in which he eliminated the possibility of a Thou-relation with nature or animals, let alone with a work of art or a decision. This entire realm of thought is alien to Ebner but seemingly central to Buber.

It is clear that these examples were so deeply engrained in Buber's

2. Lecture Four, supra, p. 65.

mind that he retained them in *I and Thou* even though they introduced inconsistencies into his masterpiece. Unwilling to abandon them, he attempted to adapt them to the dialogical principles. Those most appropriate were more fully developed; those least suitable were either shortened, obscured, or removed. Challenged on his use of these examples, he attempted to explain them further in an epilogue added to the book. Years later, he confided to Maurice Friedman that "if he were to write *I and Thou* again, he would use different categories to make clearer the distinction between these latter types of I-Thou relationship [with nature and with art] and the dialogue between man and man."[3]

One can, in fact, trace much of Buber's creative development by noting the alterations in his elaboration of the four examples in each of the following stages:

1. *Daniel* (1913)
2. Outline of 1918
3. "Religion as Presence" (January–March 1922)
4. Manuscript of *I and Thou* (May 1922)[4]
5. Galley sheets of *I and Thou* criticized by Rosenzweig (September 1922)[5]
6. Final published version of *I and Thou* (December 1922)

The evidence from these various stages is in complete agreement with Friedman's observation that Buber's development in later periods seldom involved the total exclusion of thought from earlier periods.[6] Rather, elements from earlier stages are maintained, although in an altered or abbreviated form.

In *Daniel*, Buber sought to synthesize the disparate Western realms of science, art, religion, and philosophy with the Eastern concept of

3. In Maurice Friedman's introduction to Martin Buber, *The Knowledge of Man* (London, 1965), 27.
4. In the MBA, MS Var. 350/B9.
5. The galley sheets of *Ich and Du* are no longer extant, but the reference to them in Rosenzweig's letters shows that they differed at points from the published text. See the German edition of Rivka Horwitz, *Buber's Way to "I and Thou"* (Heidelberg, 1978), Appendix D, p. 263 and Grete Schaeder, *Martin Buber: Briefwechsel aus seben Jahrzehnzen*, vol. 2 (Heidelberg, 1972–1975), 127. Buber is known to have introduced changes in his works up to the very last stage of their publication.
6. Maurice S. Friedman, *Martin Buber: The Life of Dialogue* (New York, 1960), 27.

the One. In *I and Thou* his concerns were far more biblical; and God, the Eternal Thou, is the biblical *ehyeh asher ehyeh*. But former concerns and conclusions are not discarded. Nature, aesthetics, and decision are all elements integral to *Daniel*. They become problematical when set in the framework of a theory of dialogue; yet Buber retains them in *I and Thou*. In *Daniel* Buber wrote, "In *each thing* the gate of the One opens to you if you bring with you the magic that unlocks it: the perfection of your direction."[7] In the *Hasidic Tales*, as well as in *I and Thou*, he maintained that there is no place where one cannot find Him at all times.

In *Daniel*, Buber posited the possibility of realization in every human act and stressed the central importance of the right decision for realization of God. "Religion as Presence" contains the addition of the idea of confrontation with the Thou, a position that should have precluded absolute unity, as well as the absolute I of idealism. The shift, however, was not abrupt. When formulating his concept of Thou-relation as confrontation, he continued to speak as though realization was its sole content, a seeming contradiction in terms.

In the months between the lectures and the completion of *I and Thou*, the changes introduced in the content of the four examples constituted a further, yet still incomplete, shift away from thought close to that of *Daniel* and toward more consistent dialogical-theological thinking. Thus, with regard to his first example, he stated in Lecture Four (February 1922): "I confront a human being . . . whom I love. What does that mean . . . when I actually confront this person as a Thou?"[8] After describing what it does *not* mean, he gives a definitive answer to his question: "*It is something I must realize.*" But when writing the final version of *I and Thou* (May 1922), using the lectures as a draft, he attached the element of dialogue to this very same example: "When I stand in front of a human being as my Thou *and speak the basic I-Thou to him* . . ."[9] In this first example, man's relation to his beloved, the addition of a newly acquired concept of dialogue to an existing passage on confrontation and realization gives new positive content to the relation.

However, beginning with the second example, man's relation to nature, the addition is not so easily accomplished. In a passage in *Daniel*,

---

7. *Daniel*, p. 53.
8. See supra, p. 61.
9. *I and Thou*, trans. Walter Kaufman (New York, 1970), 59.

so captivating in its detail that one suspects it is based on Buber's own experience, he wrote: "With all your directed power receive the tree; surrender yourself to it, until you feel its bark as your skin, and the force of a branch spring from its trunk like the striving in your muscles . . . yes truly until you are transformed."[10] In Lecture Four he no longer speaks of transformation but of confrontation: "What are the decisive moments in which we take something of nature into our lives? . . . Are they [not] the moments in which we *confront* nature as a Thou that confronts us and to which we have this unique, unprecedented, incomparable relationship."[11] A week later, in Lecture Five, Buber discussed nature once again. He then took the first step toward the introduction of dialogue by saying Thou to it [nature]. The idea that in a moment of confrontation one says Thou to the tree is perhaps more comprehensive than its subsequent elaboration in *I and Thou*: "I contemplate the tree. . . . The power of exclusiveness has seized me. . . . It confronts me and has to deal with me, as I must deal with it. . . . Relation is reciprocity."[12] The addition of the element of reciprocity in man's relation to a tree renders this example rather puzzling. In his criticism of the galley sheets of *I and Thou* in September 1922, Rosenzweig challenges Buber's treatment of this example, arguing that only the erroneous philosophies of the preceding centuries insist that the It—the tree—is verified only when *I* see it.[13] He takes up the same point in 1925 in his seminal article "The New Thinking."[14]

The third and fourth examples, dealing with the conception of a work of art and a decision, are the most problematical when introduced into a dialogical framework. These are what Buber called a confron-

---

10. *Daniel*, p. 54.
11. Lecture Four, supra, p. 63.
12. *I and Thou*, p. 57.
13. Schaeder, *Briefwechsel*, vol. 2, pp. 127, 137; see also Appendix B, infra, p. 230.
14. In Nahum N. Glatzer, *Franz Rosenzweig: His Life and Thought* (New York, 1961), 195–196: ". . . that a tree cannot be seen by me unless my self sees it. As a matter of fact, that ego of mine comes to the fore only—when it *comes* to the for, when, for example, I must emphasize that I for one see the tree because someone else does not see it. In that case, my knowledge shows the tree certainly associated with me, but in any other case, I know only about the tree, and about nothing else. Philosophy's [German idealism's] claim that the self is omnipresent in all knowledge distorts the content of his consciousness."

tation with spiritual beings. His example of the idea of a work of art, which a man conceives and which then confronts him as a Thou, may well have been inspired by Job's description of prophecy:

> A wind passed by me,
> Making the hair of my flesh bristle.
> It halted; its appearance was strange to me;
> A form loomed before my eyes;
> I heard a murmur, a voice . . .[15]

In the lectures, Buber attempted to show that the conception of a work of art, although it grows out of the artist's mind, is not a part of the ego but a Thou. The artist sees an image in front of his eyes, perceiving it as a form that is a not-I, as a spiritual being that is his confronter. But, as Buber explained, this idea, this being, is only momentarily a Thou, destined to be expanded, developed, formulated, and shaped as an It. He thus sees the creativity of an artist as composed of two distinct stages: that of the creative moment in which the artist receives and confronts the idea and that of the development and articulation of the work, composing it and perfecting its expression, that is, manipulating that which has become an It.

This description in Lecture Four of the creative moment[16] has clear parallels with Buber's own experience, as described by him in Lecture Seven, in the fall of 1921, when he suddenly heard words *that he had not composed.*[17] This Thou-moment, in which he was confronted by the idea that God can never be addressed in the third person, was apparently not the only event of its kind in his life. Yet to identify such creative moments with I-Thou dialogue is questionable and highly problematical.[18] Here the confronter does not have the qualities of real being; it lacks permanence or identity. Nevertheless, the example was retained in the final version of the book, but in a form so poetic that the far simpler and clearer meaning that it had in the lectures is no longer obvious.

The development of the example of a potential act upon which one

---

15. Job 4:15, 16 (New Jewish Publication Society translation).
16. See supra, p. 63.
17. See supra, p. 105.
18. See supra, p. 190, the description of the creative moment in Staffelberg.

decides is no less problematical, particularly in light of its obvious resemblance to the mystical thought of *Daniel*. There, decision is given a central importance: "Direction is that primal tension in the human soul which moves it to choose and to realize this and no other of the infinity of possibilities."[19] When developed in the framework of confrontation in "Religion as Presence," this same example takes the following form:

> The person who decides is confronted by his deed, the deed that he chooses. The deed becomes present for him as a Thou in an exclusivity that causes all other possibility of action to sink from sight. . . . Everything else is, as it were, rejected by the exclusivity of this relation, and this one thing is chosen. Even though here . . . it looks . . . like something fictive, something that is not yet there, in actuality, seen from the viewpoint of the Thou itself, it is definitely something that has being and to which I stand in relation and that I have now to actualize.[20]

Just as the idea of a work of art confronts the artist, causing all other ideas to disappear into the background, so do all other possible acts vanish when a person decides upon one exclusive act. As the idea of a work of art is momentarily present as an exclusive Thou, although it does not exist experientially, so, similarly, from the point of view of the relation, is the act truly present in the moment of decision even before it objectively exists. Yet, it must become an It in order to be realized by the person.

Even in the *I and Thou* manuscript of May 1922, Buber included a long section in which he treats the theme of decision in a manner reminiscent of his earlier pantheistic outlook. In the manuscript of this classic on dialogue, which emphasizes the religious aspect of the relationship between man and man, one finds concern for a type of decision that can be conceived only in terms of the unification of the soul. Although a part of this section was eventually excluded from the published version of the book, there is evidence to suggest that it still appeared in the galley sheets sent to Rosenzweig in September 1922. In a letter to Buber, written at a time when Rosenzweig was in possession of the major part of Book One of *I and Thou*, he alluded to a

19. *Daniel*, p. 56.
20. See supra, p. 64.

section on "permission," which followed the treatment of the examples of the tree and the work of art. In the manuscript of May 1922, this section begins: "Decision, the first born daughter of the spirit, the terrestrial comrade of grace, which loves to be beholded by your eyes. From your kingdom I have spoken time after time. Of you it is hard to speak other than in poetry."[21] A long passage follows, in which Buber does indeed speak of decision in highly poetic language. Since no such extended passage appears in the published version of *I and Thou*, it must be assumed that it was shortened and removed to its less conspicuous place in Book Two sometime after September 1922.[22]

The conclusion to this section was likewise deleted from the published version; in it Buber returned to thinking and a style more typical of the lectures: "To say to my act, Thou, means to behold it in exclusivity. . . . It confronts me and lets me know her as my Thou. . . . *Its life flows into mine.*" Rosenzweig's criticism of the galley sheets, although generally leading in another direction, may have significantly influenced Buber in his decision to exclude the greater share of this section on decision from the final version of his book.

It would be inaccurate, however, to state that there is no allusion in the lectures to dialogical thinking, meeting, or speech. There is a fleeting mention of speech in Lecture Seven and, in Lecture Six, a rare but significant example of dialogical thinking: "When we walk on a way and meet a man who comes towards us, walking his way, yet we know only our way, his comes to life only by meeting. Every true event of the spirit is meeting."[23] Indeed, this passage contains numerous elements of dialogue. But Buber did not see in these isolated lines the central expression of his thought, nor did he, at the stage of the lectures, draw the conclusions that they suggest concerning language and speech.

Unlike Rosenzweig or Ebner, Buber did not attack idealism by means of a theory of language. Buber did read Ebner's fragments prior to formulating his lectures in December 1921. It remains unclear why he adopted Ebner's concept of God as Thou but neglected the thoughts on language that were so closely tied to that concept. One might now argue that Buber found Ebner's theory of the dependence of all relation

---

21. See the German edition of Rivka Horwitz, *Buber's Way to "I and Thou"* (Heidelberg, 1978), Appendix D, p. 263; and Rosenzweig's letter in Appendix B, infra, p. 228.

22. See *I and Thou*, p. 101.

23. See supra, p. 87. This was incorporated into *I and Thou*, p. 124.

solely upon language to be too confining. He may have sought a more encompassing theory, which could include all human acts as delineated in the outline of 1918—"to create, to love, to command, etc."[24]—and which would later be defined as "love, sight, creation, decision." A concern for the direct approach to nature and to aesthetics could have led him to avoid adopting language as a fundamental principle in the lectures.

On the other hand, he may have needed an additional stimulus to propel him away from the mystical thought of *Daniel* and toward an acceptance of the central importance of speech. The adoption of dialogue as a principal element in his philosophy would obviously have demanded a far more drastic change from the philosophy of *Daniel* and his earlier speech in *On Judaism* than did his adoption of the concept of God as Thou. That he had actually considered the importance of language even prior to the lectures is suggested by the fact that in December 1921 he attempted to explain, apparently unsuccessfully, to Rosenzweig "the reality of the word."[25] Nevertheless, we still find in the lectures the dominance of realization and the four cardinal examples, none of which, with the exception of love, explicitly develops the concepts of speech or language.

Even in the *I and Thou* manuscript of May 1922, Buber still referred to his four examples as the four cardinal actions of man: "The cardinal actions are love, sight, creation, decision" (*Die Wesenakte Liebe, Anschauung, Schopfung, Entscheidung*). This sentence was, at the very end, deleted from a paragraph that was otherwise published intact. On the other hand, this manuscript shows that speech and language did have a role in Buber's thought by May 1922, especially in the first lines of Book One but also in numerous other places in the manuscript. The adoption of this basic element of dialogical thinking took place precisely in the months during which Buber maintained a close, personal relationship with Rosenzweig.

Rosenzweig had, at the very outset of their contact, sensed Buber's lack of clarity regarding the importance of language. As early as January 4, 1922, after a conversation with Buber on dialogue and on *The Star of Redemption*, he wrote to his wife that Buber did not see it quite right, adding, "Speech I will teach him in Frankfurt."[26] In these same months

24. See supra, p. 135.
25. Franz Rosenzweig, *Briefe* (Berlin, 1935), 462.
26. Ibid., p. 414.

Buber studied Rosenzweig's book, in which the importance of speech is amply treated, for example:

> Until he opens his mouth for the final act of creation and says: "Let us make man." "Let us"—for the first time the magic circle of objectivity is breached, for the first time an "I" resounds out of the sole mouth which hitherto has discoursed in creation, instead of an "it." And more than an "I." Together with the I there resounds at the same time a Thou, a Thou which the I addresses to itself: "let" "us." Something new has dawned. Something new? Is not he who speaks the same as before? And is not what he speaks the same as what was reported of him before? . . . Now it *remains* personal, now it declares "I." Really "I"? Here we come up against the boundary which warns us that even on the sixth day we are still in creation, and not yet in revelation.[27]
>
> . . . And so too we will henceforth proceed from real word to real word, not from one species of word to another as we did in describing creation. This accords with the wholly real employment of language, the center-piece as it were of this entire book, at which we have here arrived. . . . To the I there responds in God's interior a Thou. It is the dual sound of I and Thou in the monologue of God at the creation of man. But the Thou is no authentic Thou, for it still remains in God's interior. And the I is just as far from already being an authentic I, for no Thou has yet confronted it. Only when the I acknowledges the Thou as something external to itself, that is, only when it makes the transition from monologue to authentic dialogue, only then does it become that I which we have just claimed for the primeval Nay become audible.[28]

Rosenzweig had learned the importance of language, or speech, from Eugen Rosenstock a decade earlier. It served him both in his rejection of idealism and in his expression of the relation between the elements: God, man, and the world. In his exchange of letters with Buber in 1922, Rosenzweig shows how idealistic philosophy is monistic, being based on thought rather than on speech, a theme he had developed earlier in *The Star of Redemption*.[29]

---

27. Franz Rosenzweig, *The Star of Redemption*, trans. William W. Hallo (New York, 1970), 154.

28. Ibid., p. 174.

29. Appendix B, infra, p. 227; original German in Schaeder, *Briefwechsel*, vol. 2, p. 120.

At the same time that he was clarifying for Buber the central importance of language, it appears likely that Rosenzweig pointed out the
contradictions between dialogue and Buber's concept of realization, as
employed in *Daniel*, to explain man's creativity, his authentic acts of
renewal and regeneration in ecstatic moments of life experiences in
which one unites with God. In the framework of realization the emphasis had been on God as an immanent becoming arising out of the
human striving for unity. Still, one does not find in "Religion as Presence" any attempt to censor the term realization nor any suggestion
that it is inappropriate to Buber's new outlook. It appears side by side
with, and as a synonym for, the Thou-relation.

True confrontation or Thou-relation should demand, on the one
hand, a concept of God that stresses His Being and, on the other, a
limiting of the human I by the Thou, thus preventing monism or idealism. Buber's continued use of realization as a basic term in the lectures
is therefore most problematical, inasmuch as it suggests a concept of
God according to which "God becomes" only as He is created in the
human soul. In a rare instance, in Lecture Six, Buber even speaks of
the "absolute I." Discussing the stages in human development, he does
not describe the final stage as that of the attempt to return to the primary
Thou-relation but as the striving toward "a primal unity of the worlds
which were separated out of the absolute I."[30] The mystical tendency
inherent in this idealistic concept of the "absolute I" and in the striving
toward primal unity is clearly incompatible with the concept of a confronted God.

As early as 1914, Rosenzweig had attacked Buber's theory of God's
immanent becoming; the human projection of the divine involved in
realization struck him as "atheistic theology."[31] It must be assumed
that in 1922 he found Buber's continued use of realization little more
acceptable. What is certain from the written evidence is that, whereas
in January 1922 Buber uses the term realization extensively, in the final
version of *I and Thou* it appears only infrequently and has, in most
instances, been replaced by expressions of dialogue or speech. Furthermore, in the final version of the book, Buber stated clearly: "There
is no I as such."[32]

In 1923 Buber wrote a preface to a new edition of his speeches *On*

30. See Lecture Six, supra, p. 92.
31. See Franz Rosenzweig, *Kleinere Schriften* (Berlin, 1937), 278–290.
32. *I and Thou*, p. 54.

Judaism. In it he reviewed his earlier thought, indicating which elements he continued to maintain and which he had abandoned. He attempted— for the sake of Rosenzweig, I would suggest—to interpret the term realization:

> I must clarify a concept which, though ultimately neither inexact nor imprecise, has in some passages of these addresses turned out to be one or the other: the concept of "the realization of God." This term which I can justify in a fundamental sense still to be explained, becomes inexact when, as in our first address, we say that God must be transmuted from an abstract truth into a reality; for this term lures us into the glittering notion that God is an idea which can become reality only through man, and, furthermore, induces the hopelessly wrong conception that God is not, but that He becomes—either within man or within mankind. I call such a theory, manifest today in a variety of guises, hopelessly wrong, not because I am not certain of a divine *becoming* in immanence, but because only a primal certainty of divine *being* enables us to sense the awesome meaning of divine becoming, that is, the self-imparting of God to His creation and His participation in the destiny of its freedom, whereas without this primal certainty there can be only a blatant misuse of God's name. . . .
>
> We ought to understand that to "realize God" means to prepare the world for God as a place for His reality—to help the world become God-real [*gottwirklich*]; it means, in other and sacred words, to make reality one. This is our service in the Kingdom's becoming.[33]

Rosenzweig reacted very favorably: "You know how closely connected I feel to the writer of that preface."[34] After 1923, one finds that Buber virtually abandoned the term realization; it subsequently ceased to play any significant role in his philosophy.

Rosenzweig's influence was, finally, very likely discernible also in Buber's eventual exclusion of an epigraph that he had placed on the first page of Book One in the original edition of *I and Thou*. For reasons that can be understood only as the lingering effect of his earlier mystical thought, Buber quoted freely the following lines from a poem by Goethe: "So hab ich endlich von dir erharrt:/ In allen Elementen Gottes

---

33. *On Judaism* (New York, 1967), 8–9.
34. Franz Rosenzweig, "The Builders," in *On Jewish Learning*, ed. Nahum N. Glatzer (New York, 1955), 73. Buber sent this preface to Rosenzweig prior to its publication; see Rosenzweig, *Briefe*, p. 479.

Gegenwart" ("So I have got it from you at last/ God's presence is in all the elements"). These lines express not the philosophy of the I-Thou encounter, which he was establishing in the book, but his earlier pantheism. Upon receiving a copy of the book, Rosenzweig spoke strongly against the inclusion of the epigraph.[35] It cannot be proved that its exclusion from subsequent editions of the book was a result of Rosenzweig's negative attitude toward it. But Rosenzweig's candid criticism of Buber does further reveal the nature of the spiritual relationship that had arisen between them. Rosenzweig studied *I and Thou* carefully and saw its greatness. In 1923, Rosenzweig spoke of the book of Job as the biblical illustration of Buber's work.[36] There one can readily discern that there are some things "that I myself *must* say and others that no one is permitted to tell me." In 1922, Rosenzweig did not refrain pointing out questionable or unsuitable elements in Buber's thinking. This becomes even clearer in the examination of Rosenzweig's criticism of the galley sheets of *I and Thou* and of Buber's reactions to these criticisms.

35. Letter in MBA, MS Var. 350/59.
36. Rosenzweig, *Briefe*, p. 478.

SIX

September 1922

Upon receiving the galley sheets of *I and Thou* in September 1922, Buber decided to give them to Rosenzweig to read and criticize before returning them to the publisher. This afforded Rosenzweig the opportunity to scrutinize the foundations of his friend's thought.[1] The result was a frank correspondence in which Rosenzweig criticized basic structures of Buber's new thinking. In his letters Rosenzweig uncompromisingly demanded several principles of dialogical and biblical thinking that he found missing or distorted in *I and Thou*—principles that found their way into Buber's thinking in later years. The fact that Buber abandoned or altered thoughts presented in *I and Thou* and later adopted others presented in *The Star of Redemption* provides proof of the continuously dynamic quality of his thought and the influence of Rosenzweig on him.

The correspondence of September 1922 is among the most valuable contents of the Martin Buber Archive; it has only recently been published in the second volume of Buber's *Briefwechsel*,[2] Its importance for the study of modern Jewish thought is paralleled by the insights it offers into the beginnings of dialogical thinking in our century. It is, similarly, no less exciting for its revelation of the interaction of two great thinkers mutually engaged in the formulation of their basic phi-

---

1. See Appendix B, infra, p. 226; original German in Grete Schaeder, ed., *Martin Buber: Briefwechsel aus sieben Jahrzehnten*, vol. 2 (Heidelberg, 1972–1975), 124.

2. Schaeder, *Briefwechsel*, vol. 2, pp. 109–142 and, especially, 124–138.

losophies. One notes especially Buber's capacity to accept criticism sincerely; and for the study of Rosenzweig's philosophy, these letters—perhaps more so than many of his articles—provide clarification of essential points in his complicated work, *The Star of Redemption*.

For the purposes of the present chapter, it is necessary to quote only portions of the first two letters that passed between Rosenzweig and Buber.[3] Rosenzweig wrote first in an undated letter:

> . . . In your setting up the I-It, you give the I-Thou a cripple for an opponent. Truly, this cripple rules the modern world; however, this does not change the fact that it is a cripple. *This* It, you can easily dispose of. But this is the false It, the product of the great deception, which in Europe is now less than three hundred years old. Only as accompaniment to *this* It is an I—not spoken, but thought. In the *spoken* It no I resounds, at least not a human one. When I as a human being truly speak It, what accompanies the It is: "HE." The "basic word I-It" certainly cannot be spoken with the whole being. It is simply not a basic *word*; it is at most a basic thought—not even that, it is the tip of a philosophical point. If, nevertheless, It is quite real, then it must be inscribed in a basic word which *is* spoken with the whole being by the one who speaks. From His point of view, it is called I-It, from ours, He-It. Should you once say, "He who killeth and riviveth,"[4] then you have said this basic word and have said it with your whole being.
>
> From this construction to I-Thou—which, by the way, you share with Ebner—I think all the rest follows. You, like Ebner, intoxicated by the joy of discovery, throw all the rest (literally) to the dead. *It*, however, is not dead, although death belongs to It; It is created. But because you equate It with the "It"-"for"-"the"-"I"—which to be sure is dead—you *must* then raise everything which you do not want to fall into this valley of death, because it is alive, into the realm of the basic word I-Thou, which thereby *must* be enormously enlarged.
>
> . . . Dear Doctor, I am a very unselfish knight of the It, now more than ever. Behind my curtained windows[5] I am truly *interested* only in I and Thou. But, nevertheless, what will become of I and Thou if it must swallow the whole and the Creator too? Religion? I am afraid so—and shudder at the word, as always when I hear it. For *my* and *your* sake there must be something besides—me and you.

---

3. Other important letters from Rosenzweig (from September 1922) are found in Appendix B.

4. Quoted in the original Hebrew from the Amidah, a daily prayer.

5. Rosenzweig was already ill; his rapidly intensifying paralysis made it impossible for him to leave his home.

Buber responded on September 14, 1922:

> I thank you sincerely for your long and excellent criticism and ask you to keep the same kind of relentlessness and the severe unreservedness for the following proof sheets. . . .
>
> You must perhaps feel, even before reaching the end of the first part, that the injustice done to the It is less severe here. You may perhaps also see the justice done to the It when reading the second part, and almost certainly, in the third (and last) part you will see that there is also a He (and a We) as truth. A separation between actual knowledge and ability will yet remain, and in the end the speaker can only reply that he cannot do otherwise; he cannot say it otherwise than by the word for whose sake he has been such a steady and serious servant. I have already answered the question about the size of the volume and also about the number of parts. For me they are not unnamed; they bear the names, Word, History, God, but I am frightened to put these names down as titles.[6] On this point, like on some others, I am open to suggestions. Also concerning the announcement that this volume is the first of a series—I am ready to hear your advice. At present, at the end of the book and separately from the text is written: Conception of the work whose beginning is presented in this book, May 1916; first draft of this book, summer 1919; final version, spring 1922 . . .[7]
>
> Volumes II–V should treat: II—The primal forms; III—The Knowledge of God and the Law of God; IV—The person and the Community; V—The Power and the Kingdom. Thus volume III will deal only with [God as] He, and volume IV primarily with We.[8] Certainly I . . . have neither a permission to say a decisive He nor an authority to say a decisive We. Thus I must confess it, I cannot conceal my nakedness and my loneliness, and I cannot ask whether I simply carry my name, or whether I may also be called a human being. I

---

6. A detailed table of contents which Buber wrote for *I and Thou* exists in the manuscript of *I and Thou*, p. 99, presented in the German edition of Rivka Horwitz, *Buber's Way to "I and Thou"* (Heidelberg, 1978), Appendix D, p. 268.

7. For the source of the original German letter, see Schaeder, *Briefwechsel*, vol. 2, pp. 128–130. There are two versions of the Afterword, the one quoted on p. 224, supra, and the one quoted here. The dates are not the same. See the facsimile below, p. 233.

8. For Buber's plans on future volumes, see supra, p. 189, and Appendix B, infra, p. 224 (correspondence from August 1921). See also Schaeder, *Briefwechsel*, vol. 2, pp. 112–124.

would almost implore you to believe that I have not been for one moment the victim of an "intoxication"; as often as I have directed and collected myself on those things, I have always maintained a specific sobriety that can be most easily compared to the composing of a fair musician who restlessly tries to follow a heavy symphony. It was not extraordinarily successful, but the effort—I could not imagine a more sober effort.

How much and how little is there still to say! Sometimes I think that the basic difference, or as you think opposition, between us is our different attitude to the Kingdom. Otherwise you wouldn't have asked "What shall become of it." "Religion," certainly not . . .

Rosenzweig's major disagreement with Buber, as evidenced by these letters, concerns not the I-Thou but Buber's presentation of the I-It. *I and Thou* begins with the assertion that there are but two possible types of relation to the world: I-Thou and I-It. The focal point of this conception of reality is man; it is man who relates to the world *either* as a Thou *or* as an It. When a man relates to someone or something with his whole being, when he confronts it as beloved and speaks the basic word I-Thou—that is an I-Thou relation, whose light illumines the entire world. When, on the other hand, he perceives, thinks, imagines, or utilizes persons or objects in a rational and calculating manner— that is I-It. "The basic word I-It can never be spoken with one's whole being."[9] Throughout *I and Thou* Buber maintains a consistently negative attitude toward the I-It, as merely a compromise with reality: "Without It a human being cannot live"; but "whoever lives only with that is not human."[10] Buber's concern focuses on the human striving to overcome the I-It, to awaken the sense of authenticity, and to broaden the scope of I-Thou relation.

For Rosenzweig there is neither I-It nor any basic word that cannot be spoken with the whole human being. His philosophy begins, one might say, with a leap of faith and takes for its method not thought but speech-thinking.[11] It demands from the outset an orientation without which one cannot reach I-Thou; to know what is above and what is below, what is before and what is after. If one cannot accept this premise as the necessary point of departure, one cannot philosophize

---

9. *I and Thou*, trans. Walter Kaufmann (New York, 1970), 54; and *Werke*, vol. 1 (Munich/Heidelberg, 1962–1964), 79.

10. *I and Thou*, p. 85; and *Werke*, vol. 1, p. 101.

11. See Franz Rosenzweig, "Das neue Denken," in *Kleinere Schriften* (Berlin, 1937), 386–387.

September 1922

on Rosenzweig's basis, his biblical basis of faith. On other bases the
world may be grasped as one that has no beginning and no end, no
creation and no redemption. When man knows not from whence he
came and whither he goes, he may base his philosophy on rationalism,
materialism, pantheism, and so on, explaining the I-Thou as simply
an isolated affair in an infinite world. The tool of such philosophies is
thought, but that of the biblical world is speech-thinking. The latter
approach takes time seriously.

It is clear, as evidenced by these letters, that Rosenzweig's disagreement with Buber concerns both the I-Thou and the I-It. Rosenzweig argued that Buber's I-It is actually a product of "the great deception in Europe" of the last three hundred years—of the rationalism
and idealism that have typified philosophical thought since Descartes.
He notes an affinity between Buber's I-It and the *cogito* of the idealists,
that is, between those theories of human consciousness that attempt to
analyze the world only in terms of the mind. He points out that Ebner,
in his book *Das Wort und die geistigen Realitaten*, similarly makes no room
for the authentic I-It and focuses everything on the I-Thou. Neither
Ebner nor Buber offers a theory of the creation of a relation between
God and the world; for both there is either I-Thou or inauthenticity.

Rosenzweig's opposition to Buber and Ebner recalls a long section
in *The Star of Redemption* in which he criticizes Fichte's grasp of the
world in terms of I and Not-I.[12] This same issue continued to occupy

---

12. *The Star of Redemption*, trans. William W. Hallo (New York, 1970),
140–144. It is noteworthy that Rosenzweig responded with a criticism to the
galley sheets of *I and Thou* one day after he received them. This alacrity may
be explained as a result of a struggle that Rosenzweig had previously experienced and resolved. In a meeting with Rosenstock and Rudolf Ehrenberg in
July 1913, Rosenzweig was convinced by Rosenstock that his position regarding
God, creation, evil, and suffering was weak. In a letter to Rudolf Ehrenberg
dated October 31, 1913 (*Briefe* [Berlin, 1935], 762), Rosenzweig stated that once
he fully accepted Genesis 1, he yielded to Rosenstock's thinking. Rosenzweig
deduced from Genesis 1: (1) God is the Creator and the world is His creation;
(2) the world is good; (3) mankind has a common beginning. Rosenzweig perceived the above thoughts as interrelated and devoted a chapter in *The Star of
Redemption* to them. In fact, he attacked the mystics for their mere acceptance
of God and their negative attitude toward the world (*The Star*, p. 207). In a
sense, the mystic is close to the Gnostic who does not accept the idea that the
world is good. Rosenzweig attacked Islam as well, charging that it did not
understand the creation properly (ibid., p. 123). Nahum Glatzer has said that
Rosenzweig considered his chapter on creation in *The Star* to be very important
and in fact had wanted to rewrite it.

211

Rosenzweig in subsequent years. In his 1925 essay, "The New Think-ing," he again explained the difference between idealism and his own philosophy, insisting that the error of I-It philosophy stems from its basis in the fictitious omnipresent human consciousness. He envisioned the end of this traditional philosophy and, in its place, the emergence of a philosophy rooted in experience (*erfahrende Philosophie*):

> Experience knows nothing of objects. It remembers, it senses, it hopes, and it fears. One might perhaps understand the content of memory by taking it as an object; this would be then a matter of understanding, and no longer the content of memory itself. For I do not remember the content as *my* object. It is only a prejudice of the past three centuries that "I" must play a part in all consciousness: that a tree cannot be seen by me unless my self sees it. As a matter of fact, that ego of mine comes to the fore only—when it *comes* to the fore, when, for example, I must emphasize that I for one see the tree because someone else does not see it. In that case, my knowledge shows the tree certainly asso-ciated with me, but in any other case, I know only about the tree, and about nothing else. Philosophy's claim that the self is omnipresent in all knowledge distorts the content of this consciousness. . . .[13]

The certainty that the tree exists when I do not see it requires a source other than the human consciousness. For Rosenzweig the source is God, who gives nature its stability.

Within the framework of Rosenzweig's affirmation of both the first chapter of Genesis and revelation, God has two major attributes: reason and will. God is both remote and near, King and Father, He and Thou.[14] Reason is the attribute of God as Creator. In His wisdom the distant God, He, guards His world, His It, giving it order and stability; God's wisdom never changes; therefore the laws of nature remain sta-ble. Revelation, on the other hand, is an act of will, expressing the particular love of God for one particular being. Only because God loves man can man love; this, in Rosenzweig's language, is theomorphism. Love has no rules and cannot be calculated; it is the true I-Thou relation, as exemplified by the Song of Songs.[15]

From Rosenzweig's point of view, Buber places man at the center

---

13. Nahum N. Glatzer, *Franz Rosenzweig: His Life and Thought* (New York, 1961), 195–196.
14. *The Star*, p. 306.
15. Ibid., p. 199.

of his philosophy and forms a near dichotomy between God and It. If *man* relates to the world as Thou, then the tree, for example, is also related to God because "in every Thou we address the Eternal Thou."[16] But if man relates to the tree as an object, cataloging and using it, then neither Thou nor Eternal Thou is present. Of the Eternal Thou's independent relation to nature we can say nothing, for in Buber's entire treatise one finds no clear suggestion of a stable relation between God and nature.

In that regard, one might, in some sense, compare Buber's thinking of 1922 with that of Kierkegaard, as described and attacked by Buber in later years. According to Buber, Kierkegaard demands either God or world[17] and "wants Thou to be truly said only to him, and to all others an unessential and fundamentally invalid word—God demands us to choose between Him and His creation." That which is authentic is man's relation to God; of man's relation to the world, Kierkegaard says, "I have nothing more to do with the world." Rosenzweig thought that for Buber in 1922 the dichotomy was not between God and the world but between I-Thou and I-It. Nature per se does not obstruct the way to God, but man's inauthentic I-It approach to nature does. I-Thou is man's only authentic relation to nature, to man, and to the Eternal Thou. In placing the emphasis on relation rather than on the object, Buber differed from that which he associates with Kierkegaard. But he agreed with Kierkegaard in not founding his I-Thou and I-It conceptions on creation. Neither Kierkegaard, nor his twentieth-century Catholic follower Ferdinand Ebner, nor the great Pascal based his philosophy on the first chapter of Genesis.

In fragment 7, Ebner stated: "Of the relationship between God and the world we can literally know nothing." To speculate about God and His relation to the world, as do the theologians, is nothing but anthropomorphism.[18] In a similar vein, Pascal argued in his *Pensées* (no. 556) that "if the world existed to instruct man of God, His divinity would shine though every part in it in an indisputable manner; but as

---

16. *I and Thou*, p. 57.

17. *Between Man and Man*, ed. Maurice S. Friedman and trans. Ronald G. Smith, 2nd ed. (New York, 1967), 54. Interpreters of Kierkegaard indicate that the God-world dichotomy was not always so sharply presented by Kierkegaard himself.

18. *Das Wort und die geistigen Realitäten* in Ferdinand Ebner, *Schriften* (Munich, 1963), vol. 1, p. 157.

it exists only by Jesus Christ, . . . and to teach men both their cor-
ruption and their redemption, all displays the proofs of these two
truths." Ebner quoted Pascal's *Thoughts*,[19] arguing that love is more
important than creation, preceding it and succeeding it.[20] Both philosophers forgo a theory of creation and rely on Jesus, whom they
identify with the Word in the Gospel of John. "In the beginning was
the Word" echoes throughout their thinking. For them, the light is not
creation but merely the divine spark in the human soul. Creation as
such is but the darkness into which light and love shine.

Rosenzweig apparently thought that Buber followed their philosophies but emphasized the I-Thou rather than the New Testament
concept of the Word or love: "In the beginning is relation." I-Thou is
prior to I-It; love precedes reason. As a Jew, Buber of course never
viewed I-Thou as a hypostatization of the Divine; nor did he ascribe
to it the role of mediator. God alone is One, and as such He alone is
the Eternal Thou, the eternal Confronter. God's nature as Eternal Thou
is not, however, one attribute among many but *the* attribute of God.
Buber takes the negation of God as He with utmost seriousness. In the
letter of September 14, 1922, he described one of the volumes to follow
I and Thou as a work that will deal "only with God as He" and that
will treat, specifically, the knowledge of God [*Gotteskunde*] and the Law
of God. It was no doubt intended to be a criticism of theology and
religions.[21]

Rosenzweig understood the "He" otherwise than Buber. He
thought that Buber's theory of I-It was in basic agreement with the
idealist's understanding of the world as dependent on human consciousness and with his consequent denial of God's direct relation to
nature.[22] Because salvation is only in the I-Thou—yet we must always
return to the It—Buber speaks of our existence as tragic. One finds in
him a negative attitude toward the rational order of the world. The
book is, in fact, a response to the outcry of a generation suffocated by

---

19. Ibid., p. 157. Ebner used the translation of Blaise Pascal, *Thoughts* (The
Harvard Classics) (New York, 1910), p. 186.

20. Ibid., p. 199.

21. *I and Thou*, p. 161. See also the German edition of Rivka Horwitz,
Buber's Way to "I and Thou" (Heidelberg, 1978), Appendix D, "On God as He,"
p. 267.

22. *I and Thou*, p. 82. "There are moments of the secret ground in which
world order is beheld as present."

machines, institutions, sciences, and information—a generation seeking real life. Unlike Kierkegaard and Ebner, Buber replied that there is no realm of life in which the way to God is closed, for one may have an I-Thou relation with nature. Yet like them, he maintained that I-It does not and cannot lead to God. The new meaning that Buber offered to his generation is rooted entirely in the moment of I-Thou, which is the source of real and true life.

For Rosenzweig the world is related to God: "It is good" and need not be rejected. Creation depends not on our consciousness but on His mind.[23] Nathan Rotenstreich has suggested that this view of creation has its affinities with Hermann Cohen's philosophy.[24] Cohen described the God-world relation as the relation of Being and Becoming, and argued that God's most important attribute lies in His being Creator. It would seem, however, that Rosenzweig also drew on Schelling's insistence that the world can receive affirmation and meaning only through God and on his consequent rejection of Hegel's assertion that the world exists in and of itself. In his own anti-idealistic approach, Rosenzweig insisted that man may try to understand only *God's* word, to comprehend only *His* creation. At several points Rosenzweig made clear that this conception of the world as dependent on God rather than on the human mind is in fact a return to a pre-Kantian, Copernican type philosophy, to a type of He-It philosophy.[25]

From Buber's point of view, matters looked different. He appreciated Rosenzweig's criticism and therefore could say that it was "excellent" and that it should be elaborated. (In 1932, he even dedicated his *Königtum Gottes* to Rang and Rosenzweig, although neither was still alive.) Both Rang and Rosenzweig thought that Buber expanded the I-Thou too much. For Rang, it included virtually the whole world, yet it lacked the religious awe of a rare flash of a moment. Rosenzweig thought that Buber was intoxicated by his discovery of the I-Thou. Buber, however, disagreed emphatically, demanding in all *sobriety* that I-Thou should be expansive: The tree, the animal, the work of art, and the beloved must all be included. From his perspective, Rosenzweig's way appeared too systematic and too narrow, perhaps even static—

23. *The Star*, p. 114.
24. Nathan Rotenstreich, *Jewish Philosophy in Modern Times* (New York, 1968), 179, 188. See also Hermann Cohen, *Religion of Reason, from the Sources of Judaism*, trans. Simon Kaplan (New York, 1971), 60–64.
25. Glatzer, *Franz Rosenzweig*, p. 289; *The Star*, p. 152.

limiting an I-Thou relation to that between God and His beloved and perhaps also to that between two persons, even though this is not explicitly delineated in *The Star*. Buber, on the other hand, affirmed the existence of another type of I-Thou relation—speech or the I-Thou relation with the world: In a moment when will and grace are joined, one may have a relation with a tree and then the tree ceases to be an It. That tree, Buber wrote, "has to deal with me as I deal with it—only differently." The relation with the tree is, according to Buber, reciprocal. One may perhaps be reminded of Moses experiencing God in a tree.

According to Buber, in his letter to Rosenzweig, the latter's criticism was an overstatement. Whatever the differences between the two, they were not as deep as Rosenzweig had thought. Buber asked Rosenzweig for patience; he had, after all, read only the first part of the book. Buber hoped that after seeing the work in its entirety, he would agree that the injustice done to the It was not so severe or even nonexistent. Buber did not reject the world, although his acceptance of it was different from Rosenzweig's. Buber's orientation to the world was characterized by strong, pantheistic traits; he accepted the attitude of the Baal Shem Tov, who perceived the immanence of God but did not exclude a personal God or revelation. Buber was also close to the thinking of the great Hasidic figure, Rabbi Nachman of Bratslav, who claimed he saw the prayers of leaves of grass. There is in Buber's attitude exactly the tendency that is so common in Kabbalah. Mystics do not reject the personal God; still, they see God in the world. Buber wrote in *I and Thou*, "Whoever beholds the world in Him, stands in His presence." Every I-Thou hints beyond to the Eternal Thou. Buber continued the line of thinking of Hasidism (a line that Rang discerned as Neoplatonic) and would affirm the ancient Hasidic saying: "Everything in You and Thou art in everything." Rosenzweig on the other hand, emphasized the personal God, God who *is* outside the world, who guards his creatures; he rejected pantheism, which either makes the world divine or makes God worldly. God is the One above all and not the All in All. From his early attack on Buber in "Atheistic Theology" (1914), he struggled against pantheism and the "growth" of God. For him, history is the realm of the dialogue, of eternity, and of the growing Kingdom. For Rosenzweig, but not for Buber, God is outside of life in the here and now. Yet, for Rosenzweig, in the end of time when all vanished, "He is One in all the world, when He is One."

Rang and Rosenzweig also disagreed with the minor position Buber gave to the It. From their point of view, those who fail, those who have no I-Thou moments, will in Buber's theory fail altogether. The

It cannot lead to God. Buber, a Hasid at heart, was apparently more optimistic than they in his belief that God can be reached by all. Because God can be served in all ways, in the silent cleaving to Him or in brotherly love for one's fellow creature, God should be worshiped by all human beings at all times. The whole of daily life is hallowed according to Buber's Hasidic way of thinking; there is no way that does not lead to Him. The I-Thou relation has no prerequisite. In essence, then, *I and Thou* was an outgrowth of Buber's intensive work in Hasidic literature, his attempt to form a Hasidic type of philosophy.

One has to ask what Buber meant when he wrote, "He is merely a metaphor." In some ways it was certainly an attack, which Rang and Rosenzweig would support, on the old-fashioned theology. It was certainly an attack on scholasticism and the tiresome debates about Him, which substitute for a confrontation with Him in the here and now. Part of it is certainly an agreement with them. But there is more to it, as Buber wrote to Rosenzweig: "Sometimes I think that the basic difference, or as you think opposition, between us is our different attitude to the Kingdom."

This point needs to be explained further. Buber and Rosenzweig both agreed on many points in their description of the I-Thou. For both, it was a full present; for both, it was a moment of love that changes life from within; for both, disobeying or rejecting the message was not a matter of morality but a revolt against God. For both, the I-Thou contained the motif of repentance, or *teshuvah*; for both, only by responding to the Thou can the human being become I. For both, there is a similarity between the small personal revelation and the great revelation upon which religions are founded. For both, in the moment of I-Thou man finds himself and his mission in life, which means that revelation leads to redemption.

But for Buber this moment of I-Thou is disconnected from other moments: The moments together *cannot* form a line! There is a constant struggle between the chain of causality, the utilitarian tendency, and the rare moments of grace. Man has a thirst for continuity, for extension of I-Thou in time and place; he yearns for duration, for continuation. But Buber warns against this tendency; only if one realizes it anew every day can one do justice to this extraordinary relation with God or man. *Only in this lies the possibility of a fullness of reality.*

For Buber no law, no world order, no tradition, and no institution can be holy. Buber had a very low opinion of institutions and religions whose forms were frozen and of people who argued about forms and formality instead of relating directly to God. In his work on the Bible, he thought ill of the kings and idealized the time of the judges and

Samuel, when the Israelites lived in small communities and were relatively weak physically. Halakhah, Jewish law, belongs also to this category. Buber wanted man to stand free, alone or in a small group, before God. He demanded an inner, dynamic renewal free from tradition and institutions—rejecting that human weakness that leads one to flock to the synagogue and join in with others in the ways of worship or in the customs in the organized listening to an ancient prayer, a chapter of Psalms, or an ancient hymn. Whereas Rosenzweig thought there could be no Jew without Torah and had an understanding for halakhah and, like Bialik, considered the *bet-hamidrash*, the traditional synagogue, to be "the well of the soul of the people," Buber thought that institutions cannot show the way to the Kingdom. It has to be a direct way through the I-Thou relation—or through the We of the living community.

Epilogue

The foregoing historical analysis has sought to enrich our knowledge of the development of *I and Thou* and the beginning of Buber's dialogical thinking. Three periods in Buber's development are discernible.

The information concerning the early period from 1915–1920 is rather rudimentary. The historical evidence, however, while differing slightly, supports the general trend of Buber's description of a plan of 1916 and a draft of 1919: The outline we have dates from 1918, and the draft of 1919 has not been discovered. However, contemporary letters mention a philosophical work and speak of the intention to devote future years to it. The outline of 1918 departs from Buber's early mystical tendency and a consideration of God as the Confronted. The terminology of I and Thou seems basically to come from a later period; yet this plan is the thread from which his future thought would then be woven.

There was, as Buber related, a lengthy interruption in his work. He only returned to it in late 1921—the second period. Something must have occurred in the fall of that year to bring him back to those thoughts. And in December 1921, when Buber was trying to explain to Rosenzweig "the reality of the word," the latter realized that there had been a shift in his friend's thinking. At that time, Buber was involved in formulating "Religion as Presence." There is evidence, based on Buber's own testimony and upon historical and philological evidence, of connections between *I and Thou* and the work of the Catholic thinker Ferdinand Ebner. The anecdote on the train, which centers around the idea of never considering God as a He and which was dated by Buber to the fall of 1921, resulted from his reading of Ebner, where it can be found in numerous places. It is conceivable that once inspired, Buber returned to reformulate his own thinking.

The third period falls in 1922, from which we have most of the sources of *I and Thou*. These include: (1) "Religion as Presence," (2) Buber's notebook of *I and Thou* of May 1922, (3) numerous important letters, and, finally, (4) the printed book of December 1922. The lecture series "Religion as Presence" indeed demonstrates how remote Buber was in January from the final version of December.

The lectures afford us the rare opportunity to follow Buber's footsteps in that very creative and fruitful year. In 1922, there was a very intensive crystallization of *I and Thou* and, as the evidence shows, a deep friendship with Rosenzweig. Buber spoke of their dialogue as their "common and eternal" interest. The atmosphere of the Lehrhaus and the questions of the audience stimulated him too: And the form Buber finally gave to the idea of the dialogue was a breakthrough in twentieth-century thinking.

Parallels Between the Lectures and I and Thou

Lectures		I and Thou[1]	Lectures		I and Thou
Lecture Three:	p. 64	129		p. 93	78
	p. 64	129		p. 94	84
	p. 65	129	Lecture Five:	p. 102	64–65
	p. 70	153		p. 103	53, 82
Lecture Four:	p. 79	55		p. 103	60
	p. 79	55		p. 104	69
	p. 80	56		p. 104	68
	p. 81	55		p. 105	100
	p. 81	157		p. 107	65
	p. 82	54		p. 107	61
	p. 83	56		p. 107	83–84
	p. 84	59		p. 108	68–69
	p. 85	56		p. 108	68
	p. 85	59–60		p. 109	63
	p. 86	60–61		p. 109	63–64
	p. 88	60		p. 109	63–64
	p. 89	61		p. 110	76
	p. 91	77		p. 110	73–74
	p. 91	76		p. 111	77–78
	p. 92	78		p. 112	163

1. Pages refer to Martin Buber, *I and Thou*, ed. and trans. by Walter Kauffmann (New York, 1970).

Lectures		*I and Thou*[1]	Lectures	*I and Thou*
	p. 113	84	p. 166	161
	p. 115	128	p. 167	161–162
	p. 115	129	p. 167	162
Lecture Six:	p. 123	129	p. 168	162
	p. 124	124	p. 168	163
	p. 124	124	p. 170	163
	p. 124	124	p. 171	164
	p. 124	125	p. 171	164
	p. 125	125	p. 172	164–165
	p. 125	125	p. 172	167
	p. 126	125–126	p. 172	166
	p. 129	126	p. 173	165
	p. 131	135	p. 174	166
	p. 133	53	p. 175	160
Lecture Seven:	p. 153	161	p. 175	165–166
	p. 155	161	p. 176	166
	p. 159	161	p. 176	166
			p. 176	166
Lecture Eight:	p. 163	157	p. 177	166
	p. 164	157	p. 177	167
	p. 164	158	p. 177	167
	p. 164	158	p. 178	168
	p. 165	158	p. 178	168
	p. 166	158–159		

APPENDIX B

*Letters Between
Buber and Rosenzweig*

A very select number of letters has been translated in order to show the type of relationship that existed between Buber and Rosenzweig in summer 1922.

> *Letter 1:* Buber describes to Rosenzweig the themes of the second volume and the second lecture series and reveals to him his problems.
>
> *Letter 2:* Rosenzweig relates to Buber the conception moment of *The Star* and offers Buber a plan on how to construct the lecture series.
>
> *Letter 3:* Rosenzweig's criticism of Buber's *I and Thou* (the letter is quoted in part in Part Two, chapter 6).
>
> *Letter 4:* Rosenzweig continues his criticism of Buber's *I and Thou*.
>
> *Letter 5:* Rosenzweig worries over Buber's silence.
>
> *Letter 6:* Buber's reply: A meeting is preferable to a correspondence.

The original German of all these letters is found in Grete Schaeder, *Martin Buber: Briefwechsel aus sieben Jahrzehnten*, vol. 2 (Heidelberg, 1972–1975), 115–116, 117–118, 124–128, 136–138, 139. Additional letters can be found in the same vol., pp. 112–138.

Letter 1: Martin Buber to Franz Rosenzweig

Heppenheim, August 21, 1922

Dear Doctor

Thank you for sending the "Jesus" [article] by Eduard Strauss which I will be glad to publish.¹ The presentation is well done and says what it means. It is alien to me, however, in contrast to *"The Star"* in which no page is alien to me, however remote from me certain pages may be in the opinions they express. I will give you a definite example. The concept of the pagans in Strauss' essay has an admixture of cruelty, from which yours is free. [. . .] It lacks something which one could characterize in biblical terms [. . .] as the Deuters-Isaianic quality. (The older I become the more I love this prophet without name; I recognize my hereditary world.)

I would like to change the title of my course to: "The Primary Forms [Urformen] of Religious Life." ("Basic Forms [Grundformen]" is too broad a title for *this* course.) "Primary Forms [Urformen]" is a more suitable title, because one of the main aims of these lectures is to show that there are no pagans, or at least no "pagan religions." [. . .] On the content of the course, I shall just add that it leads up to the problem of "person and community," which is the subject of my third volume.² (The fourth should deal with religions; the fifth and last, with "actuality.") [. . .] The first lecture [of the series "The Primary Forms of Religious Life"] can naturally be called by a shorter name [than "Magic, the Paganism of all Nations"], but I fear that the title "Magic" would not be sufficiently set off from the three titles that follow, so that the scheme

Magic		Sacrifice ⎫	
(The Paganism of all		Mystery ⎬	The Religious Life
Nations)		Prayer ⎭	

would not come out clearly enough in the announcement. Therefore I believe that "Magic and Religion" is preferable, but if you can suggest a different way to describe it, I would be very agreeable. Perhaps I should simply say "Paganism" [das Heidentum].

---

1. An article that Strauss sent via Rosenzweig to Buber, who was the editor of *Der Jude*. The article, "Jesus von Nazareth," was published in *Der Jude*, vol. VI, p. 686 ff.

2. Buber refers to his plan for the volumes following *I and Thou*.

The rest we can discuss orally next time. I am heartily glad that I may visit you again. When I was in Frankfort last week I missed that customary route. There is something else that I have wanted to discuss with you for a long time.

Letter 2: Franz Rosenzweig to Martin Buber

August 22, 1922

Esteemed Doctor,

In Strauss' article, I do not think it is the thought which alienates you; even in the example you mention, his thought is quite closely related to mine. The difficulty lies, as always with Strauss, in the how. [. . .] I think that the "cruelty" which you sense is as far from him as from me and it is merely a matter of tone [. . .]. I would like you to return [Strauss'] manuscript to me. Perhaps one can alter [the tone of cruelty] with very little rewriting. I wrote him what you wrote and that I would ask you to send me the manuscript again for one or two days.

Now to the main subject. It seems to me that the difference between us is not in our way of dealing with life but in our view of history; that is, of the world. Therefore it is not an important difference. [. . .] For a solution to this problem [the relationship between paganism and religion] I served three years, from the spring of 1914 to the fall of 1917. I found it while stumbling at night over a horrible prickly plant on the way from the front to Prilep in Macedonia;[3] then I knew "everything". It was the moment of conception for my book (not yet as book); I knew the relationship between creation and revelation. [. . .] Until finally, at the end of 1918, in the introduction to the third part, I even, with inner jubilation, got back my clear conscience for Goethe, which I lost for the first time in high school, when one day I forbade myself, with a regular Catholic prohibition, to read Goethe, and obeyed myself for several months.[4]

That's what happened with me and the pagans.

---

3. Rosenzweig was stationed at the Macedonian front during the First World War.

4. For Rosenzweig, Goethe was a pagan; see his *Der Stern der Erlösung*, 3rd ed. (Heidelberg, a. M., 1954), 30.

It is only now that I understand the intention of your course. I do not know whether it is necessary to indicate it [paganism versus religion] in the title. The actual titles [of the lecture series] "The Primary Forms of Religious Life": Magic, Sacrifice, Mystery, Prayer already say something, at least *delimit* the material. [. . .] You want nevertheless, if I understand you correctly, to use two pedal points throughout your lectures: magic, which is the "paganism of all nations," and prayer, which is "Judaism in all religion," one decrescendo and the other crescendo. In between you would deal with sacrifice and mystery, the two specific *configurations* of religious life, (for magic and prayer are primary phenomena of religion precisely because they are not specifically religious, as are sacrifice and mystery, but primary phenomena of *all* life). This whole relationship could perhaps be expressed as follows:

The Primary Forms of Religious Life
   Magic and the Pagan
   Sacrifice: the Religious Act
   Mystery: Religious Contemplation [Schau]
   Prayer and the Jew.

I think one senses here—as much as one can sense anything in titles— the dominance of the concepts Jew and pagan. [. . .]

A very simple form of outline [of the lectures "The Primary Forms of Religious Life"] would be:

Magic
Sacrifice
Mystery
Prayer

[. . .] Perhaps that would be the best. [. . .]

Letter 3: Franz Rosenzweig to Martin Buber

Undated

Esteemed Doctor:

This is not an easy task for me. You yourself distinguish quite correctly between that which I can say to you and that which I can say about the book. Furthermore, regarding the latter I lack several things which the reader in the bookstore will know. You have to reveal to me: how long will it be, approximately? How many parts—obviously unnamed—has it? Will the reader be told that it is itself only a first part? [. . .]

All the rest that I have to say goes deeper, belongs no more to the "corrections." I will take the bull by the horns immediately:

In your setting up the I-It, you give the I-Thou a cripple for an opponent. True, this cripple rules the modern world; however, this does not change the fact that it is a cripple. *This* It, you can easily dispose of. But this is the false It, the product of the great deception, which in Europe is less than three hundred years old. Only as accompaniment to *this* It is an I—not spoken, but thought. In the *spoken* It no I resounds, at least not a human one. When I as a human being truly speak It, what accompanies the It is: "HE." The "basic world I-It" certainly cannot be spoken with the whole being. It is simply not a basic *word*; it is at most a basic thought—not even that, it is the tip of a thought, a philosophical point. If, nevertheless, It is quite real, then it must be inscribed in a basic word which *is* spoken with the whole being by the one who speaks. From His point of view, it is called I-It, from ours, He-It.[5] Should you once say "He who killeth and reviveth,"[6] then you have said this basic word and have said it with your whole being.

From this constriction to I-Thou—which, by the way, you share with Ebner—I think all the rest follows. You, like Ebner, intoxicated by the joy of the discovery, throw all the rest (literally) to the dead. *It*, however, is not dead, although death belongs to It; It is created. But because you equate It with the "It"—"for"—"the"—"I"—which to be sure is dead—you *must* then raise everything which you do not want to fall into this valley of death, because it is alive, into the realm of the basic word I-Thou, which thereby *must* be enormously enlarged.

What happens to you is exactly the opposite of what happens to your co-discoverer [Hermann] Cohen (a real story of "Four who entered the Garden.")[7] He [Cohen] discovered I-Thou as the great exception to the rule and built for its sake an additional wing to his otherwise

---

5. Rosenzweig criticizes Buber for starting with I-Thou; whereas Buber starts with the human I, Rosenzweig demands that one begin with the divine He. On the He-It, see *Der Stern*, II, p. 82.

6. Quoted in the original Hebrew from the Amidah, a daily prayer.

7. "Four who entered the garden" is a famous talmudic story (Bab. Hagigah 14b); it is also quoted in Hebrew. According to this story, four entered the *pardes*, the mystical garden, and only one came out "in peace." Rosenzweig refers to Ebner, Hermann Cohen, Buber, and himself.

already completed edifice, trying hard not to disfigure the finished one; in which he naturally did not succeed. Much too much wished to enter into this adjacent wing, which previously had found its place in the old house; thus the new wing threatened to become a house in itself, in which those who frequented the old house felt least at home [the Neo-Kantians]. You, on the other hand, erect a new building from the very start, you make of creation a Chaos, just good enough to provide timber for the new building. That which doesn't fit becomes inessential. Cohen was *alarmed* by his discovery, you are *intoxicated*. Hence many *Aherim* [those who do not believe in the God of Israel] will follow you and will "cut off the plants."[8] But in this garden there is also one who "entered in peace and went out in peace."[9] To use your language: besides the I-Thou, there are two other equally essential basic words; basic words into whose one half the whole being of the other half fits, just as much as with I-thou. One, the HE-It, the word of the "entrance," I have mentioned already. The word of the "exit"—that same exit from the garden—is called We-It (with you, surely, I can be thus formulaically brief). This is the second way of saying It "with the whole being." *I* cannot say It with my whole being but HE [God] can and We [community] can. (N. B.: in the We-It lie the answers to all those problems which philosophy attempted to answer with the pseudo-basic word I-it.) However by *Our* saying It, It becomes IT. Hence the following series arises, in which I-Thou must be the middle, because in this Garden there is a complete balance of powers, by the fact that I-Thou can unveil itself in every moment as *I*-Thou and it can equally reveal itself at every moment as I-THOU: HE-It, I-Thou, I-THOU, I-THOU, We-IT.[10] The beginning and the end of this series, linked together, yield Schelling's great word "And then pantheism will be true."

Our controversy, in all the details about which we have spoken centers on the word It;[11] not merely the tree (which by the way almost

---

8. A reference to the above talmudic story.

9. Again, a reference to the story.

10. In German, the word "I" is a three-letter word which need not be capitalized. Rosenzweig writes this word in two different ways to convey his interpretation. "Er-Es" refers to the relationship between God and the World; "Ich-Du" refers to the dialogue between man and man; "ICH-Du" refers to God's speech to man; "Ich-DU" refers to man's speech to God; "Wir-Es" refers to the acts of the community for the redemption of the world.

11. Note that the letter mentions earlier conversations between Buber and Rosenzweig on that theme.

bewitched me just now, so splendidly does it shine on page 13 [of the galleys]) and the work of art, but also the question of "law," the permission (a permission! only a permission! Birshut maranan verabotai !!!)[12] to speak of God again in the third person and through that (and through that alone) the possibility of speaking even of the Creator,—everything follows from this point. And do you not constantly pay tribute to this despised word in spite of yourself? By speaking *about* I-Thou. And by replacing Cohen's "correlation" with that not much more German word "relation" [Beziehung]. You could have selected other words, words which I can speak to You and You to Me (can I say to You: I stand in relation to You??), words that are more German, if you had not needed to squeeze into I-Thou so much (actually all authentic life) of what can be spoken complete and without compulsion only in It—of course only in the authentic It of the HE-it and We-It, not in the fictitious one of I-It.

Dear Doctor, I am a very unselfish knight of the It, now more than ever. Behind my curtained windows,[13] I am truly *interested* only in I and Thou. But, nevertheless, what will become of I and Thou if it must swallow the whole world and the Creator too? Religion? I am afraid so—and shudder at the word, as always when I hear it. For *my* and *your* sake there must be something besides—me and you.

Letter 4: *Franz Rosenzweig to Martin Buber*

September 22, 1922

Esteemed Doctor,

By now—in fact, last night—I have read the final [galley] sheets as well, in which *both* closeness and distance are heightened to an extreme. To begin with, do you think I could respond to the entire [work]? [Refers to Buber's request that Rosenzweig evaluate the manuscript.]

---

12. The first edition of *Ich und Du* contained no section on permission; it is probably the section on decision that was eventually excluded from the book, although it still appeared in the manuscript of *Ich und Du*.

The permission is not grainted by the teachers and masters but by HIM. This is another Hebrew quote in the letter; it is from the grace after meals and may be rendered in English: "Masters and teachers in HIS permission . . . (let us pray)."

13. Rosenzweig was then already sick and could not leave his home.

There is indeed no page upon which I cannot comment, but precisely for that reason—And after all it comes to the same thing, whether or not I can follow you in this or that detail. [. . .] I shall try, in this short afternoon hour, to clarify that which haunted me at night.

How do you know that the course is not cyclical [that the world does not, as the Greeks thought, consist of infinite cycles, without a creation]? Would you not have to regard this as possible? And if you do know it [that the world is created], from where do you know it? Only because it *is* so. And if there is such a Being [a Creator], why should we be unable to see and hear this Being? Why should we have only momentary flashes [of I-Thou]? Why should the continuity remain beyond our grasp? For after all, you too believe in it (the continuity). This is a bundle of questions, and yet it is actually only one question transposed from the logical to the metaphysical, the question of the It. . . . Yes, I can answer you, justice is done to the It in a few places, but this is not due to your merit but to its. These points contradict your *way of thinking:* the created, the reality which precedes all fictitious It, leaps into your concept—thank God (really!). If I still had the text here, I could mark the passages for you, one in particular. [. . .] How you would like to include Buddha in your Paradiso, that garden over which I-Thou is inscribed! How you would like to include the house-cat, all the pious pagan souls and the masters of those who know.[14] But you do not succeed; in the end they only reach a wonderfully beautiful place in the antechamber of hell—the It. But it need not have been the antechamber of *hell*; it could have been the antechamber to a real *heaven*, if you had not allowed yourself to be talked into the dia-bolical I-It of the philosophers, but had accepted the blessed He-It of the children and Goethe and the Creator. Because no one, for as long as the world has existed, has ever said: "I see the tree."[15] Only phi-losophers say that.

Right now the mail arrives and brings me your poem. [Buber had sent the seriously ill Rosenzweig a poem he had written several years earlier which included wishes for another good year.]

---

14. Quoted in Italian (maestri di coloro que sanno). Rosenzweig alludes to Dante's *La Divina Commedia*, I, 4, but changes *maestro* in the original line (which designates Aristotle) to include thinkers of a similar stamp.
15. A criticism of "I see the tree" can be found in Rosenzweig's essay, "Das neue Denken," in *Kleinere Schriften* (Berlin, 1937), 382.

It is time to end and you need your galleys. And best wishes for the New Year [. . .].

Letter 5: Franz Rosenzweig to Martin Buber

Undated

Esteemed Doctor,

Your pronounced silence on my letter of Friday makes me fear that I have offended you. If that is the case, then tell me please and don't keep silent. I am not so sensitive that I cannot take a sharp word, but neither I am so thick-skinned, that I wouldn't sense a silence more than any word, even the sharpest—and this cannot be your intention.

Letter 6: Martin Buber to Franz Rosenzweig

September 28th, 1922

Dear Doctor—

How could you think that I used a "pronounced silence" towards you [. . .]. I did not answer your letter from Friday simply because at this point in our conversation, I could, perhaps, have gone on speaking but not writing. [. . .]

Dieses Buch stellt den Anfang eines Weges, den ich weiter zu gehen und weiter zu führen versuchen will. Der erste Entwurf des ganzen Itinerars stammt aus dem Mai 1916; diese Niederschrift des Anfangs habe ich erst im Mai 1922 beendet. Möge die Ahnung eines Auftrags, die mir in dieser Zeit, nicht immer aber immer wieder, beistand, bei mir bleiben.

Erster Entwurf des Werks, dessen Anfang dieses Buch ist: Frühjahr 1916; erste Niederschrift dieses Buchs: Herbst 1919; Die gegenwärtige Fassung: Frühling 1922.

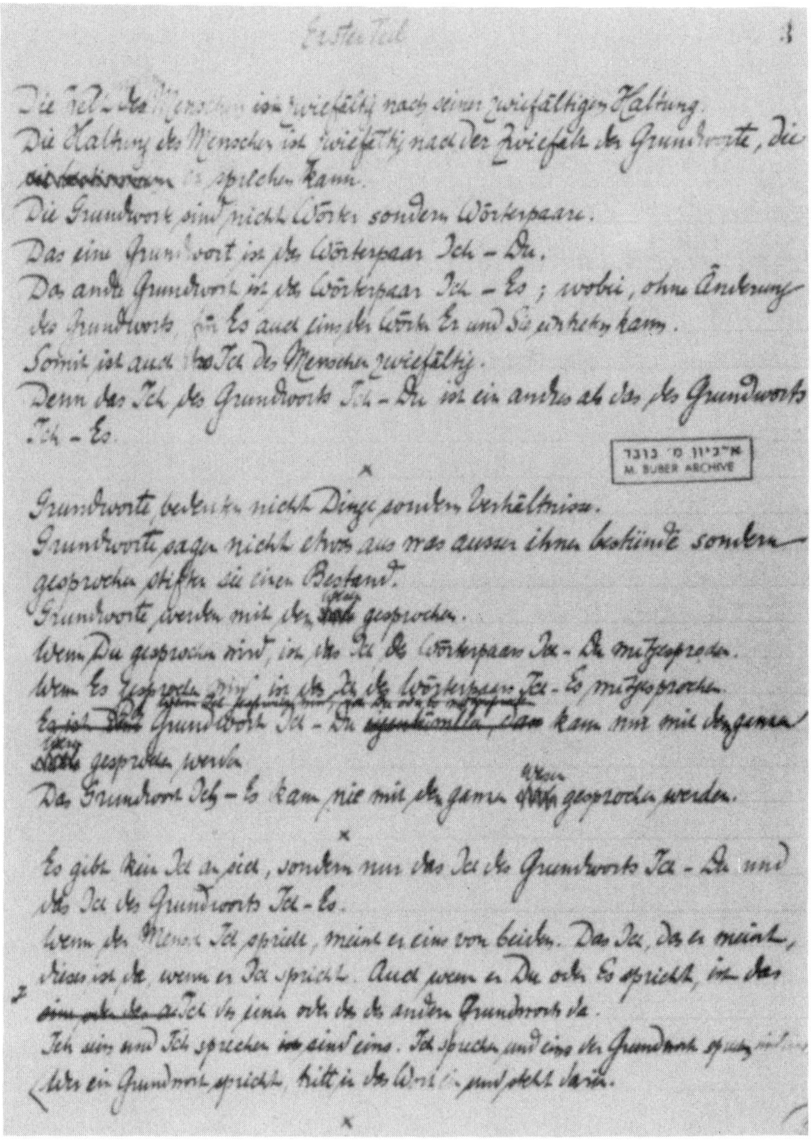

I

I. Ich und Du
1. Wort. 2. Geschichte. 3. Gott.

II. Urformen des religiösen Lebens
1. Magie. 2. Das Opfer. 3. Das Mysterium. 4. Das Gebet

III. Gotteskunde und Gottesgesetz
1. Mythus. 2. Dogma. 3. Gesch. 4. Lehre.

IV. Die Person und die Gemeinde
1. Der Stifter. 2. Der Priester. 3. Der Prophet.
4. Der Reformator. 5. Der Einsame

V. Die Kraft und das Reich

1. Ich und Du
2. Die Offenbarung
3. Die Weihe
4. Der Dienst
5. ~~Der~~ Mythus und Dogma / Die Kunde
6. ~~Das~~ Gesetz und Lehre / Die Lehre
7. Das Reich

I. Ich und Du
II. Urformen des religiösen Lebens
III. Gotteskunde und Gottesgesetz
IV. Person und Gemeinde
V. Die ~~religiöse~~ Kraft und ~~~~ das Reich

LIST OF BOOKS CITED IN THIS WORK

Bergman, Samuel Hugo. *Dialogical Philosophy from Kierkegaard to Buber* (in Hebrew). Jerusalem, 1974.

Bergman, Samuel Hugo. *Faith and Reason*. Washington, D. C., 1964 and New York, 1972.

Bergman, Samuel Hugo, *Thinkers and Believers* (in Hebrew). Jerusalem, 1959.

Buber, Martin. *Begegnung: Autobiographische Fragmente*. Stuttgart, 1960.

Buber, Martin. *A Believing Humanism: Gleanings by Martin Buber*. Translated and edited by Maurice S. Friedman. New York, 1967.

Buber, Martin. *Between Man and Man*. Edited by Maurice S. Friedman and translated by Ronald G. Smith. 2nd ed. New York, 1967.

Buber, Martin. *Between Man and Man*. Translated by Robert G. Smith. Boston, 1955.

Buber, Martin. *Bücher der Kündung*. Cologne, 1966.

Buber, Martin. *Daniel*. New York, 1965.

Buber, Martin. *Eclipse of God: Studies in the Relation between Religion and Philosophy*. New York, 1952.

Buber, Martin. *Good and Evil: Two Interpretations*. Translated by Ronald G. Smith. New York, 1953.

Buber, Martin. *I and Thou*. Edited and translated by Walter Kaufmann. New York, 1970.

Buber, Martin. *Ich und Du*. 9th ed. Heidelberg, 1977.

Buber, Martin. *Israel and the World: Essays in a Time of Crisis*. New York, 1965.

Buber, Martin. *Israel und Palästina: Zur Geschichte einer Idee*. Zurich, 1950.

Buber, Martin. *Der Jude und sein Judentum: Gesammelte Aufsätze und Reden*. Cologne, 1963.

Buber, Martin. *Kampf um Israel: Reden und Schriften (1921–1932)*. Berlin, 1933.

Buber, Martin. *The Knowledge of Man*. Edited by Maurice S. Friedman. London, 1965.

Buber, Martin. *Nachlese*. Heidelberg, 1965.

Buber, Martin. *On Judaism.* New York, 1967.

Buber, Martin. *The Origin and Meaning of Hasidism.* New York, 1960.

Buber, Martin. *Pointing the Way: Collected Essays.* Translated by Maurice S. Friedman. New York, 1957.

Buber, Martin. *Schriften über das dialogische Prinzip.* Heidelberg, 1954.

Buber, Martin. *Die Schriftwerke.* 4th ed. Heidelberg, 1976.

Buber, Martin. *The Ten Rungs.* New York, 1970.

Buber, Martin. *Das verborgene Licht.* Frankfurt a. M., 1924.

Buber, Martin. *Werke.* 3 vols. Munich/Heidelberg, 1962–1964.

Buber, Martin, and Britschgi-Schimmer, Ina, eds. *Gustav Landauer: Sein Lebensgang in Briefen.* 2 vols. Frankfurt a. M., 1929.

Buber, Martin, and Rosenzweig, Franz, trans. *Die fünf Bücher der Weisung.* 2nd ed., Berlin, 1930 and 9th ed. Heidelberg, 1976.

Buber, Martin, and Rosenzweig, Franz. *Die Schrift und ihre Verdeutschung.* Berlin, 1936.

Casper, Bernhard. *Das dialogische Denken: Eine Untersuchung der religions-philo-sophischen Bedeutung Franz Rosenzweigs, Ferdinand Ebners und Martin Bubers.* Freiburg i. Br., 1967.

Cohen, Arthur A. *Martin Buber.* London, 1957.

Cohen, Hermann. *Jüdische Schriften.* Berlin, 1924.

Cohen, Hermann. *Religion of Reason from the Sources of Judaism.* Translated by Simon Kaplan. New York, 1971.

Cohen, Hermann. *Religion der Vernunft aus den Quellen des Judentums.* Leipzig, 1919 and 3rd ed. Cologne, 1959.

Cohn, Margot and Buber, Rafael. *Martin Buber: A Bibliography of His Writings, 1897–1978.* Jerusalem, 1980.

Diamond, Malcolm L. *Martin Buber, Jewish Existentialist.* New York, 1960.

Ebner, Ferdinand. *Schriften.* 3 vols. Munich, 1963–1965.

Ebner, Ferdinand. *Das Wort und die geistigen Realitäten.* Innsbruck, 1921 and Vienna, 1952.

Fackenheim, Emil. *Quest for Past and Future: Essays in Jewish Theology.* Bloomington, Ind., 1968.

Feuerbach, Ludwig. *Philosophie der Zukunft.* Stuttgart, 1922.

Friedman, Maurice S. *Martin Buber: The Life of Dialogue.* London, 1955 and New York, 1960.

Friedman, Maurice S., ed. *The Worlds of Existentialism. A Critical Reader.* New York, 1964.

Gabe, Herrn Rabbiner Dr. Nobel zum 50. Geburtstag. Frankfurt a. M., 1921.

Glatzer, Nahum N. *Franz Rosenzweig: His Life and Thought.* New York, 1961.

Guttmann, Julius. *Philosophies of Judaism: The History of Jewish Philosophy from Biblical Times to Franz Rosenzweig.* New York/London, 1964.

Herberg, Will. *Judaism and Modern Man.* New York, 1965.

Herrmann, Leo, ed. *Treue: Eine jüdische Sammelschrift.* Berlin, 1916.

Herzl, Theodor. *Tagebücher.* Vol. 1. 2nd ed. Tel Aviv, 1934.

Heschel, Abraham Joshua. *God in Search of Man.* Cleveland and New York, 1959.

Hirsch, Samuel. *Das System der religiösen Anschauung der Juden und sein Verhältnis zum Heidentum, Christentum und zur absoluten Philosophie.* Leipzig, 1892.

Jacob, Benno. *Das Erste Buch der Tora: Genesis, übersetzt und erklärt.* Berlin, 1934.

Katchalsky, Aharon. *In the Crucible of Scientific Revolution* (in Hebrew). Tel Aviv, 1972.

Kohn, Hans. *Martin Buber, sein Werk und seine Zeit: Ein Beitrag zur Geistesgeschichte Mitteleuropas, 1880–1930.* Hellerau, 1930 and Wiesbaden, 1979.

Landauer, Gustav. *Die Revolution.* Edited by Martin Buber. Frankfurt a. M., 1907.

Landauer, Gustav. *Shakespeare: Dargestellt in Vorträgen.* Edited by Martin Buber. 2 vols. Frankfurt a. M., 1920.

Landauer, Gustav. *Der werdende Mensch: Aufsätze über Leben und Schrifttum.* Edited by Martin Buber. Potsdam, 1921.

Landauer, Gustav. *Beginnen: Aufsätze über Sozialismus.* Edited by Martin Buber. Cologne, 1924.

Maringer, Simon. *Martin Bubers Metaphysik der Dialogik im Zusammenhang neuerer philosophischer und theologischer Strömungen.* Cologne, 1936.

Mayer, Reinhold. *Franz Rosenzweig: Eine Philosophie der dialogischen Erfahrung.* Munich, 1973.

Mendelssohn, Moses. *Jerusalem.* New York, 1969.

Rang, Florens Christian. *Deutsche Bauhütte: Philosophische Politik Frankreich gegenüber.* Sannerz, 1924.

Rang, Florens Christian. *Shakespeare der Christ: Eine Deutung der Sonette.* Heidelberg, 1954.

Rosenstock-Huessy, Eugen. *Deutsche Beitrage zur geistigen Überlieferung.* Chicago, 1947.

Rosenstock-Huessy, Eugen. *Ja und Nein: Autobiographische Fragmente.* Heidelberg, 1968.

Rosenstock-Huessy, Eugen. *Judaism Despite Christianity.* University, Ala., 1968.

Rosenzweig, Franz. *Briefe.* Edited by Edith Rosenzweig. Berlin, 1935.

Rosenzweig, Franz. *Briefe und Tagebücher*, vol. 2. Edited by Rachel Rosenzweig. Haag, 1979.

Rosenzweig, Franz. *Kleinere Schriften.* Berlin, 1937.

Rosenzweig, Franz. *On Jewish Learning.* Edited by Nahum N. Glatzer. New York, 1955.

Rosenzweig, Franz. *The Star of Redemption.* Translated by William W. Hallo. New York, 1970.

Rosenzweig, Franz. *Der Stern der Erlösung.* Frankfurt a. M., 1921 and 3rd ed. Heidelberg, 1954.

Rotenstreich, Nathan. *Jewish Philosophy in Modern Times.* New York, 1968.

Schaeder, Grete, ed. *Martin Buber: Briefwechsel aus sieben Jahrzehnten.* 3 vols. Heidelberg, 1972–1975.

Schaeder, Grete. *Martin Buber: Hebräischer Humanismus.* Göttingen, 1966.

Scheler, Max. *Der Formalismus in der Ethik und die materiale Wertethik.* Halle/
Saale, 1916.
Scheler, Max. *Vom Ewigen im Menschen.* Leipzig, 1921.
Schilpp, Paul A., and Friedman, Maurice S., eds. *Martin Buber.* Stuttgart,
1963.
Schilpp, Paul A., and Friedman, Maurice S., eds. *The Philosophy of Martin
Buber.* La Salle, Ill., 1967.
Scholem, Gershom. *The Messianic Idea in Judaism.* New York, 1971.
Simmel, Georg. *Die Religion.* Frankfurt a. M., 1906 and 1912.
Simon, Ernst. *Brücken: Gesammelte Aufsätze.* Heidelberg, 1965.
Spengler, Oswald. *Der Untergang des Abendlandes: Umrisse einer Morphologie der
Weltgeschichte.* Vol. 1. Vienna, 1918.
Stahmer, Harold. *Speak That I May See Thee! The Religious Significance of Language.*
New York, 1968.
Steiner, Rudolf. *The Philosophy of Spiritual Activity.* West Nyack, N. Y., 1963.
Theunissen, Michael. *Der Andere: Studien zur Sozialontologie der Gegenwart.* Ber-
lin, 1965 and 2nd ed. Berlin, 1977.
Tramer, Hans, ed. *In zwei Welten.* Tel Aviv, 1962.
Vaihinger, Hans. *Die Philosophie des Als-Ob: System der theoretischen, praktischen
und religiösen Fiktionen der Menschheit auf Grund eines idealistischen Posi-
tivismus.* Berlin, 1911.
Wehr, Gerhard. *Martin Buber in Selbstzeugnissen und Bilddokumenten.* Reinbek
bei Hamburg, 1968.
Weiss-Rosmarin, Trude. *Religion of Reason.* New York, 1936.
Weltsch, Felix, ed. *Prague and Jerusalem* (in Hebrew). Jerusalem, 1950.

TRANSLATIONS OF *ICH UND DU*:

English: by Ronald G. Smith, Edinburgh, 1937, New York, 1958; by Walter
Kaufmann, New York, 1970.
French: by Geneviève Bianquis, Paris, 1938.
Spanish: by Horacio Crespo, Buenos Aires, 1956.
Dutch: by I. J. van Houte, Utrecht, 1959.
Italian: by Paolo Facchi and Ursula Schnabel, Milano, 1959.
Hebrew: by Zvi Woislavsky, Jerusalem, 1959.
Swedish: by Margit and Curt Norell, Stockholm, 1962 (initiated by and ded-
icated to Dag Hammarskjöld).
Japanese: by Keisuki Noguche, Tokyo, 1962.
Danish: by J. Vikjaer Andersen, Copenhagen, 1964.
Norwegian: by Hedvig Wergeland, Oslo, 1968.
Czech: by Jiři Navrátil, Prague, 1969.

INDEX

Note: Page numbers in *italics* refer to the text of the lectures.

241